THE GANGETIC WEST BENGAL

[*c.* Seventeenth-Nineteenth Century]

A Survey

THE GANGETIC WEST BENGAL

[*c.* Seventeenth-Nineteenth Century] A Survey

Soumitra Sreemani

New Central Book Agency (P) Ltd
LONDON
DELHI KOLKATA PUNE HYDERABAD ERNAKULAM

REGD. OFFICE
8/1 Chintamoni Das Lane, Kolkata 700 009, India
email: ncbapvtltd@eth.net

OVERSEAS
NCBA (UK) Ltd, 149 Park Avenue North, Northampton, NN3 2HY, UK

EXPORT
NCBA Exports Pvt. Ltd, 212 Shahpur Jat, New Delhi 110 049
email: ncbaexp@ncbapvtltd.com

BRANCHES

208B Peacock Lane, Shahpur Jat
New Delhi 110 049
email: ncbadel@ncbapvtltd.com

House No. 3-1-315, 1st Floor
Nimboliadda, Kachiguda, **Hyderabad** 500 027
email: ncbahydb@ncbapvtltd.com

Shop Nos. 3 & 4, Vinayak Towers
681/B Budhwar Peth, Appa Balwant Chowk
Pune 411 002
email: ncbapune@ncbapvtltd.com

GSS Shopping Complex, 1st Floor
Opposite College Post Office, Convent Road
Ernakulam 682 035
email: ncbaernk@ncbapvtltd.com

THE GANGETIC WEST BENGAL

First Published: January 2011

PUBLISHER AND TYPESETTER
New Central Book Agency (P) Ltd
8/1 Chintamoni Das Lane, Kolkata 700 009

PRINTER
New Central Book Agency (P) Ltd
Web-Offset Division, Dhulagarh, Sankrail, Howrah

COVER DESIGNER
Soumen Paul

COVER PRINTER
Biswanath Studio, Kolkata

PROOF-CHECKING
Subas Maitra and Kakoli Banerjee

PROJECT TEAM
Swapan Sarkar and Prabhat Jas

ISBN: 978-81-7381-642-0

Price: ₹ 295.00

To

Aditi

Contents

Preface

The present study has accrued from a recent research to dissect the happenings around the river Ganga, i.e., Bhagirathi and Hooghli during the last couple of centuries in a very rudimentary manner. It has become a settled trend for last seventy-odd years to conclude that the western part of Bengal was lagging behind its eastern part in many ways as the west was a moribund delta for the changes in the main channel of the Ganga towards east. Geographically the eastern part certainly commended more importance than the west. But one cannot ignore the fact of the economic activities and thick settlements along the course of the Bhagirathi-Hooghli—the river assumed these twin names after its bifurcation in the district of Murshidabad. During the seventeenth-nineteenth centuries this region ultimately became a focal point of many things. Being devastated by the series of Maratha Bargi raids the western part of Bengal became poorer in terms of demographic as well as agricultural resources. Then came the major upheaval—the administration and ultimately the independence of the province were acquired by a foreign trading company. A lot of natural and man-made crises hit this part time and again. But all failed to dampen the zeal of the people residing along the course of the river. One piece of settlement often washed out for the change in the river's course which was a regular feature during these years. But that was compensated very soon by another piece. The present study tries to locate the contours of such settlements.

Much kindness was bestowed upon me by several persons and institutions during my course of study. The Librarian and staff of the National Archives of India, New Delhi, and the West Bengal State Archives, the National Library, the Bangiya Sahitya Parishad, Kolkata, have been extremely cooperative throughout. My indebtedness also goes to the then District Magistrates and their staff at Malda and also at Berhampur for their courtesy and assistance during my field work in those Collectorate Offices; the National Thematic Mapping Organisation and the Survey of India, Kolkata, who issued some maps for study and their incorporation herein. The entire manuscript was put into order by my friend Sri Tanmoy Bhattacharjea. Dr Amit Sanyal, my friend and a high official in the Bidhannagar [Salt Lake] administration, had to bear a lot of trouble for this venture in various manner. Above all, Sri Amitabha Sen, Director of New Central Book Agency (P) Ltd, has taken a risk in publishing this book. My sincere and heartfelt gratitude to him as also to all the above-mentioned persons and institutions.

15 August 2010 **Soumitra Sreemani**
Kolkata

Abbreviations

B.O.R.	—	Board of Revenue
C.O.R.	—	Committee of Revenue
Dept.	—	Department
F.W.I.H.	—	Fort William—India House Correspondence
Fever Hospital	—	General Committee of the Fever Hospital and Municipal Improvement
Foreign	—	Foreign Department
Home	—	Home Department
Misc.	—	Miscellaneous
Progs.	—	Proceedings
P.W.D.	—	Public Works Department
R.B.W.C.	—	Revenue Board Consisting of Whole Council

INTRODUCTION

It is commonly believed that Bengal is the child of the river Ganga. This river carries the religious sentiments of the vast majority of the population whose ancestors had started the process of settlement along its course in Bengal thousands of years ago. Apart from religion the river for centuries has been the life belt. Agriculture, trade and artisan craft flourished, all of which allured numbers of individuals and even races in this land. Bengal's culture, its modernisations and its identity before the world outside owe to a large extent to this river. What the river Nile was to Egypt this river was to Bengal.

Between the closing decades of the sixteenth century and the closing decades of the nineteenth the Ganga changed its course number of times. In the late sixteenth the bulk of the water found its new course through the eastern direction—bifurcating the river in the district of Murshidabad. Since then the main flow of water was carried through the river Padma—now in Bangladesh into the Bay of Bengal. The original flow became meagre year after year and that ran through what is present West Bengal. This portion of the river is better known as the Bhagirathi up to the point where the river Jalangi meets it in the district of Nadia and, thereafter, as the river Hooghli. "The most fertile lands once lay along the Bhagirathi, from the area of Murshidabad southward."[1]

Being robbed of the main flow since the late sixteenth century this river had lost its glory in the eyes of the geographers and also of the common people. For this the entire region along its two banks was viewed as a moribund delta while the then eastern part of Bengal was considered as the active delta. A close examination of history reveals that reclamation and peasentisation in those regions got momentum when the main flow of the river shifted its course to the Padma.[2] Hence Bengal's wealth and strength, both originated there. Since the days of historical reckoning the western part of the Bhagirathi-Hooghli were well-settled. But the change in course in number of times altered the pattern of settlements, agricutlure and economy.

"The river's fluctuations remain unpredictable" and occurred very frequently. "The history of Rajmahal illustrates Ganga's power... In medieval times, the Muslim rulers moved their capital to Rajmahal. In the seventeenth century, it was filled with people and every kind of merchandise. Its port was jammed with vessels. Toward the end of the century, the river shifted its course three miles eastward,"[3] and paved the ultimate decline of that city. In fact, the movement of the river shaped a new history of settlement.

In the 1920s a new trend for describing the Bengal delta started taking shape. This delta was identified as a "kind of frontier area". Originating in Europe this "frontier concept has got a deep root in the intellectual world of the USA. Some scholars have projected Bengal delta on the conception of the 'ethnic frontier"'.[4] If this premise is to be sustained then one can arrive at such a conclusion, which prove the growth of peasentisation in the active delta under the leadership of a particular ethnic group.

But a close look into the contours of the events may prove this common belief wrong. Generally, the best kind of arable lands were available in the regions where the rivers were most active. Still, after the sharp bifurcation of the Ganga in the district of Murshidabad, the western course did not lose its vitality. Though the delta building movements became increasingly nominal the productivity of soil never did suffer nor did the settlements vanish. Moreover, the western course never lost its age-old place of pride in the minds of the people. The economy remained sound as ever during the Mughal rule. Though he never visited Bengal, Thomas Coryat [1612-17] knew that "Bengala, ... is a kingdom of most singular fertilite within" the empire "the midland parts thereof being watered by divers channels of the famous Ganges."[5] Hence, both economy and culture were ably patronised in the western parts. Thomas Bowrey, while presenting his travel experience during 1669-79 in this part of India, found the region thickly populated. The habitations grew chiefly for the trade along the river itself.[6] The change in the course of the principal water channel certainly had no impact. While composing the Bengali version of the epic, the *Ramayana*, the poet Krittibas Ojha had introduced himself to his readers and termed the river Bhagirathi as the original river[7] on whose banks he had come for studies.

Bengal's politics and economy during the medieval days were also centred here. The independent *Sultans* of Bengal ruled over a vast area for nearly four hundred years with their seats at Gaur and Pandua, once close to the river Ganga in the present district of Malda in West Bengal. Saptagram or Satgaon on the near defunct river Saraswati in the district of Hooghli was for long the royal port of the kingdom. At the same time Chaitanya [1485-1533] started his *Vaisanava* movement from Navadwip in the district of Nadia. Scores of scholars and seekers of knowledge considered Navadwip the sacred seat of learning and visited it.[8] This trend continued and Krishnanagar, Bhatpara and, finally, Calcutta in the nineteenth century bore that legacy with ability and pride. The entire region, the major portion of which is present day West Bengal not only carried a cherished culture but also a sound economy; however, the delta was considered a moribund one.

Bengal's history started with the spread of settlement in the western part of the river Bhagirathi that is commonly known as the *Rarh*. In the sixteenth century this portion had already been "densely populated and highly stratified agrarian order".[9] In fact, the Aryanisation of the west had been completed long ago and the Hindu society was divided by their caste system. "The west was also the region of Bengal where, at the advent of Mughal rule, Hindu civilisation was most deeply established. This is seen in the appearance of dated brick temples...[*which*] began appearing concurrently with the rise of Mughal power and proliferated throughout the seventeenth and eighteenth centuries."[10]

The settlement pattern also reflected this. The same, though not in the form of caste, remained active among the aristocracy. The aristocracy—whether during the *Sultanate* rule or during the earlier Mughal rule was consisted primarily of foreign elements. These aristocratic families maintained a strong line of difference with the local people irrespective of their status. It was to the credit of Murshid Quli Khan [1704-27] that a powerful local gentry could emerge in Bengal in the first half of the eighteenth century. This aristocracy played a very important role in the sway of the English East India Company over the province. The glory of Bengal, its vast fertile fields, its rich commerce which were the subject matter of a good number of texts—whether indigenous [the *Mangalakavyas*] or the travelogues of the Europeans—all had their roots in the Bhagirathi-Hooghli regions. Though the river was too much flood prone the people residing along its course never deserted the places which regularly were affected by severe inundations. Generally, the floods visited the banks of the river annually. After visiting this part of Bengal, Ralph Fitch [1583-91] tried to assess the role of the river in the livelihood of the people who used to reside along its course.[11]

But the Mughal rule could not bring any remarkable change in western Bengal. "As this area already possessed a monetized economy based on surplus rice cultivation and a revenue system designed to extract that surplus, the introduction of Mughal rule had little socio-political impact."[12] The inner strength of the region was deeply rooted within its economy and its culture. No doubt the Hindus of this region were divided and sub-divided into a number of castes chiefly based on trade and profession. But those divisions did not create any revolutionary change. Hence they did not adopt the religious ideology of their new rulers.[13]

Needless to say that the "Consolidation of Mughal Authority, 1610-1704" brought the province into the wider economic hinterland in the north and north-western India. "Since the overland ascendancy of Mughal influence in Bengal's eastern hinterland occurred just as Portuguese, Dutch, and English commercial interests entered the region from overseas, this...integrated into two cosmopolitan and expanding political economies, the Mughal and the European."[14] That also gave a long-standing peace in Bengal. After a strong resistance the local chieftains had to succumb to the Mughals. This helped in maintaining economic stability though the rural sector seldom had liquid currency. But that scarcity did not deter the growth of finer varieties in artisan craft and their trade. Except Dhaka, which gained an international fame for weaving *muslins*, all the places that made Bengal famous in weaving and knitting were on the banks of the Bhagirathi-Hooghli. With the growth of these industries the population also grew. The principal item, which then used to employ wider number of persons, was silk.

The foreigners in the search of silk then mostly visited the western part of Bengal, the most sought-after article that dominated the European markets for more than two hundred years. Strong competitions often amounting to physical assaults, capturing of vessels of the rival countries commenced among the European trading nations. It was the Portuguese who had initially commanded the sea-borne trade of Bengal in the late sixteenth and early seventeenth centuries. Their muscle power robbed the others of their respective trade. They were settled at Chittagong and at Hooghli, the latter being the principal one. With them a new set of population grew up in and around Hooghli town. Intermixture with the local population also gave birth to a new genre of culture. Their primary aim was to scuttle any competition but they earned such a bad name that military intervention from the imperial authority brought their ultimate doom. Following them a score of people started arriving in the Hooghli water. The Dutch who started throwing out the Portuguese vessels from the Bay, fired the first salvo of this nature. Practically, the Portuguese were paid back in their own coin.[15]

Apart from the water channels—which had connected north India with the Bay of Bengal—the long Mughal administration also secured the land routes. Their simultaneous use helped the trade to flourish beyond any calculation. Since the western part of the delta had already raised a well-settled economy through artisan crafts and their export-import trades the Mughal administration's efforts were ably utilised by this region. This region increasingly became the centre of attraction to all. Bengal then assumed a proverbial fame for her agricultural commodities and artisan produce. Silk led the list of the various articles, which were commonly exported from here. Bengal had a long tradition of silk manufacture. Under the independent *Sultans* of Gaur this trade flourished. With the progress of time finer varieties were produced Silk was such a commodity, that it involved a large number of skilled and unskilled persons—male and female alike. It was usually traded in liquid money.

In the late seventeenth to the eighteenth centuries Dhaka acquired its name producing finer variety of cotton fabric, commonly known as *muslin*. Dhaka was away from the Bhagirathi-Hooghli region. But Santipur and some places of Hooghli as well as Sutanuti [*one of the three villages—Sutanuti, Govindupur, Kalikata—which, in combine, ultimately became the city of Calcutta*] did not lag far behind in the production of cotton fabrics. But silk did never lose its prime position in trade. It was produced in many parts of the eastern India but Kasimbazar on the Bhagirathi used to dominate. Its position as a supplier of quantity silk was vindicated in the seventeenth century. The scramble for possession of best of it often involved physical force.[16] For the fast growing trade of both silk and cotton fabric the Hooghli region and the town of Hooghli itself used to command more importance. Efforts were made to induce the captains of the ships to bring their respective vessels in the Hooghli water.[17] Saltpeter was another very important article that was regularly transported through Hooghli. Though saltpeter was never produced in Bengal and had to be brought from Patna in Bihar its regular procurements by the Europeans were made through Hooghli. Huge difficulties had to be countered to bring those in Hooghli for the shallow water in the upper stream.[18] All such stories of moribund delta having lost all its previous vitalities were nullified by the activities of those foreigners. Their numbers were ever increasing though the climate was devastating.

With the coming of the Mughals in Bengal the river opened its major course downward through the east and this process continued during the next three hundred years or more. On the one hand, the eastern part became enriched with the river silt and was the core area of the active delta and, on the other, the flow of water in the Bhagirathi which arm dwindled continuously affecting the delta-building activities. Hence the peasentisation and settlements were accleratated in the eastern part of Bengal. It is a very common conclusion that the western part, i.e. the Bhagirathi-Hooghli region being bereft of the natural bounties, lost its prime position to the growing eastern and southeastern parts. But tradition as well as prevailing economic condition came in a big way in keeping the importance of the Bhagirathi-Hooghli region for more than three hundred years since the major flow of water in the river Ganga started moving through its eastern arm, i.e. the Padma.

In fact, during the major part of the Mughal rule, the eastern and southeastern parts of Bengal were not considered as parts of the province. Those were the places not within the mainstream of the administration though Dhaka was the capital of the province for one hundred years since the beginning of the seventeenth century. It had been beyond any imperial control before the initial decades of that century. Still, by 1659, Chittagong could not be brought into the imperial fold.[19] Even the social orders of both the sides differed from each other. Hence William Finch considered only "Ougolle" or Hooghli and "Pipilee" or Pipli in Orissa as the ports of the "Kingdom".[20]

In fact, the artisan products and the agricultural surplus—both helped the western parts to survive for several centuries. This region could acquire an enviable position in the eyes of the foreigners too. No doubt all those helped the western part to retain its previous position as a centre of trade and culture. The devastating raids of the Marathas in the 1740s could not make this region poor. The serial of raids undertaken by the Maratha *bargirs*[21] could not deter the town-building activities. The "city of Bengal" [i.e., *Murshidabad*] in his [*Alivardi Khan's*] reign extended over 12 kos in length and 7 kos in breadth"[22] which was not a mean achievement in those days' standard.

Still, the economic importance of the region was never appreciated by the administration. Probably collection of revenues was considered the only job. Behind all growth the role played by the river cannot be denied. This fact did not escape the notice even of the foreigners. While visiting Bengal between the years 1616 and 1619, Edward Terry found the river as the most important contributor in making "Bengala a most specious and fruitfull kingdome".[23] In fact, the Europeans could guess the real importance of the river which had all along been overlooked by the Indians. They showed their interest in the study of the nature of the river. It was they who tried to give a well-studied document on the river to help the posterity. Joao De Barros, the Portuguese, prepared a detailed note on the river in its fourth *dacad* which was published in 1613. There we find the *De scripeao do Reino de Bengalla.*[24] This was the first published document containing a map—though not so accurate which gives a picture of the then river. This tradition continued. After the English conquest of Bengal, Robert Clive and his successor William Vansittart "took such a personal interest in the compiling of an accurate survey that they incurred the displeasure" of the higher authority. The charge was that they kept those maps drawn with the fund of the English East India Company for their personal use.[25] The better use of the river and to have a wider knowledge of the surroundings were the prime motives. But to the people of Bengal the river meant a sacred channel only. There was not a single work of geography or a single piece of cartography produced by them. This has made the construction of settlement pattern difficult.

However, the works left by the Europeans help us to understand the pattern along the course of the river. In the 1770s, Major James Rennell started producing his well-researched survey sheets covering wide areas of Bengal. From the very beginning Rennell's eyes were fixed in the details. His first maps under the title *An Actual Survey on the Provinces of Bengal Bahar S.C.* were published by Andrew Dury in London in 1776 when Rennell was in India. "It was on a scale of twelve miles to an inch and was the first map to be based entirely on measured distances and survey in the field." Another map drawn by Rennell of the country between Bengal and Delhi was published by the same publisher in the very next year. But the minute details were missing in it which became a cause of displeasure to Rennell himself. Hence he redrew his entire map and published the rectified maps in 1778. This collection was popularly known as *Bengal Atlas*[26]. But this *Atlas* could not reach India. Those were despatched to India on a East India Company's ships which was captured by the Portuguese. The entire cargo was lost. But this could not dampen the zeal of Rennell and his masters in London. Soon after another set was prepared in which the river Ganges along with other navigable routes were prominently displayed. Those maps were so popular that starting from their first edition in 1781 those were printed and sold a number of times till 1829. In January 1780 Rennell read a paper at the Royal Society of England on the Ganges and Brahmaputra rivers. First, the lure of wealth and, secondly, the availability of well-informed atlas, enhanced enthusiasms among scores of English who started flocking into Bengal in increasing number. After 1757 the bulk of these people settled in Calcutta, which was ultimately made the seat of highest authority.[27]

Between the late sixteenth and late nineteenth centuries the entire region witnessed several changes touching the daily livelihood of the people, their economic activities and their cultural settings. During the period the capital of Bengal was first transferred from Gaur to Rajmahal, on the bank of the Ganga, now in Jharkhand. From there it was shifted to Dhaka in the heartland of the expanding delta in the beginning of the seventeenth century where the seat of administration remained for hundred years. Again, the capital returned on the banks of the Bhagirathi-Hooghli. First it was Murshidabad and then Calcutta. The latter place was well nourished by the English. Similarly, the river was thoroughly studied by them. With the growth of the political power of the foreigners the economy of this region was transformed. First, the wealth of the region was squeezed and secondly, capital was invested in raising industries conducive to the need of the English.

This trend continued even during the nineteenth century when industrialisation—though in a very limited scale, started taking place in India. Coal, the most important article of this process was discovered in Burdwan and that was transported to many parts of the country through the river Ganga.[28] In 1823, a regular freight service between Calcutta and Allahabad became popular. Industries came up. In place of agriculture a new brand of employment was undertaken. A continuous flow of immigration enriched a new type of settlement. The English, as the ruler, was never ignorant of the situations and future possibilities. The first railway communication was laid between Calcutta and Mirzapur in the district of Hooghli as the region had already been highly commercialised with the help of the river connections.[29]

The rise of Chaitanya in the initial decades of the sixteenth century as the celebrated leader of the *Bhakti* unified the caste-torn Hindu society to some extent. Chaitanya with his vast number of followers, travelled very widely and followed the course of the Bhagirathi-Hooghli from his birthplace, Navadwip, to the mouth of the Hooghli. The chroniclers[30] of Chaitanya's life give a detailed picture of well-settled habitations in the entire stretch of the route. Since the Hindus saw the river Ganga with religious reverence its attraction was tremendous. Even after the shrinkage in water-flow this arm of the river was considered the original one. "Here the Gentiles hold the water of Ganges in great estimation, for having good water neere them, yet they will fetch the water of Ganges a great way off, and if they have not sufficient to drinke, they will sprinkle a little on them, and then they thinke themselves well."[31]

Whatever might have been the changes in the course of the principal channel of the river Bhagirathi-Hooghli, it had no impact on the growth of population and economic prosperity of the region. There were as many as forty-seven towns including the cities like Calcutta and Howrah among the seven western districts comprising Malda, Murshidabad, Nadia, Hooghli, Burdwan, Howrah and the 24 Parganas while the seven districts like Rajashahi, Rangpur, Pabna, Faridpur, Jessore, Maimansing and Dhaka in the active delta had only twenty-one towns.

The growth of Calcutta under the Company's rule surpassed anybody imagination. Within less than one hundred years of its coming into urban set-up Calcutta was viewed as the only modern metropolis in this part of the globe. The introduction of the English language as a medium of administrative dealings and then as a medium of instruction opened the western world to the people, primarily along the river Hooghli. Calcutta acquired a prime seat in imparting the western education. Calcutta also witnessed the growth of a urban English educated middle class who was then commonly called as *Bhadralok.* This *Bhadrolok* initiated the trend of a new westernised urban culture and taste. They not only gathered education from the west but also, gathered the western social behaviour and political tendéncies. This ultimately kindle the huge masses in the later part of the nineteenth century. India started demanding the political rights and some privileges which was the part of life of an Englishman.

No doubt the growing economic acivities and the wider scope of modern education helped to construct this pattern. Ultimately, the world outside came to know Bengal for her growth and achievements, which chiefly originated along the banks of the Bhagirathi-Hooghli.

NOTES

[1] Steven G.Darian; *The Ganges in Myth and History.* (Honolulu, 1978), p. 135

[2] R. K. Mukherjee; *The Changing Face of Bengal: A Study of Riverine Economy.* (Calcutta, 1938) is one of the primary studies and also Richard M. Eaton; *The Rise of Islam and the Bengal Frontier, 1204-1760* (New Delhi, 2000), ch. V

[3] Darian; *op. cit.,* p. 136

[4] Ralph W. Nicholas; 'Vaisanvism and Islam in Rural Bengal' in David Kopf ed. *Bengal:Regional Identity* (Michigan, 1969)

[5] Quoted in Sir William Foster ed.; *Early Travels in India.* (New Delhi. 1985), pp. 246-247

[6] Thomas Bowrey; *A Geographical Account of the Countries around the Bay of Bengal, 1669-79* (London, 1905), pp. 132-133

[7] Krittibas; *Ramayana* in Bengali. S. C. Majumder ed. (Calcutta, 1987) chiefly the Introduction

[8] Brindaban Dass; *Chaitanyabhagvat:* In Bengali. Sukumar Sen ed. (Sahitya Akademi, 2003)

[9] Eaton; *op. cit.,* p. 186

[10] Eaton; *op. cit.,* p. 184

[11] Foster ed. *Early Travels...* p. 24

[12] Eaton; *op. cit.,* p. 186

[13] *Ibid*

[14] Eaton; *op. cit.,* p. 151

[15] Sir William Foster ed.; *The English Factories in India, 1637-41.* (Oxford, 1912) p. 65, pp., 76-77

[16] In the 1670s the English East India Company started employing "more peons, who were needed to look after the weavers". See Sir Charles Faweett ed.; *The English Factories in India, 1670-77.* (Oxford, 1952) New Series Vol. II., p. 331

[17] Faweett ed.; *op. cit.,* p. 325 and p. 329

[18] Foster ed.; *The English Factories in India, 1668-69* (Oxford, 1921)

[19] Eaton; *op. cit.,* p. 199

[20] Foster; *Early Travels...* p. 182

[21] For details, *Maharashtrapurana* in Bengali Magazine, *Jhar;* September, 2004, pp. 181-18

[22] Karam Ali, *Muzaffarnamah* in J. N. Sarkar ed.; *The Bengal Nawabs* (Calcutta reprint, 1985), p. 58

[23] Foster; *Early Travels....* p. 295

24 C. R. Wilson; 'Note on the Topography of the river in the 16th Century from Hugli to the Sea as represented in Da Asia of De Barros' in the *Journal of Asiatic Society, Bengal.* Vol. I

25 Susan Gole; *India within the Ganges* (New Delhi, 1987), p. 81

26 Susan Gole; *op. cit.* p. 86

27 P. J. Marshall; *East Indian Fortunes: The British in Bengal in the 18th Century* (Oxford, 1976). Chiefly the introduction

28 *Marine Dept. Progs.* 22 May, 1839

29 *P.W. (Railways) Progs.* 17 September, 1848

30 See, Brindaban Dass, *Chaitanyabhagvat;* Jayananda; *Chaitanyamangala,* Biman Bihiri Majumdar and Sukhomoy Mukhopadhyay eds. (Asiatic Society of Bengal, Calcutta, 1971) etc.

31 Foster; *Early Travels....* p. 26

1

THE RIVER

For centuries the Indians are known as the worshippers of the river Ganga or Ganges. A lot of myths and legends are connected with it. A large number of holy places sprang up along its course. The people also knew the importance of the river when the question of farming was involved. It is one of the very few rivers, which had and still has water in it throughout the year. The river Ganga has been occupying a prominent place in the topography, geology and history of Bengal. The river with its two arms has shaped and reshaped the course of history of Bengal. The Bhagirathi or Hooghli flows through the western part of Bengal while the Padma flows through the eastern part, now known as Bangladesh. By its movements the river built, destroyed and again re-built landmass mainly in the southern and eastern parts of Bengal. "Bengal is literally a child of the Ganga"[1] for such activities. The river Ganga has come down from a Himalayan glacier and traverses a long route covering a major area of northern and eastern India.

When the river touches the plain lands in the present day western Uttar Pradesh the entire region from there to present day Bihar and a part of Jharkhand is known as the Gangetic Plain. Soon after the river starts its downward journey it enters the western boundaries of Bengal. Bengal was built by the silt carried down by the river from the Himalayas.

Until probably the twelfth century the river Bhairab—now flowing through Bangladesh and until the middle of the sixteenth century the Saraswati on whose bank once lay Satgaon, the port of Bengal, were the chief rivers of western Bengal. In fact, a number of rivers acted as distributaries of the Bhagirathi in the lower Bengal, which were called the Nadia Rivers in general. In the sixteenth century, the Bhagirathi rose, but after a century or so it began to decline along those Nadia rivers. The Englishman, Ralph Fitch, during his visit between 1583 and 1591, had noticed this character of the river. From Patna he came to Tanda near Gaur in present day Malda district. "Tanda standeth from the river Ganges a league because in times past the river flowing over the banks, in time of raine did drowne the country and many villages." Fitch could identify another channel of the river, which "remaineth drie, which is the occasion that the citie doeth stand so farre from the water".[2] Hence, the erratic movements of the river had a long history. This very change in the course of the main channel was seen by some, as the beginning of doom for central and western Bengal.[3]

The Ganga and then the Bhagirathi-Hooghli entered Bengal near Gaur, once the capital of the independent *Sultans* of Bengal. Until the sixteenth century, the river was in flourishing condition. There was a severe earthquake in 1505, and shortly after it, the Ganga left its old course past Gaur and retreated southwards. This tectonic movement along with the junction of the river Kosi with the Ganga helped it to move eastward by turning the Padma its main channel. But the people, in general, did not consider the Padma as the main channel, nor sacred. Still, from Gaur to Sagar Island, the following channels are considered sacred, "(a) Gaur to the Ganges near Shibganj. (b) The Bhagirathi from its present take-off from the Ganges to Calcutta. (c) *Adi* Ganga [*Tolley's Nullah*] at Calcutta via Garia, Baruipur and Rajganj to Diamond Harbour. (d) Diamond Harbour to Saugor island roughly by the present Hooghli channels".[4]

On the junction of the river Kosi with the Ganga in the middle of the eighteenth century, the united mass of water opened a new passage through the eastward channel, the river Padma. Siltation of the Bhagirathi started. The distributaries of that river such as the Ichhamati, the Jalangi and also the Mathabhanga, all Nadia Rivers lost touch with the Bhagirathi and within a very short span of time these rivers themselves became main channels.[5] For centuries the drainage system of this region is constituted by the tributaries and distributaries of the Ganga and the Brahmaputra, along with some insignificant river systems discharging into the Bay of Bengal. "Conspicuously enough, the Padma and the Bhagirathi, both distributaries within the fork and that of the tributaries outside it."[6]

Sudden changes in the river systems affected seriously the course of the rivers in the lower Bengal. But those were not the culmination of the topographic changes. The river Teesta joining the Padma till 1787 suddenly drifted eastward to join the Brahmaputra. That also affected the movements of the river Ganga. The quantity of water in its channel declined considerably.

Since the mid-sixteenth century "the old channel of the Bhagirathi began also to decay, the decline being especially manifest after the southern detour of the Damodar in 1770".[7] The river Damodar once fell in the river Hooghli near

Satgaon on the river Saraswati in the present Hooghli district. Now, by changing its course, that river found a new passage, 129 km below from its former meeting point and met the Hooghli near its mouth at the Bay. In the last three decades of the eighteenth century frequent changes took place in the courses of a number of channels. "This revolution in Bengal's river system was due to the cumulative effects of changes in the up-river areas, the catastrophic inundations of 1769-70 and 1786-88 and the earthquake of 1762".[8] It is commonly believed that for such revolutions the western part of Bengal suffered since the main flow of the river Ganga shifted towards the east.

The Bhagirathi was still accepted as the river of Bengal, an offshoot of the main channel, which it leaves in the district of Murshidabad in 24°35″ N and 88°5″ E; tributaries from the eastern fringe of the Chota Nagpur plateau also feed it. After flowing through Murshidabad, it constitutes the boundary between Burdwan and Nadia districts till, after a total course of 140 miles, it unites with the Jalangi in 23°25″ N and 88°24″ E to form the river Hooghli. The chief tributaries of the Bhagirathi are: in Murshidabad, the united waters of the Bansloi and Pagla, and the Chora Dekra, and, in Burdwaṅ, the Ajay and Khari—all on the right bank. The Bhagirathi throws open the Nadia rivers from its left bank which play a very important role in the flow of water. The most westerly and for commercial purposes the most important channel by which the waters of the Ganga enter the Bay of Bengal is being formed by the confluence of the three western distributaries of the great streams–the Bhagirathi, Jalangi, and Mathabhanga. The Bhagirathi's tributaries in the Chota Nagpur drain an area of about 8700 sq. miles "the Bhagirathi joins the Jalangi at Nabadwip, in 23°25″ N and 88°24″ E, and the distinctive name of the Hooghli is by some assigned to the united rivers from the point; according to others the river does not take this name till just above Santipur, 24 miles further down the stream. The united stream is joined by the Mathabhanga 15 miles below Santipur, and it thence proceeds almost due south to Calcutta".[9]

"So far as can be ascertained from early traditions, the existence of old beds, and towns with old histories on the bank of the river, the main Ganges stream from the dawn of history in Bengal … flowed south down the course of the present Bhagirathi to about the vicinity of Tribeni … This was the most natural and direct course to the sea. At Tribeni the Saraswati branched off south-westward, entering the present Hooghli at Sankrail and then according to … [*some*] flowed through Garden Reach and Tolley's Nullah [known as the *Adi* or original Ganga] and past Baruipur into the Sattramukhi and Channel Creek … to Ganga Sagar."[10] An alternative route of the river as suggested is that "at Tribeni the Ganges divided into three streams: (1) the Saraswati flowing south-westward past Satgaon and emerging into the present Hooghli at Sankrail, with a main branch running past Amta into the Damodar and probably also the Rupnarayan and so into lower Hooghli; (2) the Jabuna [Jamuna] following the direction south-eastward along the route of the decayed stream of that name; (3) a middle branch, which was the Bhagirathi proper, flowing south along the present Hooghli Channel to Calcutta and then through Tolley's Nullah [*the Adi* Ganga] to the sea".[11] Probably this second route was mostly frequented and human settlements sprang up along this course.

Dhanapati, the legendary merchant of the *Chandimangala* written by Mukundaram Chakraborty in the second half of the sixteenth century, sailed Singhal [*present day Sri Lanka*] along the Bhagirathi or the present Hooghli. Dhanapati could find a good number of well-populated places e.g. Tribeni, Khardaha, Konnagar, Kotrong, Kalighat, Baruipur, and Magra on the *Adi* Ganga. As this channel was gradually filled up and the delta-building function of the Ganga and the system of distributaries connected with it finished "its activity ... and it sought a new channel towards the east, where a new tract of the country became the scene of its creative activity".[12] Hence the flow of water diminished in the original one and gradually shifted towards the east apparently in the sixteenth century. The shift of the Damodar accelerated silting of the Hooghli channel, which had already suffered owing to the eastward migration of the main channel. The Bhagirathi-Hooghli system, taking off at the obtuse angle probably occupies a weak zone, perhaps resulting due to the change in the basin axis.[13]

In these ways the river Bhagirathi-Hooghli lost its earlier position. The river may be divided into two sections, the first being 64 miles from Santipur to Calcutta and the second of 80 miles from Calcutta to Sagar Islands, where it becomes an estuary. "The influence of the tides is felt strongly as high up as Navadwip, especially during the dry season; and it is estimated that the tidal inflow during the four months is more than double the total fresh-water discharge of the year".[14] It has been argued by some that for such daily tidal inflow the regular flow of water in the Bhagirathi-Hooghli suffered. Moreover, the river-bed increased gradually which also failed to maintain the flow. The changes also occurred in the upper stream resulting in certain topographical changes in the location of the town of Gaur, the capital of Bengal between 1202 and 1576, except for 60 years. Gaur once stood on the river Ganga but it gradually receded westward leaving this place totally unhygienic. Here in 1575 a severe epidemic spread out killing a number of men including Akbar's victorious general Munim Khan. Gaur was ultimately abandoned forever and a new provincial capital, Rajmahal, came up on the other side of the same river. Here the average width of its bed is about 3 miles "but the stream does not fill its channel in the hot weather, and almost invariably overflows it in the rains".[15] A severe flood sometimes in 1640, washed out the entire town of Rajmahal. But the river deserted Rajmahal and, in 1666, Tavernier found the place roughly one and a half miles away from the Ganga. Though the river again came closer to the town and it was found in 1860 that it ultimately left for its orignal channel three miles away.[16]

The changes in the course of the other rivers, which had connections with it were also affected seriously. For such happenings the pattern of human habitations and traffic movements underwent numerous changes. No doubt, the most noteworthy changes used to occur in the river Ganga itself. A great change occurred in the course of the river Brahmaputra during the latter half of the eighteenth century when it entered the Padma at Jaffarganj near Goalundo, now in Bangladesh. Since then the bulk of water took this passage for its journey towards the sea. Similarly, considerable changes occurred in the Nadia group of rivers. The Jalangi and Mathabhanga-Churni are comparatively new rivers, "the modern Churni having opened out since Rennell's time at the end of the eighteenth century. They carried the spill from the Ganges in the region south-westward into the Hooghli instead of south-east into the Bay, as was the trend formerly".[17] For such changes the Bhagirathi-Hooghli failed to maintain the flow of water which it could some 400 or 500 years ago. Those are the major premises commonly used to show that for the moribund nature of the river during the last couple of centuries the western part of Bengal failed to flourish in comparison with its eastern neighbour.

The Delta

Almost the entire area of present day western Bengal and Bangladesh "is in popular sense deltaic. It has been succinctly described as 'new mud, old mud, and marsh'—and if we take in all areas of generally deltaic aspect, including the Surma Valley, it is probably the largest delta in the world".[18] Still there has been a debate to identify the exact area of the delta. Without going into details of the various arguments in respect of those it can be said that the lands between the Bhagirathi-Hooghli, the Padma-Meghna and the Bay of Bengal are the actual delta. However, there has been another debate to locate their moribund, mature and active sections. About 200 miles from the sea "but 300 reckoning the windings of the river commences the Delta of the Ganges".[19] For last couple of centuries the Ganga's tendency for a tilt toward the east made the Bhagirathi-Hooghli region a moribund delta. A lot of discussions have been made to identify the actual reasons and period for such shift, "it is at least clear that the Bhagirathi or one of its several branches (Hooghli, Saraswati, *Adi* Ganga or Tolley's Nullah) was the most important distributaries in the seventeenth century, but has been silting at least since 1770, when the Damodar, which helped to keep it clear, shifted its mouth 80 miles [*129 km*] to the south".[20] However, the lower reaches of the river retained their vitality being fed by the Damodar and Rupnarayan.[21] For such erratic movements of the main channel of the Ganga and some of its distributaries too and often the settlement pattern along their respective courses also changed. But the uniqueness of the Gangetic delta lies in such changes and "their effects upon drainage, soil fertility, and the configuration of land, with all their concomitant reactions on agriculture, sanitation and the movements of population".[22]

In Bengal the river has contributed in many ways as it continuously built and re-built landmass. For the recurring floods the top soils used to receive exhaustive fertility. Though it has been argued by some that, when the flow shrank, the delta-building prospect also reduced to nothing. But the labour of man and the nature's bounty simply changed the economy of this part of Bengal with the changes affected in the landmass. The drainage systems of the region when "analysed chronologically, which is necessitated to correlate the evolution of landform in such an area of shifting river courses, reveals that the whole of the Bengal Delta had two distinct systems, i.e. the Ganga system, skiriting the Meghalaya Plateau and joining the Bay a little north of Chittagong. It is also believed that before the Rennell's drainage survey [1765-73] the Bhagirathi lay further west and flowed through the deserted channel, the *Adi* Ganga".[23]

In general, the deltaic rivers have a particular character of their own. When those rivers reach the delta the force of their current is checked, and "owing to the slight slope of the country" the rivers cannot carry their heavy burden of silt, which is deposited in the river-beds and on the banks.[24] But as soon as lower lands are leveled up completely "there is bound to be a change in the course of the main river ... This tendency is strikingly illustrated by the onward sweep of the Ganges successively through the different tracts of the Delta from west to east. Emerging from the upper levels round the Rajmahal hills and prevented by their rocky barrier from flowing further to the west, the main waters of the Ganges originally flowed along the general course now indicated by the Bhagirathi. As the channel was gradually filled up and the delta-building function ... was finished ... and it sought a new channel towards the east".[25] In this way the lands on the west of the Bhagirathi lies outside the true delta, which consists of the land between the Bhagirathi on the west and the

Madhumati on the east. It is probably the largest delta in the whole world. The region [21°25″-26° 50″N; 86°30″-89°58″E] embraces an area of about 80,968 sq. k.m.[26] Hence the measurements of the delta were universally accepted.

In fact the delta was more active in the eastern part of Bengal during the sixteenth and seventeenth centuries. For the shallowness of the river the bed levels increased which failed to cater the annual floodwaters. But the floods brought more relief than the damages caused by them. The entire region covering the districts of Nadia, Hooghli and the 24 Parganas was much benefited for the "yearly deposit of sand and ooze, and the Ryots may almost rejoice on beholding the rich layer of mould which remains after the deluge has passed away".[27] But the western half of the river did not usually receive the same benefit. Still "in the areas which are subject to tide the silt which passed down to the tidal creeks from the rivers, carried upwards by the flow tides thus having spread out produces a lessening of the current, and deposits silt in this spill area". The Sundarbans were the best example of these natural changes.[28] Often by the oscillation of the rivers in the deltaic region the entire landmass up to Murshidabad was well fed by them. All the rivers acted erratically. "A river can attack its banks … and carry off the spoil: but the still water seizing the silt, forces the river to deposit it exactly where it is most useful in forming a barrier against the further incursions".[29] The delta proper is "relatively low-lying region comprising Murshidabad, Nadia, 24 Parganas, Calcutta, Howrah and Hooghli, and parts of Burdwan and Midnapur… Bils, swamps, *chars*, levees, Dangas and costal dunes are the only features of physical prominence".[30] All these regions have a long history of human settlements. "Except for *bils* and a few patches of jungle there is comparatively little waste land"[31]. Traditionally the principal occupation of the people here had been "agriculture in season".[32] Nature's bounty helped the human settlement as that had helped the delta in taking its shape.

What the River Was

To the indigenous population, the river Ganga was and still is one of the rarest gifts from heaven. They used to worship the river and those settled along its course considered themselves the most blessed creatures on earth. Generally the local people never ventured to go outside and for this they never tried to assess the importance of the waterways. Besides, they did not try to understand the river in any geographic point of view. There had never been any cartographic interest or any history of survey. The credit goes to the Europeans who made the river known to the people away from India. Their primary interest was trade and for its stake they decided to explore this country. Fifteenth century onwards the nations in Europe started competing each other in exploring the hitherto unknown lands. Since ships were the only vehicles the knowledge of waterways was essential. It was the European sailors and travellers who first drew the maps relating to India. Bengal did not escape their interest. The arrival of Vasco da Gama in the western coast in 1498 inspired the Europeans to look into the minutes within this vast land. They started mapping various parts of this land. But the majority of those maps in the initial years were drawn on conjectural ideas though some of them were the reflections of the travelogues of the European travellers. Since the Portuguese sailors outnumbered their competitors and since they had the monopoly in the eastern waters the pioneering works are all in the Portuguese language.

Sixteenth century onwards Europe was passing through the process of reformation. They excelled not only in science and technology but also implemented their inventions in practical work. In this way the age of discoveries started unfolding. Their principal aim was to fetch wealth. Hence the scope of trade and commerce suddenly multiplied. The Europeans had for centuries looked the Arab traders at askance as these people had a monopoly on the eastern trade, chiefly originating from India. The lure of this trade brought the Europeans into this land. The Portuguese sailors' interest in Bengal was manifest from the initial decades of the sixteenth century. It goes to the credit of those people to explore the river Ganga and to draw a map of it as perfect as possible. Joao de Barros [*c.*1496-1570] was the pioneer in this field. Barros' map of Bengal [*c.*1550] "is, perhaps, the earliest map showing the imaginary river Ganga in peninsular India. The map is east oriented and gives details of the delta region of the Ganga".[33] The map is full of inaccuracies. It does not have any longitudes. "It covers the territories between 21° and 27° latitude from Orissa in the west to the Arracan in the east. River Ganga is shown entering Orissa and meeting the western channel of the Ganga's delta, known as Hooghli".[34] Very mention of Hooghli and some of the places including Satigam [Satgaon] prove the importance of them as the trading centres and ports with which the Portuguese had already been familiar. Some other places like Xore i.e. Dakhineswar on the Hooghli and in the north of Calcutta did also find place in it. The map was certainly drawn for the use of the explorers and for this the watercourse commended more importance. But the villages and towns along its course did also have their places though not properly.

In his footsteps some others continued the process of cartography. Among them Giacopo di Gastaldi or Jacobo Gastaldi of Venice was famous. In 1554, he drew his maps, which also were not at all perfect. After the arrival of Sir

Thomas Roe in 1615 the officials of the English East India Company became increasingly interested in exploring the details. Hence their process of cartography started taking shape. In 1619, William Baffin, the first mate of the ship 'Anne', drew the first map for the English sailors. Though his map also failed to reflect the actual geography, the course of the Ganga, and its fall in the Bay[35], this presented some settlements along its course.

What Did Rennell Find?

The first proper survey of the river was made by Major James Rennell between 1764 and 1767. He also tried to compare his findings with those of earlier few which were then available to him. He writes that about 220 miles from the sea but 300 reckoning the windings of the river commences the head of the delta. "The two westernmost branches, named the Cossimbazar and the Jellinghy Rivers, unite and form … the Hoogli River ... The Cossimbazar River is almost dry from October to May, and the Jellinghy River … is in some years unnavigable during two or three of the driest months".[36] He sailed through the river and reached Amboa or present day Katwa in the district of Burdwan. He compared his findings with the map drawn by Van den Broucke, drawn in 1660. Van den Broucke had found a large set of habitation between Kalna and Katwa on the same side of the river. But Rennell could only see "a few poor Huts".[37] Rennell observed that the shrinkage in the river was caused by such desertations. His experience was not good. In several places he found the river very shallow and not at all fit for the sail of bigger boats. "The Cossimbazar River at its conflux with the Jellinghy appears to be very narrow … The people informed … that it is now navigable for middle-sized Boats".[38] In the earlier decades of the eighteenth century Cossimbazar or Kasimbazar was still a very important outlet for silk, chiefly towards the European markets.

Not only the river Bhagirathi declined from its earlier position, the branches and tributaries also followed its fate. Hence, to Rennell, the river Mathabhanga at its head-water seemed just a "Nullah [or Creek]" which was only "2 Cubits* deep".[39] The principal cause for such decline of the river was siltation. In the districts of Nadia and Murshidabad, this siltation appeared to be the major hindrance to the normal flow of water. At Kaliganj the "River is divided into 2 channels by a Sand Bank of 5 miles long …". The embankments were not sound: "The Banks are now near 30 foot high, and are continually falling".[40]

*1 cubit = 18 – 22 inches = 46 – 56 cm

Moreover, the river took serious turns often upwards in some places like Kasimbazar for which the natural flow faced sudden obstructions. In the village of Raita "the River takes an ESE Course for 5 or 6 miles, and is all the way divided Into 2 Channels by a large Sand Bank".[41] These sandbanks and the shoals in many places prevented the big boats to sail.

"In places where the current is remarkably rapid, or the soil uncommonly loose, as would astonish those who have not been eye-witnesses to the magnitude and force of the mighty streams occasioned by the periodical rains of the tropical regions". This, Rennell, thought was the cause behind "a gradual change in the course of the river".[42] Sudden fluctuations in the course created "steep and a shelving bank" who in turn were "induced in all the winding parts of the river".[43] Rennell was not sure how long the river would remain navigable. During eleven years of his "residence in Bengal" Rennell saw "the outlet or head of the Jellinghy River was gradually removed three quarters of a mile further down". The movements in the rivers were so erratic that Rennell calculated "a mile in ten or twelve years being the usual rate of incroachment," and the intensity was bigger in the places of junctions of two rivers.[44] Viewing these Rennell apprehended that many places along the course of the river Bhagirathi would either change their respective locations or would simply be vanished.

For last few centuries, prior to the survey made by Rennell, the river Ganga had left a number of large lakes or marshes [called commonly *bil*] which were actually its old bed of flow. Those lakes could be found in many places. During the heavy rains and floods in the river which was nearly an annual affair multiplying the problems also flooded those lakes. Rennell was sure of his conclusion that "the inundations in Bengal are as much occasioned by the rain that falls there, as by the waters of the Ganges."[45] Rennell's survey had certain effects. The government of the English East India Company was seriously interested in keeping the river Ganga navigable throughout the year. But the changes in the river-course were very much evident.

The Changes in the River between 1658-64 and 1764-76

One of the mostly used maps was drawn by Van den Broucke during the years 1758-64 wherein the Ganga was shown divided into a number of channels near Rajmahal. But Rennell could distinctly locate only two such channels forming an island between Sakrigaly in Malda district and Rajmahal. Hence, within a hundred years, the siltation in the river was such that it could create an island that, in turn prevented the normal flow of water. The position deteriorated gradually and in 1805, Major Colebrooke found a number of islands between Rajmahal and Udainalla.

Van den Broucke had noted the existence of two large islands on the river Ganga, east of Rajmahal and also on the north of Murshidabad. Rennell did not find them. In Murshidabad, as shown in Van den Broucke's map, the river was divided into two channels surrounding a very large island. During Rennell's time the said island became much smaller in size. Van den Broucke found another big island between Satgaon and Calcutta on whose west the river Saraswati and on the east the river Bhagirathi used to flow. The Bhagirathi, after crossing Calcutta, took a right turn and traversed down the sea. This channel was nothing but the *Adi* Ganga of today. Rennell did not mention that island nor the existence of Saraswati. Two most important changes can be visible in these maps. Van den Broucke had recorded two streams falling into the Bhagirathi. The Damodar reached the Bhagirathi from the west and the Jalangi from the east near Kalna. These are absent in Rennell's drawing.

In Van den Broucke's map, the river Damodar is shown falling in the Bhagirathi near Kalna. But Rennell found the Damodar meeting the river Hooghli at Gaonkhali, a hundred miles down Kalna. Van den Broucke had noted the presence of only Jalangi river in the district of Nadia. But in Rennell's time there were several rivers in the said district. But the most important change took place between those one hundred years in the Bhagirathi itself. The river was much bigger in Van den Broucke's map. But in Rennell's Map the Bhagirathi was a mere insignificant stream.[46]

Since the later half of the eighteenth century when the principal channel of the Ganga entered the Padma at Jaffarganj near Goalundo, now in Bangladesh sufferings of the Bhagirathi began. The bulk of water took this passage for its journey towards the Bay. Similarly, considerable changes occurred in the Nadia group of rivers. The Jalangi and Mathabhanga-Churni are comparatively new rivers, "the modern Churni having opened out since Rennell's time at the end of the eighteenth century. They carried the spill from the Ganges in the region south-westward into the Hooghli instead of south-east into the Bay, as was trend formerly".[47] For such changes the Bhagirathi-Hooghli failed to maintain the flow of water which it could some 400 or 500 year ago.

In fact, topography of the region had undergone a vast change within a period of a few hundred years. Since the Mathabhanga "opened up the Churni distributary to the south-west into the Hooghli, the lchhamati has deteriorated the Jabuna, the relic of the old Jabuna branch of the Ganges," given off from the left bank of the Hooghli near Bansberia which met the Ichhamati lower down, has closed in its upper course. Since the "main stream of the Ganges having in the course of ages raised the land surface on the extreme western side of the delta may by this process [*of deltaic changes*] have been naturally diverted gradually into the comparatively less developed regions to the eastward. It may have been further influenced in this direction by the change of course of the Kosi river".[48] For the shrinkage in the stream during the period under study it was often believed that the river itself was nothing but a mere canal. Bernier in the 1660s also shared this view. In 1930, Sir William Wilcox put this canal theory very strongly. To him, the Bhagirathi had been cut by the ancient Hindu rulers of Bengal.[49]

Since the major flow of water was through the Padma channel the Bhagirathi-Hooghli used to suffer in many ways. The inundation and subsidence along the course of the river used to change the landscape in regular intervals. For such damaging nature of it the Bhagirathi had earned respect and subordination. The Padma was separated from the Bhagirathi at Biswanathpur in Murshidabad. From here to Navadwip the length of the river, in 1913, was 141 miles, though it was 161 miles not in a very distant past.[50] The change in the windings were very sharp. "With a bed level from 55 to 63 feet at the entrance, at the end of the flood season, it will be seen that as the Ganges level falls, the depth over the bar is reduced until the dry sand emerges" and this was a major reason for slower flow of water in the Bhagirathi.[51] What Bernier had seen was confirmed by Rennell though more than a hundred years after. This proved that during the entire period under study the Bhagirathi's fordability was never uniform.

In the latter half of the nineteenth century this river attracted some minute attention from the government. A regular monitoring of the flow of water was done. "Records of the varying river level are kept at Geria [*in Murshidabad*] and various other places and continuous gauge curves for Berhampur since 1861 and for Jangipur [*also in Murshidabad*] and Katwa [*in Burdwan*] since 1890. The levels deteriorated constantly. The "small depth at the height of the flood season is not" unique. In 1851, the maximum depth was only 12 feet and in 1853 only 14 feet 6 inches.[52]

However sacred the river was, the shallowness was constantly complained of during the period. But how the river actually behaved during all those years is still a subject matter of fierce debate. The Portuguese documents of the earlier decades of the sixteenth century were full of references of Chittagong as the principal port of Bengal. The *Sultans* then had their capital at Gäur on the banks of the Ganga and that place stood in the near vicinity of Satgaon, another port. Jao da Barros made the first reference of the shallowness of the river in the port of Satgaon in 1540. da Barros writes that the majority of ships avoided Satgaon though it was "a great and noble city."[53] This decay continued uninterruptedly and Caesar Frediricki found that the heavy vessels could not proceed beyond Betor, a place near present Sibpur in the district of Howrah. One thing was by then clear that the vessels had become bigger in respect of the earlier ones. Another very important reason for the decadence of the Hooghli was the sudden shift of the Damodar in the later part of the seventeenth century. More or less at the same time, the Jalangi met the Hooghli flowing down the southwest. In 1787, the Teesta was diverted from a southerly course into the Ganga at Goalundo. A few years after, the Mathabhanga-Churni opened south-westward into the Hooghli. These frequent changes not only affected the watercourse but also shaped and re-shaped the delta itself. Probably the Bhagirathi, "or true Ganges, always flowed very nearly in the direction it now does [i.e.; *in 1863*], the extension of the delta on the left bank being about sufficient to counter-balance the repulsive action of the More, Adjie, Damodar and Rupnarayan, on its right bank".[54]

"The ancient river has been slowly silting up ever since. Its reduced current further increases shoaling at the mouth of its larger feeder streams, such as the Damodar and Rupnarayan. English logs of the seventeenth century record chilling moments when their ships passed the dangerous bars near the river's mouth. The most treacherous of these is the James and Mary Sands, a constantly shifting silt deposit formed by the Damodar and Rupnarayan. The name is taken from the Royal James and Mary, a ship sunk on this spot in 1694".[55] "between the Damodar elbow and the Hooghli is a most typical dead delta zone. Here the small streams, some formerly spill channels of the Damodar, have lost their headwaters by silting or shifts of the river, while the Hooghli has probably been pushed to the east by the detritus of the plateau streams."[56]

"The Bhagirathi is a typical alluvial spill stream flowing through a bed of its own formation and carrying a charge of very fine sand and silt … which is rapidly transported to a spilling ground where the slope is much reduced. In these cases a rise of bed level may possibly be expected".[57] The earliest reference of such obstruction was made by Tavernier. In 1666, both he and Bernier reported that the Bhagirathi head was dry. Similar was the experience of Rennell in the dry season of the 1760s. Again, in 1797, Captain Colebrooke stated that the river was not navigable during the lean months.[58]

In the 19th Century

The map drawn by Rennell clearly shows that "the only portions of the Bhagirathi channel, which have persisted apparently unchanged are the straight sections from Jiaganj to Murshidabad and at Berhampur [*towns*]. The permanency of the channel in these places is probably due to the Bhagirathi embankment on the left bank," but the changes between these places and Palasi, a few miles below, could not be averted in spite of the presence of embankments. "Katwa was apparently always been on the river bank, but between this town and Nadia [*or Navadwip*] which in Rennell's time was on the left bank, lay on the right bank of the river" in the later part of the nineteenth century.[59] From a comparison of the survey map drawn by Rennell with the others of later date it can be seen that the only portion of the Bhagirathi which had flowed unchanged was the straight section from Jiaganj to Murshidabad town. This was chiefly due to the presence of the Bhagirathi embankments on its left.

For the changes in the course of the tributaries and also for the raising of the river-beds the capacity in them was gradually diminishing. During the rains these rivers seldom were able to carry the excess water. In the earlier decades of the nineteenth century at least 13 feet [4 metres] depth in the river Mathabhanga was not available[60] at its junction with the Bhagirathi. The maximum discharge of all the tributaries of the Bhagirathi with abnormally high floods was about 450,000 cusecs.[61] The problem of flood aggravated though often there were certain efforts to arrest the damages. In 1865, it was calculated that from the western tributaries like the Damodar, Rupnarayan etc., the united discharge during the high flood was over 70,000 cusecs.[62] These wide variance forced the river to behave erratically. Moreover, the slope of the Bhagirathi was "variable and it is difficult even to determine the general slope with any accuracy" and the "total general fall of the river from Geria [*in Murshidabad*] to Nadia may be estimated at about 43 feet, giving mean slope of 3.66 inches to the mile".[63] As the foreign rulers decided to see the river as the main waterway from Calcutta to the northern India and vice versa their principal aim was to keep the river-bed as deep as possible. They found that the "general and progressive deterioration of the rivers involves two factors influencing their discharge and those are the general raising of their bed levels in relation to the parent stream, the Ganges".[64] "The progressive general elevation of bed level may also be determined by its effects on the river levels at high and low stages and particularly on the latter".[65] First, the slope and then the bed level both put obstacles in the normal flow.

The river Hooghli had some other problems too. It was affected by the sea-tides daily. "The river is tidal throughout during the dry season. During ordinary spring tides in the dry season, a flood current is perceptible as far as Samudragarh [*in Burdwan*], about 7 miles below Nadia, and in the highest spring tides of the year a slight upward current is sometimes felt at Nadia."[66] "During the height of the freshet season, tidal influence ceases above Guptipara owing to the raised level of the river, but the limit varies naturally with the height of the freshets and the strength of the tide."[67] To the English the importance of the Hooghli was too much. To understand the character of it the river was divided into three portions (i) the Upper Hooghli from Nadia to Hooghli town, a distance of 60 miles; (ii) the Lower Hooghli from Hooghli to Kantabaria in the south 24 Parganas at the head of the estuary, 78 miles; and (iii) the estuary from Kantabaria to Sagar, 36 miles. A few centuries back the Kunti Nadi, an old channel of the Damodar had entered on the right bank near Nayasarai and contributed in the flow of water. There had been another insignificant stream namely, the Kharia Nadi, used to flow in the Hooghli near Mirzapur. Entire portion of the river here was tidal. Due to the slower and mild flushing of the river the bed became gradually higher. The shoals and sandbars appeared in different points starting from the downstream shores of the Sagar Island to many places in the upstream. Barrackpur, Chinsura, Ichhapur were a few to be mentioned. Still in the first quarter of the nineteenth century the river channel from Calcutta to Chinsura or even higher was in good condition.[68]

The East India Company's interest in maintaining the flow in the river was evident in 1789. On 25th March of that year Captain Kyd, the Superintendent of Works, in his report to the Governor General in Council observed that the "navigation is stopped about nine miles above Sooty [*in Murshidabad*]; here I found a Soal [*sic*] of Sand about one mile in length and the whole Breadth of the River, a Stream of about four Inches in Depth flowing over the deepest part". The encroachments by the river were fast and vast. Captain Kyd measured the distance between the Bhagirathi at Sooty and the Ganga at Saddiganj [*also in Murshidabad*], which appeared to be only two miles and 271 yards. While the map drawn by Rennell "makes this distance upwards of five miles," three miles of the Bank must have been destroyed since that Survey was made.[69] Between Rennell's time and 1789 i.e. a mere twenty odd years the nature of the streams changed very substantially. Kyd also noted that "the water which enters the Bagruthy from the Ganges at Mohungunge [*in Murshidabad*] runs with considerable force to Sooty during the rainy season, the distance upwards of twelve miles, but from thence passes in rapid stream again into the Ganges at Soddegunge". In Rennell's map the current is shown to run from Soddegunge

[Saddiganj] to Sooty. If this change had really taken place since the survey was made it certainly indicated that a great portion "of water will pass that way in the event of the Ganges encroaching as far as the Bagruthy."[70] Kyd was hopeful and thought that by making a "Dam across the channel at a cost of four thousand rupees would keep the river full of water. The river be kept free from shoals. It is the lifeline of economy in this part".[71] Hence, the problems of the river were somehow understood. To augment the flow in 1793, a proposal for opening the old mouth of the Damodar above Calcutta had been made.[72] Till 1818 the flow in the downstream was more or less good as the Mathabhanga still carried enough water. But in 1818, its flow suffered terribly and the merchants of Calcutta appealed to the government to take action for augmenting supply in the Bhagirathi. To maintain a steady flow often a particular portion of the river was kept separated from the other portions so that the major flow could get a much deeper area. Usually bamboo fencing was raised to facilitate the said flow. This was called *bandhalling*. In some cases those *bandhals* were raised which could render relief for only a few years. In 1823, the Bhagirathi head in Murshidabad shifted about half a mile to the east of its former position, which paved the way for larger supply of water. The dredging boats were also deployed[73] to maintain the maximum possible flow.

But at the end of 1824, the entrance of the river shifted five miles farther west. The intake of water rose sharply and its breadth was enlarged from 250 feet to half a mile. In the very next year, the river Ganga altered its course and the entrance of the Bhagirathi shifted eight miles to the southeast. "The river became wholly unnavigable as early as November, and it was found that it would be a useless expenditure to attempt to improve it. In spite of a second dredging boat ... all the rivers became closed at the beginning of March 1826".[74] During a flood in 1829, the entrance of the river at Murshidabad "was removed three and a half miles" from its previous position and the "old channel of 1823 re-opened".[75] For heavy rains in the Rajmahal hills in 1831-2, the Bhagirathi was again inundated. That cleared away the shoals below Berhampur and re-opened easy communication by small boats. The chief aim was to keep the river navigable at least for a couple of months in a year so that merchandise could be brought and sent. As many as 359 *bandhals* were raised between 1832 and 1835 in different parts of the Bhagirathi and occasional dredging were carried. But the results were not coming. Hence the dredging operations were stopped in February 1835.[76] Again, between 1837 and 1840, the flow of water in the Bhagirathi was good. But in 1842-43, "it was found to be in a worse state than at any time during the previous five years". Serious efforts were made for maintaining the regular flow of water. In 1845-46, the river could be kept open throughout the dry season. But that lasted only for a year and in February 1847 the river became unfordable. As a result, the dredging operations resumed. Suddenly a fresh opening was made from the Ganga to the Bhagirathi. In May, the rains set in and the flow was more than substantial which gave the depth from 5 to 10 feet.[77] Meanwhile the Saraswati on which once stood Satgaon—was "filled up". The lowland which lay between the villages and towns, situated on the west bank of Hooghli on one side, "the now-filled up Surrusutty on the other, extending in length many miles from north to south [*i.e. from the southwest of the town of Hooghli to the vicinity of Sulkea*]" being regularly flooded. Why did those happen? "... The tides of the Hooghli cannot act so powerfully as to keep the channel clear of new accumulations; the consequence is that the beds of these khalls have been raised over the level of the surrounding Country".[78]

For such changes and inundations lands along the course of the river eroded very frequently. Problem of encroachments was another cause of rivers' woes. The district of Murshidabad was regularly affected. In 1790, the height of water in the Ganga "exceeding anything ever known before and the great havoc made on the natural Banks of the river". Soon after that a lot of discussions took place to find out a plan for the safety of the cantonment and Murshidabad town. The Superintendent of Works mooted two proposals viz. to turn the course of the river at Lalbag, a few miles above Murshidabad, and, a strong embankment from Rangamati to Jangipur, both in Murshidabad district.[79] In some places *chars* or land full of clay and sand above the water level used to appear. Similar to the Bhagirathi the river Hooghli also suffered from the same problem. The appearance of *chars* in that river at, Balagarh, Hooghli, all in the district of Hooghli and at Palasi in Nadia, were frequently complained of.[80] The river, even at its lower stream near the mouth at the Bay, also experienced the same problem.[81] A *char*, measuring 238, *bighas* in the middle of the Hooghli between Salkia and Ghusury in Howrah district and a few miles below Calcutta on the opposite side of the river appeared. Some people from nearby areas used to make bricks from the earth, which was being regularly deposited there.[82] These *chars* were the major obstacles for the movements of vessels in the river.

Efforts for Improvements

From the very initial days after the assumption of the *Diwani* of Bengal in 1765, the offcials of the East India Company had been enagaged in maintaining the normal flow of water in the river. In Malda, the Ganga "Once washed the walls of Gour, but it now flows sixteen miles further east".[83] This could happen within two hundred or some more years. The Company's government made occasional surveys of the river in different points to assess the actual fordability in it. From the survey report of G.A. Princep it was known that in the month of April the river "discharges at Sekreegali [*in Malda*] about 21,500 cubic feet of water in a second. The average width of the river…5,000 feet there."[84] Hence, the principal object was then to maintain at least that position.

To augment the flow of water in the river the government instituted a committee, called, the Rajmahal Canal Committee, in the early 1840s. The report and suggestions were presented on 15th February 1841, where the Committee advised for cutting a canal between Rajmahal and Mirzapur in the district of Hooghli. The total length was computed more or less at 129 miles.[85] That the canal with a depth of 6 feet, and having a breadth at bottom of 50 feet was proposed. It was designed to carry 1,178,284 cubic feet of water in an hour.[86] "The comparatively great difference of level between the Bhaugirruttee at Cutwa, and the Hooghli at Mizapur … explains the great tortuosity of its intermediate bed, and the cause of its constant shallowness in the dry season."[87] In the closing decades of the nineteenth century the river was fordable below Katwa in the months of February and March only.[88] It is evident from the keen interest shown by the foreign rulers in keeping the waterways open throughout the year that they wanted to use the channel chiefly for communication purpose. But the people residing along its banks did not share this view. They used to fetch water for irrigation purpose only, which was not to the liking of the rulers. The foreign masters were too keen to maintain the fordability only.

In his evidence before the "Hooghli Commission" in 1853, Major Lang submitted that "when the head of the Bhagirathi was near its present position [*as during Rennell's time*], that river was obstructed annually early in the dry season to such an extent that cargoes were landed in the neighbourhood of Suti, conveyed thence by land to Jangipur and thence taken down the river in small dinghies." [89] The condition did not improve in the earlier decades of the nineteenth century, as we have seen. The fordability could only be maintained by the erection of the *bandhals*. This system of *bandhals* was first introduced in Nadia group of rivers in 1820. A *bandhal* "is a permeable, oblique weir, or spur, placed so as to narrow a wide shallow channel and to guide the current into the channel selected which it improves by the scour which takes place along the face of the bandals [*bandhals*], owing to the rush of water under them".[90] Dredging was also frequently resorted to keep the mouth of the river open. Dredging machines drawn by the bullocks were used by Mr May in

1823 and 1825 and stream power was employed. "Rake dredgers and spiked rollers were also employed to stir up the sand and open the channels, but apparently with little success." Often hand-dredging with the help of spades and shovels were also done.[91] "As a matter of fact the conditions in the Upper section of the Hooghli cannot be said to have altered" since 1750s.[92]

Attempts were made to avoid the difficulties of navigation, particularly, at the James and Mary bar by erecting subsidiary ports lower down the Hooghli from Calcutta. The river route between a point at New Harbour started by Benjamin Lacam in 1795 and the sea was very "intricate and dangerous". Land was sandy and clayey.[93] In 1847, another abortive attempt was made for a dock at Diamond Harbour. One Mr. Leonard placed the first comprehensive scheme in 1865. He proposed for narrowing the channels at Moyapur and Royapur at the mouth of the river by training walls. Those were to guide the ebb and flood currents on to the middle-line of the crossing. As a result the effects of the tides could be restricted.[94] Another proposal was put forward by Sir Charles Harley also in 1865. His scheme was for an "isolated, half-tide training wall in mid-river about 10,000 feet in length" and he disapproved Leonard's proposal.[95]

The Company's officials also assessed the importance of the river channels passing through the Sundarbans. The river Hooghli falls through these forests. A large number of small streams also join the Hooghli here. The Company made a massive drive for clearing the forests. The Sagar Island is one major island in this region. Through this portion tidal waves had been inundating for many centuries. Since big vessels were increasingly unable to enter the port at Calcutta, a new anchorage at the northern extremity of the Sagar Island was established and better embankment was raised to prevent subsidence. The Island was leased out to the Sagar Island Society who had taken all the measures. Upon the pleadings of the Society the government sanctioned funds for raising the *bund* or embankments having a 9 feet base with 5 feet wide top and 4 feet height.[96] Another sum of 3,080 rupees was also sanctioned for making embankments along seven miles between Diamond Harbour and the Baratala river.[97] It could not be made sure whether all the channels of the river Hooghli falling into the Bay were navigable or not. But the pressure on the river was increasing steadily. Calcutta had already occupied a place of prominence in international trade. Hence, entire sea-front of the Sundarbans from Chittagong on the east to Hijli in Medinipur district in the west was surveyed.[98] Still, the human efforts failed to achieve the desired results. When all such works were undertaken Walter Hamilton visited this part of India and produced a book. He saw that the lower parts of Bengal around this river "are overflowed" during the later part of July. That "from an inundation of more than 100 miles in width, nothing appearing but villages and trees, and here and there the artificial site of an abandoned village appearing like an island".[99]

The government officials understood that unless the waterways directly connected with the river Hooghli, were not properly maintained that river would suffer. The major problem was posed by the daily tides of the sea. The tidal bores seriously affected the navigability. Since the flushing depended on the flow of waters from the upper streams their availability was unpredictable. To resist the flood water in some places "insulated habitations and fields considerably raised above the level of the country, exhibit the effects of patient industry".[100] During the Mughal rule rising of embankments and their maintenance had been a serious duty of the *zamindars* in the province. Those embankments were used in two ways, viz., protection from inundations and from subsidence. Apart from these, the embankments used to provide overflow irrigation. But to the English officials this system appeared to be the major cause of the subsidence. By cutting the embankments the farmers used to collect water for irrigation. The officials never favoured that.[101] Their primary objective was to keep the water channels as free as possible.

NOTES

1 P.G. Steven Darian; *op. cit*, p., 135

2 Sir Willian Foster; *Early Travels in India*, p. 24

3 R.K. Mukerjee; *op. cit*., pp.7-8

4 Government of West Bengal, State Gazetteer; *The Rivers of Bengal*. (Calcutta, 2001) Vol. I, p. 37

5 *The Imperial Gazetteer of India: Provincial Series*; *Bengal*. (Calcutta, 1909) Vol. I, p. 6.

6 R.L. Singh ed.; *A Regional Geography* (National Geographic Society of India, Varanasi, 1971, reprint, 2000), p. 258

7 R.K. Mukerjee; *op. cit*., pp. 8-9

8 *Ibid*.

9 *The Imperial Gazetteer..., Bengal*. Vol. I, p. 222

10 "Report on the Hooghly River and its Head-Waters". in the *Rivers of Bengal*, Vol. II, p. 30

11 *The Rivers of Bengal*, Vol. II, p. 31

12 B.N. Ganguli, *Trends of Agriculture and Population in the Ganges Valley*. (London, 1938), p. 205

13 R.L. Singh, *op. cit*., p. 259

14 *The Imperial Gazetteer..., Bengal*. Vol. I, p. 223

15 L.S.S. O'Malley; *Bengal District Gazetteer, Santal Parganas* (Calcutta, 1910), p. 8

16 *Ibid.*

17 *The Rivers of Bengal.* Vol. II, p. 35

18 O.H.K. Spate and A.T.A. Learmonth with A.M. Learmonth; *India and Pakistan: A General and Regional Geography,* (Delhi, 1984), p. 571

19 Walter Hamilton, *Geographical, Statistical, and Historical Description of Hindostan and the Adjacent Countries*, (London, 1820), Vol. I, p. 9

20 O.H.K. Spate etc. *op. cit.*, p. 574

21 *lbid.*

22 B.N. Ganguli; *op. cit.*, p. 203

23 R.L. Singh; *op. cit.*, p. 259

24 B.N. Ganguli; *op. cit.*, p. 203

25 B.N. Ganguli; *op. cit.*, p. 205

26 R.L. Singh; *op. cit.*, p. 252

27 "The Plains of the Lower Ganges" in the *Calcutta Review*. Vol. IX, Jan. 1848

28 Rai Gopal Chandra Chatterjee Bahadur, "Overflow Irrigation in Bengal" in the *Modern Review*, May, 1935

29 J. Ferguson; "Delta of the Ganges" in the *Quarterly Journal of the Geographical Society of London*, 1863. Proceedings of 1 April, 1863

30 R.L. Singh; *op. cit.*, p. 297

31 B.N. Ganguli; *op. cit.*, P. 215

32 B.N. Ganguli; *op. cit.*, p. 245

33 P.L. Madan; *River Ganga*: A *Cartographic Mystery* (New Delhi, 2005), p. 47

34 *lbid.*

35 Madan; *op. cit*, p. 57

36 James Rennell; *An Account of the Ganges and Burrumpooter Rivers* (London, 1781) pp. 7-8

37 James Rennell; *The Journals of Major James Rennell, the first Surveyor General of India: Written for the Information of the Governors of Bengal during the Survey of the Ganges and Brahmaputra Rivers, 1764 to 1767*, T.H.D. Latouche ed. (Calcutta edition, 1910), p. 11

38 *The Journals of Major Rennell* … p. 11

39 *The Journals of Major Rennell* … p. 13

40 *The Journals of Major Rennell* … p. 14

41 *lbid.*

42 Rennell; *An Account* … p. 11

43 Rennell; *An Account* … p. 12

44 Rennell; *An Account*… pp. 12-3

45 Rennell; *An Account*… p. 20

46 R.K. Mukerjee; *op.cit.*, pp. 184-86

47 *The Rivers of Bengal*, Vol. II, p. 35

48 *The Rivers of Bengal*, Vol. II, p. 37

49 *The Rivers of Bengal*, Vol. I, p. 54

50 *The Rivers of Bengal*, Vol. II, p. 62

51 *The Rivers of Bengal*, Vol. II, p. 63
52 *The Rivers of Bengal*, Vol. II, p. 64
53 Quoted in *The Rivers of Bengal*, Vol. II, p. 32
54 Ferguson; *op. cit*
55 S.G. Steven Darian; *op. cit.*, p. 144
56 O.H.K. Spate etc. *op. cit.*, p. 587
57 *The Rivers of Bengal*, Vol. II, p. 82
58 *The Rivers of Bengal*, Vol. II, p. 58
59 *The Rivers of Bengal*, Vol. II, p. 54
60 *B.O.R. Misc. Progs*, 2 May, 1826
61 *The Rivers of Bengal*, Vol. II, p. 70
62 *The Rivers of Bengal*, Vol. II, p. 71
63 *The Rivers of Bengal*, Vol. II, p. 73
64 *The Rivers of Bengal*, Vol. II, p. 80
65 *The Rivers of Bengal*, Vol. II, p. 81
66 *The Rivers of Bengal*, Vol. II, p. 115
67 *The Rivers of Bengal*, Vol. II, p. 116
68 *B.O. Misc. Progs*, 15 March, 1824
69 *B.O. Misc. Progs*, 7 April, 1789
70 *Ibid.*
71 *Home Dept.* (*Public Branch*), 21 March, 1792
72 J.H. Garrett; *Bengal District, Gazetteer, Nadia*, (Calcutta, 1910; Reprint 2001), p. 17
73 *Gazetteer, Nadia*, p. 9
74 *Ibid.*
75 *Gazetteer, Nadia*, pp. 9-10
76 *Gazetteer, Nadia*, pp. 10-11
77 *Gazetteer, Nadia*, p. 11
78 *Railway Dept. Progs.*, 1 April, 1852
79 *B.O.R. Misc. Progs.*, 31 Jan. 1791
80 *B.O.R. Misc. Progs.*, 17 July, 1827; 11 Sept., 1827; 9 Oct., 1827; 15 Jan., 1828; 8 Aug., 1828
81 *B.O.R. Misc. Progs.*, 9 Jan., 1829
82 *B.O.R. Misc. Progs.*, 15 March, 1825
83 *Census of India. 1901*, Vol. VI, pt.1, p. 67
84 *Foreign Dept. (Secret Branch) Progs.*, 15 Dec., 1831
85 Col. D. Macleod and Major W.N. Forbes; *Report on the Rajmahal Canal, dated 15th February, 1841*
86 *Report on the Rajmahal* … pp. 6-7
87 *Report on the Rajmahal* … p.15
88 J.C.K. Peterson; *Bengal District, Gazetteer, Burdwan*, (Calcutta, 2001), p. 5
89 *The Rivers of Bengal*, (Calcutta, 2001) Vol. III, p. 89
90 *The Rivers of Bengal*, Vol. III, pp. 91-92

91 *The Rivers of Bengal*, Vol. III, p. 92

92 *The Rivers of Bengal*, Vol. III, p. 122

93 *Home Dept. (Public Branch) Progs.*, 21 Nov., 1788

94 *The Rivers of Bengal*, (Calcutta, 2001) Vol. III, p. 180

95 *The Rivers of Bengal*, Vol. III, p.181

96 *Foreign Dept. (Public Branch) Progs.*, 8 Feb., 1822

97 *Foreign Dept. (Public Branch) Progs.*, 25 Feb., 1822

98 *Marine Dept. Progs.*, 18 Sept., 1839 and 29 April, 1840

99 Walter Hamilton: *op. cit.*, p. 10

100 Hamilton; *op. cit.*, p. 21

101 *The Rivers of Bengal*, Vol. I, p. 120

2

EMBANKMENTS OF THE RIVER

For the movements and regular erosion of the river Bhagirathi-Hooghli a rich tradition of embankment helped the people residing along the course of the river in arresting those phenomena. Abul Fazl's description on the topography of Gaur, the long time capital, can be used as an example of the embankments in existence. Since the city was situated between the Ganga and the Mahananda there existed a constant threat to it. "Thus occupying, as is the case in all Deltaic lands, the lowest site; and east of it: lies the Kallak Saja marsh, called in the Ain, Chuttia-pattia, into which the drainage of the town opened. Every increase in the waters of the Ganges caused the marsh, which is connected with it to rise, and 'if the (earthen) embankment broke, the town was under water', and the drainage was driven back into the town".[1]

The Mughal administration used to grant remission under the head of *poolbandi* to those *zamindars* who undertook embankment work of the rivers and canals in their respective areas. While visiting Bengal in the 1660s Francois Bernier reached to the conclusion that the river from Rajmahal to the sea was nothing but canal cut by human beings.[2] Bernier drew his conclusion after his visit of Kasimbazar.

The principal embankment of the river Bhagirathi extended in a single stretch from Bhagbangola in the district of Murshidabad to Palasi in neighbouring district of Nadia. Its length was nearly 57 miles.[3] Here "embankments had been erected by zamindars, along the east of the Bhagirathi mainly to protect interior lands from floods".[4] Sir William Wilcox expressed similar views in 1930. To him the "Bhagirathi and other rivers in Central Bengal were originally really canals excavated by the old Hindu rulers of Bengal for the purposes of overflow irrigation".[5] "The Bhagirathi is a typical alluvial spill stream flowing through a bed of its own formation and carrying a charge of very fine sand and silt." Hence " a rise of bed level may possibly be expected, should the deposit be restricted to the river channel by embankments".[6] The Bhagirathi-Hooghli continued to maintain this tradition even in the latter half of the nineteenth century. It was rather a serious omen that substantial portions of land were encroached by it regulary.[7] Hence the length and the process of maintenance of the embankments during those days were commendable. It has also been claimed that the sixteenth century was the time when "the Padma became considerably enlarged, it seems not improbable that the erection of embankments, at any rate on a large scale, dated from that century."[8] As the river water was essential for agriculture that was to be fetched in whatever manner possible. But this often became the source of trouble. The common practice was to cut the mud embankments at convenient places for creating channels to carry water in the nearby fields. This enhanced the possibilities of erosion and then floods. Hence the making and breaking of embankments were common features in the life of Bengal. In majority of cases the damaged embankments caused inundations resulting into loss of life and property. But the " Bhagirathi embankments have been in existence for a considerable number of years and in the circumstances, the rise in flood level cannot be ascribed solely to them".[9]

Bengal also used to receive sufficient quantity of rainfalls every year. The rains in the catchments were a major source of water that was compounded by tidal bores. "... the inundations ... are as much occasioned by the rain that falls there, as by the waters of the Ganges; and as a proof of it, the lands in general are overflowed to a considerable height long before the bed of the river is filled." But the land along the immediate adjacent to the river-banks were nothing but natural embankments which "is considerably higher than the rest of the country, and serves to separate the waters of the inundation from those of the river until it overflows".[10] These portions were highly fertile and their fertility was regularly enriched when the flood water receded. "When embanked, the material from the sea banks in suspension is carried up the channel and should the river have no spilling *bil*, or fresh head-water supply, to reinforce the downward swing of the current, it is deposited in the bed and the river naturally deteriorates."[11] It was argued by some that for the presence of such very strong embankments the delta forming process suffered in the Western Bengal. "The extension of the embankments on the Hooghli has not counteracted ..[*the*] effects [*of the changes in the course of the Damodar and such other rivers falling within the Bhagirathi-Hooghli system*], as the Hooghli's spill has apparently for a long period been restrained by its high and well-formed banks with the ordinary zamindari banks".[12] Those "Zamindari banks were only flood-protective works, and that they were kept up solely for that purpose".[13]

The flow of water in the Hooghli was largely dependent on the discharge by the Nadia rivers. The Nadia rivers were very much flood-prone. But the "only regular embankments on the Nadia rivers are the protective system along the left bank of the Bhagirathi, known in the upper part as the Laltakuri embankment and the Kachikata embankment for a short distance on the left bank of the Mathabhanga". The Laltakuri system was extended above Lalgola to Akriganj.[14] But it will be wrong to conclude that these embankments could always withstand the attacks of high floods. "In addition to the main embankments, there are numerous zamindari bunds of about 3 feet in height, protecting land at threatened points from inundation, and preventing spills from disseminating freely."[15]

The *zamindars* used to take care of the embankments—whether natural or artificial—in their respective areas. Loss of land due to floods or any type of erosion was the principal reason for the loss of revenue. In 1815, Hamilton travelled through Howrah, Hooghli and Burdwan and was surprised to find the production of high quality grains in huge quantities. He came to the conclusion that the better irrigation network was the prime reason for such success. "Though the Mahratta-Afghan wars had thoroughly disorganized the more difficult irrigation on the Ganges Bengal's problem was of different nature." Hamilton thought that "by 1815 the zamindars and tenants of Central Bengal had neglected the clearing of the canals and repairing of the banks …, a work known as pulbandi … This negligence began in Bengal in the troublous Mahratta-Afghan wars, and the early English who were traders and sailors knew nothing about irrigation. Seeing many waterways neglected and unused after the wars, they thought the canals [called by them rivers] were only for navigation and they left them alone".[16]

One of the principal motives behind the raising of those *zamindari* embankments had been irrigation though Sir William Willcocks contested this view. To him those embankments were "only flood protective works, and that they were kept up solely for that purposes".[17] He also held that "embankments had been erected by zamindars, along the east of the Bhagirathi mainly to protect interior lands from floods".[18] "The necessity for embankments … has long been recognised, and they date back to a period anterior to British rule."[19] While placing the reports on the findings of the survey conducted on the Nadia rivers in 1915, Major Hirst came to the conclusion that "perhaps from about 1550 A.D. the spill waters of the Bhagirathi have been practically restricted, by handmade embankments".[20]

The government primarily maintained this and the East India Company followed the practice. The best available evidence of embankments one can gather from certain regions. The districts of Murshidabad and Nadia were two principal districts in western Bengal where the embankments of the Bhagirathi had helped people to save lands from erosions. During the Mughal rule the officials showed least interest in dissecting the anatomy of the rivers. But for the sake and safety on the lands at least one measure was adopted. The principle behind such measure was to have a secured source of revenue.[21] In the later years, particularly in the late eighteenth and nineteenth centuries the government of the East India Company also followed the said tradition. The Company established a separate department to look after those three principal rivers of Nadia under the name of the Nadia Rivers. After repeated surveys the Company found the causes for the decay of the river Bhagirathi. To augment the flow of Bhagirathi, chiefly during the dry-months, the Company's officials took several measures for maintaining the flow of water in the Nadia Rivers. For this, the water channels were to be kept properly.[22] That required constant embanking of those rivers so that normal flow of water did not get obstructed. Murshidabad had one of the best traditions of embankments. Apart from this major one there were also a number of marginal embankments raised and maintained by the *zamindars* "in order to prevent the rivers overflowing their banks ... They are occasionally breached, but great as is the immediate injury caused by such accidents they are often accompanied by compensations. Fresh and rich deposits of silt are usually brought in by the inundation, fertilising and raising the soil."[23]

But floods were never welcome. The officials of the Company were all acquainted with the outfall of such a calamity. Floods meant loss of lives; loss of cattle and crops and, above all, loss of land. The loss of the last item was intolerable. They put their utmost towards the maintenance of the embankments. Often the required number of workmen could not be gathered. The demand of wages was high[24]—the fact itself was a testimony of the scarcity of even unskilled labour in the following years of the famine of 1770. In December 1773 it was estimated by the Governor General in Council that at least 30,000 rupees was required to do some works. But the sanctioned amount was only 8,000 rupees which was considered totally inadequate at that moment.[25]

Despite all types of endeavour and surveillance the regular breach could not be averted.[26] The primary motive was to provide protection to the city of Murshidabad. But all the programmes could not be executed for the lack of adequate fund.[27] Sometimes the effects were severe. As the consequence of the sudden desertion of the prevailing route by the Bhagirathi in 1813, all the embankments along Kasimbazar were breached. Hamilton in his *East India*

Gazetteer of 1815 stated that "in 1813, a canal was dug between the Bhagirathi and great Ganges [*here it was the Padma*], to ameliorate the unhealthiness of the town [*of Murshidabad*] ... by maintaining a permanent stream of wholesome water."[28] The district of Mursidabad attracted constant attention in this regard. The officials of the East India Company never waste any chance for the protection of the riverbanks. Since 1787 repairing of "Pooshtahs" [*i.e.; high embankment*] at Lalbag "City", Bolaukbag and Domcol was regularly undertaken. In 1789, the Governor General in Council deputed an engineer for the repairs of the embankments in the district. He was also asked to report upon "the expediency of Shutting up the River at Lollbaug".[29] In the same year a "modest" amount of 30,000 rupees was spent to arrest the encroachment of the river that had destroyed huge properties during the previous few years. The total length of the works done was 3,743 yards.[30] This work continued for long. But the floods of 1798-99 made havoc.[31] In 1800, some huts on the riverbank were removed at Bolaukbag for strengthening the embankment there.[32] To protect the city of Murshidabad a permanent brickwork instead of usual mud was undertaken. For this the old mint house was demolished and 59 lac pieces of "fine Bengal" bricks were procured.[33] Still the city was threatened on many occasions by the river. The embankments were breached even during the winter of 1799-1800.[34] The "pooshtah" or the high embankments was repaired on a war-footing. That failed to deliver the results on a permanent basis. But there had never been any comprehensive plan though the river Bhagirathi could never be tamed. Particularly the districts of Murshidabad and Nadia had to bear the burnt most.

The officials of the English East India Company and then the other officials had been engaged in saving the lands along the river in Murshidabad also for the presence of the army cantonment at Berhampur. In 1804, the then district Collector was asked by the government to take appropriate measures for permanent solutions so that there would no case for loss of revenue in future.[35] In 1818, the embankments were proposed to be raised suitably in Berhampur.[36] There had been constants demands for allotment of regular funds for the said purpose. Though the demand could not be met, allotments were made sometimes.[37] Brigadier Colin Mackenzie, the then agent of the Company at Murshidabad, in his report of 27 May, 1858 noted that "the Bhagruttee river at present threatens ... a portion of the town of Murshidabad, of various mosques," burial grounds and even the Nawab palace.

Still the river threatened the city of Murshidabad and there had not been any urge on the part of the English Company to take appropriate measures for the safety of the said town.[38]

When the *Nawab* himself cut the embankments of the Moti Jheel or the famous Pearl Lake of the days of Alivardi Khan in Murshidabad city to facilitate the drainage of floodwaters stagnated there, the Collector of the district took serious exception. He was apprehensive of frequent floods in consequence to that act. But he failed to prevent the said act.[39] The Moti Jheel faced other problems too. The head of the Moti jheel was also asked to economise the expenditure in relation to maintenance.[40] Similarly, it was stated that all repairs must be done in accordance to the funds available.[41] Needless to say that the officials of the Company had only money in their considerations and they ignored the actual necessities time and again.

Mushidabad had a long tradition of embankments that was lacking in the remote areas of the south 24 Parganas. Since the 1770s the Company's officials started a systematic reclamation of forestlands in the Sundarbans. The Mughals had no idea about the deep mangrove of the area. From Nadia downward the entire southeastern part of Bengal was *bhati* i.e.; the lowlands, and they had never ventured to move towards that direction. The Company's officials were not of that type. It was these people who could realise the importance of the Sundarbans. First, its location as a place between the sea and the port of Calcutta and, secondly, the lure for land revenue and forest-products made the entire area too important. This was the the prime cause for which the Company ventured into the areas. For its close proximity to the sea the entire southern face of the 24 Parganas had to suffer from daily tides of the sea. Often those tides could reach up to a height of 20 feet.[43] For the absence of proper embankments the river encroached a good portion of land in the neighbouring areas of Calcutta starting form Dakhineswar in the north to Ballia, Medanmall etc. in the south.[42]

Hence embankments assumed importance. In 1781, the annual grant for maintenance of the embankments was not less than rupees 16,300. But this amount was not sufficient as reported in the official quarters. Condition of embankments in the Sundarbans was then deplorable.[43] The question of security for the port of Calcutta from any impending attack from the mouth of the river Hooghli was also resolved. The Company could assess the importance of the Sundarbans. For the sake of the port at Calcutta they earnestly required a free and safe passage up to the mouth of the river at the Bay. The draft of the river Hooghli was to be maintained throughout the year so that the vessels had smooth sailing. Any erosion would cause immense harm. Hence, the river 'bunds' i.e., embankments should be regularly checked. [44]

In the district like the 24 Parganas—where the rivers and several other channels used to criss-cross each other the official attitude here was to maintain those for. communications and drainage purposes. To arrest land-erosion, a special stress was put behind the maintenance of the embankments too.[45] In the southern portion of the district the matter was better focussed. But certain immediate necessities often led to certain actions, which, consequently, helped deterioration.

In this field, the Sundarbans presented a uniqe pattern. There the embankments were necessary for two purposes; (1) for extension of cultivation, and (2) for maintenance of the water channels. How those reclaimed lands could produce good harvest had never been known. The Company's officials had taken several measures in distribution of lease to enthusiast persons in big 'lots'. The 'lot' was very common since each of those had thousands of *bighas* in them. The story of such reclamations is no less interesting than any adventure. Here spread of agriculture and process of embankment were linked with each other. The farmers showed their skill while arresting the salty tidal waters, which inundated the lowlands of the forests twice daily. The Company's only interest was to reap the maximum possible monetary advantages in way of rents and revenues.

Lands in Bandypore under Pargana Ballea in the 24 Parganas were taken from Baranasi Ghose—the then *Diwan* of the President of the Board and one of the most influential Bengalees in Calcutta—for the construction of the Budge Budge fort.[46] The construction of the fort and the embankments went side by side. Within three years more lands were taken from the same Baranasi which was used for embankments.[47] The problems in this part of Bengal differed from those in the districts of Murshidabad and Nadia. The effects of the tides were too serious. Tides arrived at least twice daily. The high tides generally flooded a large area for nearly two to three hours and soon after the low tide reduced the supplies of water to a very considerable amount. To cope with such situations the embankments were very strong in structure. Regular mud filling and close attention were basic points. Here new embankments were raised as and when lands were reclaimed for habitation as well as cultivation. The progress of the work was reported satisfactory from the initial days.[48]

Another very important thing was also associated with such work. The sea-face from the districts of Khulna to Medinipur was full of salt manufacturing pans. Those were called salt *khalary* which were leased out for rents. Any damage to them meants a loss of income. Since trade in salt was then purely the Company's monopoly it had a special interest in keeping them in working conditions.[49] So the embankments must be of permanent nature.

The Sundarbans presented the best possible example for embankments. Through the wide-scale embankments of nearly all the water channels including the river Hooghli the process of land reclamation started there in the earlier decades of the nineteenth century. The reclamation process was very fast and the leaseholders' interest to reap maximum benefit accelerated it. Since the riverbanks were daily flooded by the tidal waves the embankments were raised to such a height to prevent the water from entering into the fields. In the Sundarban forest area embanked low lands were farmed out for making salt.[50] In the district of Nadia, the principal purpose for embankments was to save land form erosion. Any loss of land meant loss of revenue. But in the Sundarbans, lands were embanked for the purpose of reclamation. It was the official policy that no part of reclaimed forestland would remain fallow.[51] The results were positive in majority of cases. Cultivation in the Sagar Island increased rapidly.[52] Facilities along the embanked lands were reaped. The district of 24 Parganas and the Sundarbans in particular—was greatly benefited. Agriculture was carried behind these protective embankments.[53]

It was felt at the official quarter that security and prosperity both depended on better communications. On 9th May 1800, all the district magistrates were asked by the supreme authority to adopt measures for "facilitating the communication between the principal Cities and Towns throughout the different Districts". They were especially asked to maintain the embankments for better road communications.[54] From Murshidabad down towards Sagar Islands the entire course of the river had to be embanked. Diamond Harbour was built in the earlier decades of the nineteenth century and Sagar Island was leased out. A new anchorage for better movements of ships came up at the northern extremity of Sagar. From Diamond Harbour to the new anchorage a strong embankment was raised. That also helped the "Dak Runners" for their speedy movements. These runners were the carrier of postal articles during those days. The embankments having a 9 feet base with 5 feet wide top and 4 feet height were sanctioned.

Though the Company always endeavoured to shift the financial burden on others it could not avoid the responsibility and had once allotted money at the estimated expenditure of 1,000 rupees per mile.[55] Another sum of 3,080 rupees was sanctioned for the protection of Diamond Harbour.[56] Not only these embankments but all others in the nearby areas including the Sundarbans were maintained in such a way that tidal waves could not enter the fields.[57]

But the river was always unpredictable and there were complaints for the breach in the bank. In 1830, the condition of those was reported very serious.[58]

The Company's government put the responsibility on the *zamindars*. "It was, in fact, considered to be a duty of the zamindars 'to secure their lands from inundation by repairing the embankments'. The cost of repairing the *bands* was known as *poolbandi* and was realised by the zamindars from the tenants".[59] A special contract with Burdwan *Raj* was drawn for better maintenance of the entire river and the canal embankments in the districts of Hooghli and Burdwan where the *zamindari* of the *Raj* was spread.[60] As this *zamindari* was considered the most prosperous in terms of agricultural produce, better provision of water and prevention of land-erosion were the prime motive of the government.[61]

A new department was created to monitor the works on a permanent basis and not in a piecemeal manner. "As late as 1833, there was no reliable record distinguishing Government from the *zamindari bands*; and in May 1835, the Superintendent of Embankments remarked that, owing to the gradual disrepair and decay of the latter, every successive flood did more and more damage."[62] Embankments also helped to extend the Diamond Harbour. Lands were purchased and, in some cases acquired for it in the 1830s.[63] Instead of protective embankments often the river and other channels were embanked for only irrigation purpose. The district of 24 Parganas witnessed those. "It was on the 13th February 1838 that Government took over the embankments on the Hooghli at which time much of the water found its way on to the land on both banks." In general estimation the height of the tide had constantly been rising which necessitated the work.[64]

The East India lrrigation Company was engaged to irrigate fields though the Secretary of State in London disapproved the scheme for introduction "of canal irrigation" as that could "affect" the revenue assessments. It was a common apprehension that for the digging of canals the government would lose revenue as cultivable lands were to be dug to extend the canals. By the Act of Government of the India in 1863, the government reserved its right to increase revenue due to the increase in income for "any other cause than irrigation from" the East India Irrigation Company's canals. Still the government expected to distribute the profits arising from irrigated fields among the farmers in way of investments in irrigation.[65]

The Collector, 24 Parganas, in his letter dated, 24th August, 1870 to the Executive Engineer, 24 Parganas, observed, "several embankments have been cut by the ryots for irrigation purposes". This was a very common picture in the whole of Bengal though there had already been a law passed in 1855 which made it punishable as and when an embankment was breached for irrigation.[66] But "The Embankment Act is not, and never has been, in force in the Nadia district, and there were no embankments which are maintained from

Government or public funds. In 1868, the Collector urged the necessity of action by government in the way of repairing existing, and constructing new bunds, as the zamindars could not be relied on". Only after this some funds were allotted but not for embanking any portion of the river Hooghli.[67] The official apathy towards raising embankments of the river in this portion was astonishing. In an article under the title of 'A River of Ruined Capitals', which apperared in the journal *The Nineteenth Century* of January 1888 Sir William Hunter noted that the Hooghli was the "creator and destroyer" of the province in its western part "each autumn, too, the network of currents rend away square miles from their banks".[68]

With the coming of the railways the process of embankments got a new momentum. In the 1840s a railway connection between Calcutta and Mirzapur in the present district of Hooghli was first envisaged. Then some experts expressed their opposition to the said proposal since the proposed line was designed to pass along the course of the Ganga itself.[69] But for the populous nature of the entire region the railway connection was ultimately allowed. Then came, in the forefront the issue for its safety. It was specifically resolved to put up the embankments and to maintain those in proper way.[70]

Being alarmed Mr. Mackenzie, entrusted for the work sought the opinion of Col. Arthur Cotton, then an expert on river irrigation in India. Cotton's suggestion was to raise bamboo works to embank the river on the side of the cities to arrest the immediate encroachments. But he was apprehensive of the success of that project since there was every possibility of the river encroaching the opposite side. To complete the entire work and for its annual maintenance a recurring expenditure of three lacs of rupees per annum was the budget. But for the reluctant attitude of the government nothing could be done.[71] It was once lamented in the official circles that the people here were very timid. They did never protest against the official negligence towards the maintenance of the embankments, and when threatened by the river, they simply shifted their places of residence.[72]

In 1859, the state of the river was a matter of alarm to the Superintendent of the Nadia Rivers. In his letter of 11th April 1859 to the Agent of the Governor General at the Murshidabad Court he wrote that, for the flood of the river entire Jaffergunge area, where once the palace of the *Nawab* stood had been threatened. After the month of May in each year the water level used to rise and without permanent preventive measures those places could not be saved in future.[73]

No doubt the railways helped to extend the embankments but those often put serious obstructions to the natural flow of the rivers. As the primary motive was to connect Calcutta with the rest of India the western part of the river Bhagirathi-Hooghli was affected. This caused stagnation of waters in several pools and marshes, some of which were the creations of that venture. Those pools were the happy breeding grounds of malarial mosquitoes. These types of mosquitoes spread the disease and those were viewed by many as the cause for decline in productivity in the western Bengal in the mid-nineteenth century.

NOTES

1 H. Blochmann; *Contributions to the Geography and History of Bangal* (Calcutta, reprint, 2003), p. 5

2 F. Bernier; *Travel in the Mogul Empire A.D. 1656-1168* tr. A.Constable, revised by V.A. Smith. (New Delhi, reprint, 1989), p. 442

3 L.S.S. O'Malley; *Bengal District Gazetteer, Murshidabad.* (Calcutta, 1914; Reprint 1997), p. 118

4 *The Rivers of Bengal.* Vol. III, p. 45

5 Quoted by S.C. Majumdar in *The Rivers of Bengal.* Vol. I, p. 54

6 *The Rivers of Bengal.* Vol. I, p. 82

7 *Political Dept (Police Branch) Progs.* July 1869. No. B.1/2

8 *The Rivers of Bengal.* Vol. III, p. 45

9 *The Rivers of Bengal.* Vol. ll, p. 82

10 Rennell; *An Account of* … p. 20

11 *The Rivers of Bengal.* Vol. ll, p. 45

12 *The Rivers of Bengal.* Vol. ll, p. 44

13 *The Rivers of Bengal.* Vol. lI, p. 120

14 *The Rivers of Bengal.* Vol. I, p. 59

15 *The Rivers of Bengal.* Vol. I, p. 61

16 *The Rivers of Bengal.* Vol. I, p. 119

17 *The Rivers of Bengal.* Vol. l, p. 120

18 *The Rivers of Bengal.* Vol. III, p. 45

19 L.S.S. O'Malley; *Bengal District, Gazetteer, Hooghly.*, (Calcutta, 1912, reprint, 1997), p. 164

20 *The Rivers of Bengal.* Vol. III, p. 45

21 *B.O.R. Misc. Progs.*, 17 May, 1796

22 *Sudder B.O.R.; Lower Provinces Progs.*, 27 Feb., 1834

23 *Ibid.*

24 *C.O.R. Progs.*, 27 Dec., 1773

25 *Provincial Council of Rev. at Murshidabad Progs.*, 18 Dec., 1773

26 *B.O.R. Misc. Progs.*, 7 Oct., 1800; July 1807 and 26 Feb., 1808

27 *B.O.R. Misc. Progs.*, 9 Aug., 1805

[28] Quoted in *Gazetteer, Murshidabad,* p. 11

[29] *B.O.R. Misc. Progs.,* 31 March, 1789

[30] *B.O.R. Misc. Progs.,* 8 Feb., 1790

[31] *B.O.R. Misc Progs.,* 7 March, 1800

[32] *B.O.R. Misc. Progs.,* 24 Jan., 1800

[33] *B.O.R. Misc. Progs.,* 22 Aug., 1800

[34] *B.O.R. Misc. Progs.,* 24 Jan., 1800

[35] Ber[hampur] Coll[ectorate]; *Letters Received, 1804.* A letter dated 29 May, 1804 from the Board of Revenue to the Collector

[36] Ber. Coll.; *Letters Received,* 1818. A letter dated 16 Feb., 1818 from the Secretary Govt. of Revenue to the Collector

[37] Ber. Coll.; *Letters Received,* 1820. A letter dated 10 March, 1820 from the Secretary, Govt. of Bengal to the Committee of Embankments, Murshidabad, informing about A sanction of Rs. 12,165 and 3 *annas*

[38] Ber.Coll.; Govt. *Letters from May 1797 to1799 on Nizamat Affairs.* A letter dated 1 Aug. 1797 from the Persian Serestadar to the Collector; *Letters Received,* 1809. A letter dated 3 May, 1809 From the Board of Revenue to the Collector.

[39] Ber.Coll.; *Letters Received,* 1823-4. A letter dated 26 Jan., 1824 from the Collector, Murshidabad to the Agent of the Governor General at Murshidabad

[40] Ber.Coll.; *English Correspondence; Nizamat Dept.* A letter dated 15 Aug., 1838 from the Secretary, Govt. of Bengal to the Agent, Governor General at Murshidabad

[41] Ber. Coll.; *English Correspondence; Nizamat Dept.* A letter dated 22 Sept. 1842 from the Commander, 2nd Division to the Agent of the Governor General

[42] *R.B.W.C. Progs.* 19 Sept., 1774

[43] *C.O.R. Progs.* 6 July, 1781

[44] *Presidency Commissioner of the Sundarbans Records.* 19 May, 1832

[45] *B.O.R. Misc. Progs.,* 10 Dec., 1805

[46] *C.O.R. Progs.,* 10 Nov., 1783

[47] *C.O.R. Progs.,* 2 Feb., 1784

[48] *C.O.R. Progs.,* 29 Aug., 1785

[49] *B.O.R. Misc. Progs.,* 15 Oct., 1789

[50] *B.O.R. Misc. Progs.,* 16 Feb., 1830

[51] *B.O.R. Misc. Progs.,* 3 July, 1818

[52] *B.O.R. Misc. Progs.,* 16 July and 30 Nov., 1824

[53] *Census of India, 1951. West Bengal District Handbook, 24 Parganas.* p. lvii

[54] *B.O.R. Misc. Progs.,* 9 May, 1800

[55] *Foreign Dept.* (*Public Branch*) 8 Feb., 1822

[56] *Foreign Dept.* (*Public Branch*) 25 Feb., 1822

[57] *B.O.R. Misc. Progs.,* 24 Jan., 1829

[58] *B.O.R. Misc. Progs.,* 26 Oct., 1830

[59] *Gazetteer, Hooghly,* p. 164

[60] *B.O.R. Misc. Progs.,* 9 April, 1824 and 27 July, 1824

[61] *B.O.R. Misc. Progs.*, 4 Feb., 1817

[62] *Gazetteer, Hooghly*, p. 165

[63] *Sudder B.O.R. Lower Provinces Progs.*, 2 Nov., 1835

[64] *The Rivers of Bengal.* Vol. II, p. 243

[65] *Lt.Governor of Bengal in Revenue Dept. Progs.*, March, 1867

[66] *Judicial Dept.* (*Police Branch*) *Progs*., Nov., 1870

[67] *Gazetteer, Nadia*, pp. 17-8

[68] *Quoted in Gazetteer, Nadia*, p. 15

[69] *P.W. Dept. (Railways) Progs.*, 3 Sept., 1845

[70] *P.W.Dept. (Railways) Progs.*, 25 March, 1846

[71] *Foreign Dept. (Political Branch) Progs.* 7 Jan., 1859

[72] Ber. Coll.; *Books of Letters Issued, Jangipur* vol. 29. A letter dated 31July, 1885 from the Asstt. Magistrate, Aurangabad to the Commissioner, [*probably the Superintendent*] Nadia Rivers

[73] Ber.Coll.; *Miscllaneous Letters Received in 1859*

3

ECONOMIC ACTIVITIES

Under the independent *Sultans* Bengal's agriculture, artisan produce and economy as a whole flourished in many ways. As the control from the then centre i.e.; the Delhi *Sultans* was always nominal, Bengal had no obligation to remit annual tributes to it. This was one of causes for accumulation of wealth here. Moreover, the absence of any history regarding peasant revolt also confirmed the easy life of the common people. This ultimately maintained the power of consumption acquired by the common people.

Now the question is, who were those people of whose livelihood we are talking about? Bengal—as its political boundaries were then assumed—was ruled from Gaur, and, for sometime, from Pandua. The control over the lands far east of the river Bhagirathi-Hooghli was nominal. Even the Mughal might was not able to bring order in those lands. The Mughals had the intention in curbing the Portuguese pirates in the deep of the eastern delta where their writ ruled everything. The Mughals shifted the capital to Dhaka in the beginning of the seventeenth century for this purpose. For one hundred years these arrangements continued. Dhaka and its surroundings were hubbing in activities.

But the shift could not rob the Bhagirathi-Hooghli regions of their economic importance. However 'dead', the western part did never lose its prime position in trade and commerce. Agrarian production could keep its balance with the population in the region. Moreover, sowing of newer varieties helped in changing the crop patterns in many ways. Again, any loss in agriculture was always compensated with artisan produce. Bengal gained its name and fame in producing various types of such articles, possession of which was the bone of contention among the European trading companies from different countries.

Majority of the produce originated in the places along the rivers Bhagirathi-Hooghli. The strong economic activities helped the people residing along their course. The population structure there remained more or less same for a couple of centuries. It was not merely the conjectural compositions of the medieval poets who devoted thousands of words in describing the flourishing trade of a legendary merchant named Chand. The travelogues left by the Europeans can be placed as proof of such buoyancy. The change in the course of the river; diversion of its main water flow to its eastern channel could not minimise the scope of settlement in the region. The availability of easy labour contributed in the economic activities. Not only the manual labour or personal skill of any individual artisan, but also the skill for adaptation of foreign technology made this portion most sought after region in the whole of India in the nineteenth century.

Between seventeenth and nineteenth centuries the history of Bengal was more or less shaped by the people residing along the course of the Bhagirathi-Hooghli. Their life-style can be understood from the chronicles of the economic activities of the region where agriculture and industry were so closely knit that one cannot be treated separately from the other.

A. AGRICULTURE

For long it has been an established fact that the Gangetic delta is rich in agriculture. For the availability of water and for regular visits of floods, often as an annual event, the fertility of the lands along the course of the river Bhagirathi-Hooghli was enviable. It has been suggested that "agricultural development as determined by the extension of cultivation in Western Bengal, which stands second in order of density amongst the natural division of the Ganges Delta". The regions west of the river Bhagirathi had a long history which eventually dates back to the Aryan civilisation.[1] The river helped the entire region in the extension of agriculture, which also received enough rainwater from time immemorial. In fact, the rich agrarian products of this region brought Bengal's prosperity in the medieval period.

The independent *Sultans* of Bengal had either no control or a minimum in the eastern part of the growing delta. Hence, the economic activities of the province in the records of history had emanated from the Bhagirathi-Hooghli region. Needless to say that the river played the most important role in generating such prosperity. For centuries together agriculture depended on this river alone. From an estimate prepared in the 1930s it can be concluded that artificial irrigation in the central and western Bengal covered a very limited quantity of cultivable lands. In Murshidabad it was 28 per cent, in Burdwan 42 per cent and in Hooghli it was 44 per cent of the total arable land.[2] The movement of the Ganga in Bengal was such that for its behaviour the crop pattern varied in Malda. "The rate of rise of the rivers and the time that they remain in flood determine for the rest of the district [*except highlands of the Barind, east of the river Mahananda*] the character of the cultivation, ..., whether a quick-growing crop of rice"... or any other variety,[3] The *Diara* or alluvial river land "are formed by the deposition of river silt in the beds and on the banks of rivers and are most sought after by cultivators. They are renovated every year during the rains by a deposition of silt, and require no measures. They are the most suitable for winter and spring crops, pulses, wheat, barley, oilseeds and vegetable. These also grow the most luxuriant indigo".[4]

But the character of land farther west from the river channel was not so fertile. This zone, better known as "typical dead delta zone"[5] could not produce the same type of crop as available along the close banks of the river. For the eastward march of the main course of the river the western part has been robbed of its natural bounties. This premise has been put forward by a number of researchers for last couple of decades. It is a commonplace observation that for last couple of centuries the delta has been active in the east and not in the west. Since the level of the main channel has risen gradually it failed to receive the entire flow of silt-laden water from the tributaries.

But peasentisation occurred in the western part much earlier than the eastern." "Except for *bils* and marshes and a few patches of jungle there is comparatively little waste land" in Burdwan-Nadia regions. "Even the beds and banks of the *nullahs* and *bils* as they dry up are almost exclusively devoted to the production of rice. There is even terraced cultivation on the slope of the undulating lands".[6] "At the height of the rainy season, when the river comes down in flood, the flood-water with its heavy load of silt flows through the distributaries which overflow their banks and cover the adjoining lowlands with a rich layer of silt. Although the silt, which the Ganges deposits annually, has a large proportion of silica, mica, and argillaceous earth yet it contains a good deal of fertilising properties".[7]

The Ganga alluvium was and is "rich in plant nutrients and organic matter and is alkaline in reaction ..., though the uplands, i.e., the older alluvium, is somewhat neutral in reaction. The riverine tracts are prone to frequent siltation, which mars the proper development of profiles. The grayish colour owes to the existence of fine sands. The interfluvial zones are covered by soils, clayey to sandy in texture depending on the location".[8] For centuries together this silt helped this region to grow its agricultural productions.

There are two main paddy crops. The *Aman* variety is transplanted in May and June, harvested in November-January, thus corresponding to the *kharif*; the *Aus* or *Bhadoi* is a quicker crop, sown with the pre-monsoon rains of April, harvested in July-September. "The rabi crops do not possess the same importance in the Ganges Delta as in the comparatively arid regions of the Upper and the Middle Ganges Valley." A vast quantity of land in the Bhagirathi-Hooghli region was used both for the *Bhadoi* and *Aghani* or aman crops.[9]

The western part offered a variety in crop production for long. The periods of sowing and reaping of each type also differed from one another,which, ultimately, helped the farmers to work in the fields roughly throughout the year. The principal reason behind such diversity was the varied nature of lands themselves. In the Ganges *diara* or the tract along the river in the district of Malda, "the rapid rise and fall of the river level only permits *bhadoi* crops..., whilst in the *tal* [*north of the Kalindri river, which floods deeply and drains by meandering streams into swamps or into the Kalindri*] *aman*."[10]

The southern portion of the district where the Ganga flows is still extremely fertile. Apart from these main crops jute was in serious competition with rice for last few centuries. Ratua, Kaliachak and Manikchak along the course of the river Ganga in Malda has a long history of crop production. The demobilised soldiers of Sher Shah chiefly populated these areas. All those—men and later their descendants—were commonly called *Shersabadias*. They were very good agriculturists and spent much time and labour on the reclamation of land which the ordinary cultivators could never attempt to clear. "In cultivating methods they are superior in every respect to their neighbours.... Generally they make their plots very long and rectangular in shape, so that no time is wasted in continually turning the plough".[11]

The major area of jute cultivation was confined in the eastern portion of Bengal where the availability of water was more in comparison with the western one. But it is wrong to conclude that jute was never grown in the western Bengal. Malda is a part of the *Barind*, or the Ganga-Brahmaputra *Doab* and the lands along the course of the Ganga were extremely fertile. A variety of crops including sugarcane, oilseeds and pulses could be found there.[12]

It has also been a commonplace observation that the rate of growth of population in the active delta, i.e., the eastern part of the river and particularly the present Bangladesh, was much higher than that in the western part since the late sixteenth century. But the growth in the west, though meagre, actually helped in keeping the land-man ratio in a favourable condition. Moreover, the coming of the modern industries since the beginning of the nineteenth century also created a new set of employment not dependent on agriculture.

"The Lower Ganga Plain is endowed with vast stretch of flat lands of fertile soil whose fertility is often revived through frequent siltations and which naturally becomes the most potent resource of the region. The soils in association with climate and surface features have contributed to the development of an agricultural landscape dominated by rice-jute culture".[13] Both Malda and Murshidabad can be placed as examples of varieties of crops. Malda could also provide a good number of employments in the fields. In the last few centuries the lands along the river Ganga had attracted regular immigrations from neighbouring Murshidabad and also from Nadia.[14] Hence the southern portion of the river had been densely populated.[15]

But the erratic movements of the Ganga had their effects both on settlement patterns and on agriculture. "Owing to the changes in the main channel, an estate is often washed away and re-forms on the opposite bank. In this way some estates have been thrown to and fro like a shuttlecock between Malda and Santal Parganas".[16] In Murshidabad, the *Bagri* or eastern half is "as a rule, low and subject to inundation, but the alluvial soil is very fertile. The principal crops are *aus* or early rice and jute, and when they are off the ground, abundant cold-weather crops are raised; but in the lowlands to the south-east, over the tract known as the *Kalantar*, practically the only crop is *aman* …, which depends on flood for successful cultivation. In the *Rarh* or western portion …, the land is generally high, but intersected with numerous *bils* and old beds of rivers. Winter rice is the main staple…, sugar-cane, mulberry, tobacco, potatoes and various vegetables are also grown".[17] "Artificial irrigation is practiced only in the *Rarh* tract owing to the peculiar conformation of the country."[18] For years together artificial irrigation in the *Rarh* had helped to grow more crops.[19] Probably the crop production did not suffer any drastic change in the years 1768-69 and 1769-70 in the lower Bengal covering the Bhagirathi-Hooghli region. But the "deficiency of the currency are so common" that all transactions were affected. The agents of the Company "could not procure sufficient silver to make the customary advances for the investment, while private persons, finding it impossible to recover even good debts on account of the debtors' inability to obtain coin to pay them in, refused to have any commercial dealings".[20] Hence the famine of 1770 was not the real offshoot of any crop failure.

This state of affairs helped the officials of the Company to look into the land settlement process deeply. The rural life of the entire province experienced a sea-change. Huge casuality of both human and livestock was recorded. Similarly, peasant vagrancy[21] changed the pattern of farming as well as settlements. After the famine, Bengal suffered for want of labour for long. The peasant was then very precious. The landholders started searching capable persons who could till lands. New areas were to be found out which could produce enough crops.

The *Char* lands [*the sandy lands which come out above the water level*] in the middle of the river Bhagirathi in the places like Bhagbangola, Islampur, Palasi were all known as most fertile places and the annual revenues generated from these places were much better in comparison with other neighbouring places.[22] A good number of people used to hold lands in newly farmed areas as *paikast* or non-resident holding, the practice which had been prevalent since the Mughal rule. During the farming system [1772-77] in "Hooghli quite a large number of proposals for farming the lands made it possible to accept the most advantageous offers. The *talukdars* and petty *zamindars* engaged to pay government increased revenue in their hereditary possessions".[23] As soon as the Permanent Settlement came into force those lands attracted indiscriminate increase in revenue.[24] In some cases the dead rivers and the *chars* within them also present a vast fertile tract. Though the rains and floods often put hindrance they ultimately helped in fertilising the topsoil. In turn these topsoil was used in reaping winter crops.

How much the river Hooghli was used in the western tract can be judged from the crop pattern in the region—whether that was in Murshidabad[25] or in the present district of Hooghli. In bringing new varieties the Portuguese in Hooghli had a major contribution. While visiting Hooghli between the years 1669 and 1679, Thomas Bowrey was surprised to find a good variety of agricultural products with which the foreign companies used to trade. The volume was so big that consignments towards Persia, Arab, China, and the countries around the South Sea apart from India were too regular.[26] Probably the lands that witnessed the arrival of the foreigners found new crops hitherto unknown. Even once cultivation of coffee was tried in the district of Hooghli.[27] Many new varieties were introduced. Since the land-man ratio was tilting heavily in favour of and a large amount of fields remained uncultivated for long. New settlement and farming started taking place in the region very fast notwithstanding those sufferings. The English brought a large variety of new crops in these regions. The officials sometimes encouraged the indigo planters and such other men to offer advance to the cultivators for sowing *ganja* or *cannabis sativa* for higher profit.[28]

The crop pattern used to vary in the entire zone. The most noteworthy area was Burdwan. "In 1815 Hamilton passed through Burdwan, Hooghli and Howrah [*the original Burdwan raj.*]. Here is a description of this tract by him.

'In productive agricultural value in proportion to its size in the whole of Hindustan, Burdwan claims first rank and Tanjore the second."[29] Though the district suffered for the outbreak of malaria since the second half of the nineteenth century it was famous for its agricultural products. "Burdwan is separated from the Gangetic delta by an important branch of the Ganges ... The soil of most parts of the district differs considerably from that of central Bengal, both chemically and physically."[30] The land formation helped agriculture to grow in huge proportion. " Paddy and sugarcane are the principal crops. They grow both in the laterite clay and the red sand."[31] "The Ganges, in the course of its eastward march, has left long loops of disused channels all along its western banks, and the soil here is waterlogged and swampy. The whole of the eastern tract is extensively cultivated, there are no large uncultivated pastures here, and the density of population is high."[32]

Though the western tract along the river Bhagirathi-Hooghli was less fertile in respect of the eastern, the varieties in crop pattern there could not be ignored. During the Mughal rule wheat was nearly a foreign element in Bengal but in the middle of the eighteenth century its production became increasingly popular along the Bhagirathi. The districts along its course were chosen for its cultivation.[33] Another important crop was sugarcane. The Europeans introduced advanced technologies to refine sugar and exported the product to the western India, which then usually imported sugar from Java as well as China, and to prepare rum.[34] Later on, the Europeans made serious attempts to grow sugarcane in the 24 Parganas.[35] Similarly, potato was a new variety in India and the said crop was initially introduced in these regions. The Company's officials had the view that the Europeans should be involved in increasing the productivity and increasingly agricultural lands were allotted to them to achieve the target.[36]

In the case of fertility and agricultural produce the district of Burdwan presents one of the brightest pictures. But "The Bagri is a unique area for its remarkable distribution and sitting of rural settlements." Certainly the Padma-Bhagirathi tract "with relative heights between 6 m and 9 m are the favourite sites ... Numerous linear settlements hug the Jalangi levee [Murshidabad] as also Malda, 24-Parganas etc".[37] Chiefly starting from Murshidabad down to the Bay of Bengal the eastern tract of the river has long been treated as a store-house of agricultural crops. Murshidabad—though never very famous for productivity—was also known for cotton, indigo and jute cultivation even in the middle of the nineteenth century.[38] Jute and fibres of similar nature were grown for making paper. This crop-variety was introduced by the foreigners in large number. The districts like Murshidabad, Burdwan, Hooghli, the 24 Parganas and Howrah had a good contribution.[39] Often agriculture flourished for the deep interest shown by the traders as well as landholders. "Production of cash crops like oil seeds, mulberry and sugar cane was more than usually expensive and almost entirely based on advances from the traders to cultivators ... In the *zamindari* of Nadia, situated very near Calcutta and linked with the metropolitan market by river, cultivation was almost carried on with the grain and seed advanced to the peasants by petty *mahajans*."[40]

With the progress of time new varieties of crops were also introduced. Apart from jute the new introduction was indigo in the first half of the nineteenth century.[41] Similar was the picture in Nadia where the East India Company's officials constantly encouraged people to grow new varieties.[42] Since the beginning of the 1820s the experiments got momentum. "The country is flat and the general aspect is that of vast level of alluvial plain, dotted with villages and clusters of trees and intersected by numerous rivers, back-waters, minor streams and swamps. The soil is agriculturally classed as highland, and bears cold weather crops as well as rice." The western portion of the district of Nadia is called *Kalantar*, lying between the Jalangi and Bhagirathi rivers.[43] For the system of *utbandi* holding in place of lease the high rate of productivity could be imagined. This system was widely prevalent in the *Bagri* and *Kalantar* areas of Murshidabad and in Nadia. "Under it the tenant pays rent only for the land which he cultivates each year, and he cannot acquire occupancy rights unless he tills the same land for twelve years consecutively, which, in fact, he rarely does. Meanwhile the landlord can raise the rent at his pleasure, and if the tenant refuses to pay, he can be ejected." It is clear that regular cultivations were not possible in those lands. Since the lands of this region were sandy, those often were left fallow to recover productivity.[44] But this observation sounds absurd when one goes to the very next lines in the same text. The *utbandi* rate was higher than the general rate of rent prevalent then. " In 1872,..., the rate of rent for *utbandi* lands was about twice as high as that for leasehold lands."[45] In such tracts indigo and jute were the principal crops. The crop patterns were nearly similar in the nearby areas. Cultivation of indigo at Naihati-Bhatpara area in the 24 Parganas[46] was started in the closing years of the eighteenth century. No doubt those along with other such crops and fruits were introduced during the last two or three centuries.

The lowest portion in the region covers the district of the 24 Parganas that, incidentally, presents a very complex structure. Here the arable lands may be divided into three main classes: (1) the comparatively high-land along the banks of the rivers;(2) the low-lying depressions that stretch away below the river banks;(3) the lands adjoining the Sundarbans.[47]

The Sundarbans covering a vast tract–300 *kos* from east to west and 200 *kos* from north to south was and is the rarest kind of mangrove forest in the entire globe. The writings of Abul Fazl are clear evidence that the Mughals were aware of the forest but certainly not of its potentialities. They failed to appreciate the worth of the resources hidden in the forest. History says that the Mughals did never venture beyond the present Nadia for any reason. Probably the marshy lands, innumerable rivers and channels of various size, jungles and bushes, and above all, damp as well as sultry weather in combine failed to attract the Mughal nobles and their retainers. All of them were men from the dry belt of northern India. There is very little reference of the Sundarbans in the contemporary Mughal records of the sixteenth or seventeenth centuries.

It has been argued that for nearly three centuries the northern boundaries of the forest remained unchanged.[48] Certainly land reclamation was tough job and the principal obstructions came from the nature. But the presence of the Portuguese pirates within the vicinity of the Sundarbans also had serious bearings. It was the credit of the English East India Company to take a vigorous undertaking for the reclamation of lands within the deep of the forest. They were guided both by their financial as well as security outlook. Their first object was to secure the position of Calcutta port. After procuring the *Diwani* of the province in 1765 they started the process at their ease. Meanwhile, Mir Jafar had awarded the *zamindari* of the 24 Parganas to Robert Clive soon after the battle of Palasi in 1757. Clive was not inclined to keep the award for himself and he transferred the right to his masters. Hence both Calcutta and also the adjoining 24 Parganas were easily brought under the administration of the Company.

For the safety of the Calcutta port and also for a regular safe passage to and from it the Company built the fort of Budge Budge, a few miles down from the port on the riverbank. Then it initiated a well thought-out plan for the spread of agriculture and also settlement in the Sundarban area. In 1770 forest areas in the vicinity of Calcutta had been leased out for reclamation. They were known as *Patitabadi Talooks*. From the time of Claude Russell, the Collector General in 1771, grants of lands were made form the forest areas and these grants required first reclamation and then cultivation.[49] Then Mr. Tilman Hinckel, the judge and magistrate of the district of Jessore, accelerated the process of reclamation for agriculture.

The topography of the area was not very congenial for the works. Besides the Hooghli a number of medium and small channels ran criss-cross within the forest and nearby areas. There were the problems of recurring tides also.

Daily at least twice the area was flooded by high tides—often the height of which was twenty feet or more. When the tides started receding they left a huge quantity of silt. In some parts "marsh cultivation"[50] was introduced which induced farmers to settle in those areas. To prevent their accumulation high embankments were necessary and agriculture had long been carried in that region behind the protective embankments "which have to be continuously maintained in order to shut out the ingress of salt water to lands which were brought under cultivation".[51]

In the 1780s the Company put its stress on the fast allotments of forest-lands that were developed as arable fields.[52] The *Patitabad* or the fallow lands were brought under cultivation chiefly on the close vicinity of the rivers Hooghli and Matla.[53] Big quantities of land were leased out to the lessees, who were officially termed as ' lotdars'. Lands were farmed out in 'lots' for very attractive considerations. Cultivation increased in a very considerable manner and the numbers of transfer were also heavy.[54] Contemporary documents are full of such demands.[55] The growth of cultivation was also considerable. To sell the agricultural produce, demands for markets also gathered momentum.[56]

The first systematic rules for the grant of forest lands were made in 1830 which enjoined that 1/4th of the land should be brought under cultivation within five years from the date of the grant of lease. The lease was for twenty years.[57] It was then the earnest endeavour of the Company to bring as much land as possible under cultivation.[58] Rent-free allotments were also prevalent.[59] Mr. Henckell, of Jessore, "perhaps exaggerated when he said that the *ryots* paid at the rate of 3 rupees per bigha for a nominal 5 bighas but actually one rupee per bigha for real 15 bighas. But Henckell also admitted that a *ryot* who held 10 bighas of land never cultivated above 5 bighas,... This was also the practice in Nadia."[60]

To neutralize the effects of the salty water, which regularly flowed with the tides, an extended canal network connecting the Tangrakhali River with the Hooghli was spread.[61] For such activities the demand for land was constantly increasing.[62] To help the new settlers and to have smooth communications with Calcutta all-weather roads were laid.[63]

To offer better terms in 1853, the grants were made for 99 years with rights to perpetual holding; renewal for each period was of 30 years. The revenue assessed then was six *annas* [*an anna = 1/16th part of a rupee*] per acre and did not become payable until the 51st year after a very long and gradual enhancement commencing from the 21st year. The grantees were required to reclaim 1/8th of the area for cultivation in five years, 1/4th in ten, 1/2 in twenty and practically the whole in thirty years.[64] Other allied facilities were also offered to the lessees. One of the primary obligations of those 'lotdars' was the maintenance of the embankments. Later, in 1879, there was an express injunction to maintain at least 3/4ths of the land in a fit state of cultivation.[65] But the yield of paddy was higher than the average yield elsewhere in Bengal.[66] Attraction of lands was such that people from different parts started arriving in numbers. They began to reclaim on their own which was never encouraged by the government.[67] For the high fertility, agriculture flourished and new varieties were experimented as and when those were possible. Even cottonseeds imported from Brazil were sown here.[68] Probably the said experiment failed to yield expected results. Barring one or two such failures growth of agriculture was really noteworthy.

As the government decided to establish a new port on the river Matla not very far from Calcutta and named it Port Canning the growth rate on this side was much higher than other parts of the Sundarbans and their adjacent areas. The reclamation process of the forestlands for agricultural purposes was remarkable. New settlements sprang up and the entire area became vibrant of several activities.

The usual term used to describe the cultivating tenants' holdings was *mourasi* and sometimes, *mourasimokarari* i.e.; a right for perpetuity. Nearly all such tenants possessed registered documents.[69] A new pattern in agrarian life was ushered in through the Sundarbans.

In fact, this part of Bengal witnessed a vast change in the field of agriculture, which spread form a period of no less than three hundred years. Under the Mughals the long days of tranquility helped the economy in several ways. Growth of agriculture helped in the spread of settlements. New areas were populated and new types of crops were often experimented—as and when possible. The legacy was carried on under the English—though the interest of the latter was vastly different from that of the former. Still, the English could be given certain credit for introducing new crops hitherto unknown and for creating newer opportunities in consequence.

NOTES

1 B.N.Ganguli; *Trends of Agriculture and Population in the Ganges Valley*. (London, 1938), p. 223

2 Ganguli; *op. cit.*, p. 267

3 *Gazetteer, Malda*, p. 40

4 Ganguli; *op. cit.*, p. 91

5 Speat and Learmonth; *op. cit.*, p. 587

6 Ganguli; *op. cit.*, pp. 214-5

7 Ganguli; *op. cit.*, pp. 203-4

8 R.L.Singh; *op. cit.*, p. 264

9 Ganguli; *op. cit.*, p. 256

10 *Gazetteer, Malda,* p. 40

11 *Census of India*, 1951; *Dist. Handbook, Malda,* p. xviii

12 Spate and Learmonth; *op. cit.*, p. 582

13 Ganguli; *op. cit.*, p.266

14 *Census, 1951; Dist. Handbook, Malda*, p. xv

15 *Ibid.*

16 *Census, 1951*; *Dist. Handbook*, Malda, p. vl

17 *Gazetteer, Murshidabad*, p. 98

18 Ganguli; *op. cit*., p. 265. *Even in the late 18th century the region used to have certain canal irrigation.* See *C.O.R. Progs*. 2 July, 1781

19 *Gazetteer,Murshidabad*. p. 98

20 *A letter dated 25 Sept. 1769 from the President and Council to the Court of Directors para* 39; quoted in W.W. Hunter; *The Annals of Rural Bengal*. (Calcutta, reprint; 1996), p. 39

21 For details see A. Nag Choudhuri-Zilly; *The Vagrant-Peasant: Agrarian Distress and Desertion in Bengal, 1770 to 1830*. (Wiesbaden, 1982)

22 Ber[hampur] Colle[ctorate]; *The Malikana Register for the years*, 1891-2 and 1894

23 N. K. Sinha; *The Economic History of Bengal* (Calcutta, 1968) Vol. II., p. 70

24 Ber Coll.; *Letters Received*. Assorted bound vol. Extract of a letter dated 19 Feb.,1796 from the Governor General in Council to the Board of Revenue

25 *Gazetteer, Murshidabad*, p. 98

26 Bowrey; *op. cit.*, pp. 132-3

27 *B.O.R. Misc. Progs.* 16 March, 1824

28 Ber. Coll.; *Correspondence in relation to Post Office and others,* 1852-5. A letter dated 24 Jan. 1853 from the Jr. Secretary, Board of Rev. to the Commissioner of Rev. 14th Division, Murshidabad.

29 *Rivers of Bengal.* Vol. I, p. 119

30 *Gazetteer, Burdwan,* pp. 89-90

31 *Gazetteer, Burdwan,* p. 91

32 Ganguli; *op. cit.*, p. 226

33 *C.O.R. Progs.* 1 Dec.1783

34 A. Das Gupta; *Malabar in Asian Trade, 1740-80*. (Cambridge, 1967), pp. 100-02

35 Marshall; 'Private British Investment in 18th century Bengal' *in the Bengal Past and Present*. Diamond Jubilee no., p. 61

36 *B.O.R. Misc. Progs.* 2 March, 1829

37 R.L.Singh; *op. cit.*, p. 277

38 *B.O.R. Lower Provinces; Land Rev.Progs.* 2 Sept.1858, 1 Oct.,1858

39 Hem Chunder Kerr; *Report on the Cultivation of, and Trade in Jute in Bengal and the Indian Fibres available for the Manufacture of Paper.* (Calcutta, 1874) p. 36

40 Ratnalekha Ray; *Changes in Bengal Agrarian Society.* (Delhi, 1979) p. 62

41 *Gazetteer, Murshidabad*, p. 104

42 *B.O.R. Misc.Progs.* 7 March 1828

43 *Gazetteer, Nadia*, p. 4

44 *Gazetteer, Nadia*, pp. 86-7

45 *Gazetteer, Nadia*, p. 87

46 *B.O.R. Misc. Progs.* 10 June, 1800

47 *Census, 1951; District Handbook, the 24 Parganas.*, p. Iiii

48 For details see W. W. Hunter; *A Statistical Account of Bengal Sundarbans* (Calcutta reprint 1999)

49 *Census, 1951; District Handbook, the 24 Parganas*, p. xc

50 Hunter; *Statistical Account....Sundarbans*, p. 21

51 *Census, 1951; District Handbook, the 24 Parganas*, p. lvii

52 *C.O.R. Progs.* 26 Feb., 1784

53 *C.O.R. Progs.* 29 April, 1784

54 *B.O.R. Misc. Progs.* 29 Nov., 1825, 20 Dec. 1825

55 *B.O.R. Misc. Progs.* 23 Nov., 1827

56 *B.O.R. Misc. Progs.* 15 June, 1827

57 *B.O.R. Lower Provinces, Land Rev. Progs.* 25 June, 1850

58 *B.O.R. Lower Provinces, Land Rev. Progs.* 11 Nov., 1851

59 *B.O.R. Misc. Progs.* 9 Dec., 18117

60 N. K. Sinha; *The Eonomic History,* Vol. II, p. 135

61 *B.O.R. Misc. Progs.* 23 Feb.,1807

62 *B.O.R. Misc. Progs.* 23 Jan.,1827

63 *Sudder B. O.R. Lower Provinces Progs.* 5 Dec.,1836

64 *Census, 1951; District Handbook, the 24 Parganas*, p. 1vi

65 *Ibid.*

66 *Census, 1951; District Handbook, the 24 Parganas*, p. 1vil

67 *B.O.R. Lower Provinces, Land Rev. Progs.* 5 July, 1850

68 *B.O.R. Lower Provinces, Land Rev. Progs.* 31 March, 1858

69 *Census, 1951; District Handbook, the 24 Parganas*, p. xci

B. TRADE AND INDUSTRY

Bengal's trade in the medieval and late-medieval period had become proverbial.The economic activities of the entire "province" roughly centred on the Bhagirathi-Hooghli regions. The agricultural prosperity—though slowed down in comparison with the eastern part of the delta—did not lose its importance. Trade was closely related to agriculture. The people got several new avenues for the sharp growth in artisan produce and commercial ventures.

A lot of researches have been done and detail mention of them would sound redundant. Bengal's fertile fields, rich agriculture and excellent river system helped it for centuries to generate and accumulate wealth in various manners. One of the earliest written documents is *Travels of Ludovico di Varthema*, written around 1508, where Varthema, writes on the rich merchants of Gaur with whom none could be compared.[1] Similar was the descriptions in The *Book of Durate Barbosa. Barbosa*, a Portuguese official was in India between 1500 and 1516/17. He could notice the presence of a large number of merchants "strangers from many lands, such as Arabs, Persians, Abexis and Indians All of these were great merchants and they possess great ships after the fashion of Meca; others there are from China, which they call *'Juncos.*"[2] The fine and white cotton cloths were mainly produced for exports. Barbosa could even find some cotton fields in and around the "city."[3] The entire region from Malda down to Sutanuti [*later a part of Calcutta*] and Betore on the western side of the river Hooghli [*presently in Howrah*] had a long history of trade and manufacture. It is claimed that with the sack of Gaur by Sher Khan in 1537 the fortune of this place started declining. "Whilst at the same time a period of development of trade and commerce in Bengal were commencing with the coming of the Portuguese and other traders from the west. This trade gradually introduced a good deal of wealth in the form of specie into Lower Bengal."[4]

Though a pestilence and that too for the recession of the river Ganga in 1573 had its toll, the effects did not last long. There was seldom a reference of shortage of cash currency. Rents were collected mostly in cash.[5]

The trade of silk further enriched the process of monetisation. Malda had been famous even prior to the Muslim conquest for rearing the silkworm. "The Mahomedan conquest is traditionally reported to have caused the manufacture to dwindle away, owing to some religious prohibitions against the wearing of silk. Soon after the desertion of Gaur the industry revived.... It is also recorded that in 1577 one Sheik Bhik, who used to trade in Maldahi cloths, set sail for Russia with three ships laden with silk cloths".[6] Malda had a large number of rearers, chiefly from the *Puro* caste of the Hindus who had colonised some places, English Bazar being the foremost one. The silk generated different types of employments and the labourers were paid in cash. Practically, entire families of rearers or weavers were wage-earners.[7] As Tavernier found a large quantity of silk was consumed locally[8] one can imagine the purchasing capacity of the people. Bengal's wealth was generated in the way where agriculture and artisan craft had nearly equal contributions. The entire region was dotted with several trading marts, majority of which survived for many long years.

The Bhagirathi-Hooghli river system used to connect all those trading marts and manufactories situated on the banks with a larger hinterland, which included the Gangetic valley. Even the introduction of faster and modern devices like railways could not diminish the importance of the said waterways in fostering a growing trade.[9]

Bengal's artisan produce along with its agricultural surplus had made it affluent under the *Sultanate* rule. Commerce used to fetch huge profit and trade balance had been favourable. Years together "....apart from Bengal the sources of silver supply in India were scanty".[10]

Under the Mughal Rule

After the conquest of Bengal by the Mughals the said tradition continued. Under the Mughals, Bengal was seen as a paradise on the earth. For more than 150 years this *subah* or the province witnessed a peaceful atmosphere without any sign of dissent. Though the Mughals were invited with violent oppositions from the local chieftains and there was an armed rebellion against Akbar in 1579-80 the latter years did not experience any of the upheavals of those type. This environment helped Bengal in many ways. There was no administrative oppression, no tariff barrier and, above all, there was no incidence of war. All those combined made the waterways peaceful and movement of commercial traffic smooth. During the rule of Jahangir, .the river Ganga was usually full of trading boats owned by the *beparis* or the traders.[11] Though Malda—where Mirza Nathan stayed for some time was known for its silk, the cotton fabrics were no less important as a manufactory. Nathan purchased a piece of cloth from the mart at Pandua [*sometimes the capital of Bengal under its Sultans*] at the exorbitant price of 4000 rupees.[12] Similar was the experience of Thevenot, the French. He was astonished to find the price of a gold-adorned turban was not less than several Toman [*a currency of Iran; 1 Toman =29.5 Rupees*].[13]

But it is commonly believed that with the changes in the course of the main channel of the river Bhagirathi in the late sixteenth century the western part of the delta gradually lost its earlier vitality. Being moribund, the area failed to generate resources—as a consequence of which agriculture stagnated. But the volume of trade and the artisan produce of various kinds along both sides of the Bhagirathi-Hooghli speak differently. The legendary merchant, Chand, of many *Mangalkavya* fame can be considered as the representative of the era. Chand's vessels carried a number of articles including fenugreek seeds, pigeon-pea, a kind of pulse, oil, ghee or butter-oil, caraway, evergreen variety of pumpkin, coconut, corns, black cummins, cotton cloths.[14]

Chand's story is not history but it presents the picture of trading world of the then Bengal. Moreover, the routes Chand followed covered the Bhagirathi-Hooghli river course, which had a number of urban settlements on its banks. Those included Katwa, Amboa or Kalna, Fulia, Guptipara and Tribeni.[15] Raw silk from Kasimbazar and saltpetre from Patna were the major export items, which were carried by the European merchants. Bengal's *moslin*'was yet to get a strong foothold in the European markets.[16] In the sixteenth century this sea-bound trade was dominated by the Portuguese. For their highhandedness and piracy on the sea the Portuguese attracted the attention of the Mughal emperor. They were ultimately wiped out from the Indian waterways.

Soon after they were succeeded by the Dutch. The "Dutch bring up ships of six and seven hundred Tonns to ride before their Factory at Chinsura".[17] Since the bigger ships failed to reach the port at Hooghli, often goods had to be collected from nearby places and then were sent to Pipli in Orissa on the Bay. Hooghli still was the principal port in Bengal outsmarting its rival Chittagong. "Not long after the campaigns of the Mughal general Munim Khan [1575-76], one observes too the thift of most trade from Satgaon to Hughli[17A] While visiting Bengal in the 1670s Thomas Bowrey noted that out of a number of arms of the Ganga the Hooghli was the most-important. "Up and downs the same a very Considerable Merchandize is drove, and very beneficial".[18] In fact,-the economic activities of the Mughal Bengal were chiefly concentrated around the course of the Bhagirathi–Hooghli channel. "It will be remembered that the active development of the trade of Bengal began when the Dutch and English settled at Hooghli".[19] It is not improbable to conclude that the huge amount of bullion, which was the common import item here, was circulated in this region comparatively in higher degree in respect of others.[20] The frequent arrivals of foreigners in different times have produced a large quantity of information. Their travelogues and diaries help to reconstruct the history.

With the capture of Chittagong from the Arakans the trading arena spread and got the active delta as a hinterland. No doubt, for this, artisan crafts in the traditional centres received required boost in the seventeenth century. The Mughal might was felt and the Portuguese, Magh and Arakan piracy chiefly in the eastern waters was effectively suppressed. "While it has been usual to ascribe the decline of Chittagong to the shift of Portuguese attention westtward-to Hooghli and Pipli-and to the decay of Gaur, one may note in addition that the fading importance of this part of eastern Bengal occurs simultaneously with the rise of the Arakan Port and capital of Mrank-u.... This could be an additional factor to be borne in mind while analysing to reorientation of Bengali external trade.[20A] Bengal's trading empire spread throughout the East and South East Asia. It was a long period of buoyancy. "Bengal attracted migrant merchants from western India. Finally...... Mughal nobility and members of the Bengal, Orissa and Oudh administrations participated actively in trade from the 1640s."[21] In usual course all these helped commercialisation of agriculture and creation of new job opportunities.

With the establishment of the Mughal administration, Satgaon was one of the very important *sarkars* or district which was extended from near the Sagar Island in the mouth of the Bay in the south to a little above Palasi in the present district of Nadia in the north, and from the Kabadak river [*now in Bangladesh*] in the east to beyond the river Hooghli in the west. Hooghli itself was the foremost port then. Under the Portuguese it had already assumed importance as the door to the western commercial world. For enrichment of trade and for domestic works they used to bring a good number of slaves here regularly from the Maghs of the Chittagong hills.[22]

The Mughal administration brought a long-standing peace and order in the entire province. Very soon the status of Hooghli enhanced and other foreign companies from Holland and England started their trade from here. "Up and downe" the Hooghli river "a very Considerable Merchandize is drove.... Especially to the English and the Dutch Nations."[23] This trend continued for long. The nature of articles were also various. The bulk of rice in the seventeenth century found their way towards the Coromandel Coast and also to Sri Lanka and other littoral countries of the Indian Ocean. Bengal stood out for low prices and had a large surplus in provisions available for exports. "There was a regular costal trade in rice, sugar and butter, carried to Coromandel and around Cape Comorin to Kerala. Sugar was shipped to Gujarat and even to Persia while opium was chiefly exported to Kerala. Sometimes wheat was also sent ... to southern India and the Portuguese possessions. Opium, long pepper, ginger and tobacco were exported on Indian 'trading shipping', and gunny bags sent by sea to Persia".[24] Hooghli town was increasingly populous. Thomas Bowrey was surprised that the "great towne" " is a famous and Sumptuous place, adorned with many fine structures and very populous" with a "very large Bazar".[25]

The cotton cloths, white as well as coloured, manufactured in Bengal had a constant demand outside of India. In the opening decades of the seventeenth century the directors of the Dutch company asked for dispatch of 2,000 to 3,000 pieces of Bengal *taffechelas* [*a type of cloth*] regularly.[26] There is a strong point to believe that goods from different parts were regularly brought in the said ports through the innumerable waterways linked with the river Bhagirathi-Hooghli. During the sixteenth century the export items of Bengal were chiefly drawn from as far as place like Allahabad through the river Ganga[27] and the tonnage of the barges ranged up to 400 or 500 tons.[28] "by reason of its Rivers" observed Careri "Bengala is accounted the most Fruitful" province in the Mughal India.[29] But it is a matter of debate whether Bengal had any port other than Hooghli in the beginning of the seventeenth century. However disturbed for piracy, the Hooghli estuary was most frequented then. In 1618 Sir Thomas Roe, the English envoy in the Mughal Court, wrote that "Bengal had no ports but such as the Portuguese possessed for small shipping" and that was no other than Hooghli.[30] During the Mughal rule the Hooghli and its distributaries were most frequented water channels. They also facilitated smooth communications not only within the province but also, with the outside. Though sufficient data regarding Bengal's waterways were scanty still "the river systems of the Ganges....carried a much heavier traffic than" what they carried in the opening decade of the twentieth century.[31]

The tradition continued for long and without any interruption though Bengal had to face number of turbulence and ultimately, became the colony of a foreign trading company. The river routes of which the Bhagirathi-Hooghli remained prime, ably sustained its trade network. In the 1840s the scene remained the same. "The assemblage of these various steamers...of the great leviathans.., and the little iron vessels which paddle away to Allahabad week by week—gives an air of life".[32]

What Hooghli as a port during the major part of sixteenth and seventeenth centuries used to command that importance was shifted to Calcutta.The vast hinterland in the northern India was connected with the outer world primarily through Calcutta. Goods were brought and sent regularly from and to Allahabad. The rise of the English in Bengal had a major contribution in building up a river traffic network. A distance of 850 miles was the river route, which finally could cater the wider, hinterland along the river Ganga. "Other than increased volume and better protection from pirates, which lowered transportation and insurance costs, there were no major changes in river transport in the period 1757-1857."[33]

Calcutta was connected with Rajmahal, Mongyr, Patna, Benares in one hand and Murshidabad, Pabna and other places in the deep east in other hand.[34] The officials of the English Company were able in assessing the importance of the water course. To protect the entire route form its mouth at the Bay the Company employed a good number of police-boats for guarding the river.[35] Hence the economic roadmap which had been laid in the sixteenth century on the banks of the river Hooghli was strengthened with the progress of time. One of the principal aims in laying the railways along the river Hooghli was to tap the industrial items that were then produced on both sides of the river.[36]

European Connections: Early Phase

The Portuguese connected Bengal with the wider Asian as well as Mediterranean trade network chiefly in the earlier part of the sixteenth century. After initial resistance from the local Muslim rulers ultimately the Portuguese had their fortified establishments at Chittagong which was named *Porto Grande* and at Hooghli, *Porto Piquino*. Since Chittagong was largely away from the administrative control of the Bengal *Sultans* the port at Hooghli could be viewed as one of the major ports of Bengal. Satgaon, a few kilometres away from Hooghli on the river Saraswati had been the royal port of Bengal. It was linked with Gaur as well as Pandua, the then capitals under different dynasties of Bengal through the river Bhagirathi or Ganga. For its location no administrative control from Delhi could be possible. Except Gyiasuddin Balban [1266-86] no ruler from Delhi could ever try to impose imperial authority over this part of India. Only Firoz Shah Tughlaq [1351-87] after him ventured to attack Gaur though without a tangible result. This independence from any superior control for long days helped Bengal in accumulating wealth. It is well-known that by his sack of Gaur, the then capital of Bengal in the 1530s Sher Khan, later Shah, acquired huge booty. Hence in the late sixteenth century, Bengal's wealth had become an open secret to all.

Bengal's wealth was generated and the surplus was enjoyed by one large section of people. It was often claimed that the traders of Satgaon were privileged class who did not require travelling to any other place for vending their products.[37] The arrival of Diego Rebello, the factor of Coromandel pearl fisheries in Satgaon in 1535 and his formidable opposition to the Arab ships, prove the growing nature of trade centring around the said port. In the very next year the Portuguese acquired permission from the ruler of Bengal for raising fortified factories both at Chittagong and Satgaon. Later their principal settlement was transferred to Hooghli in 1579-80 as Satgaon faced trouble due to the siltation in the river there.[38] In the 1580s "the Portuguese private traders shifted their settlement to a town much further up the river, which later became

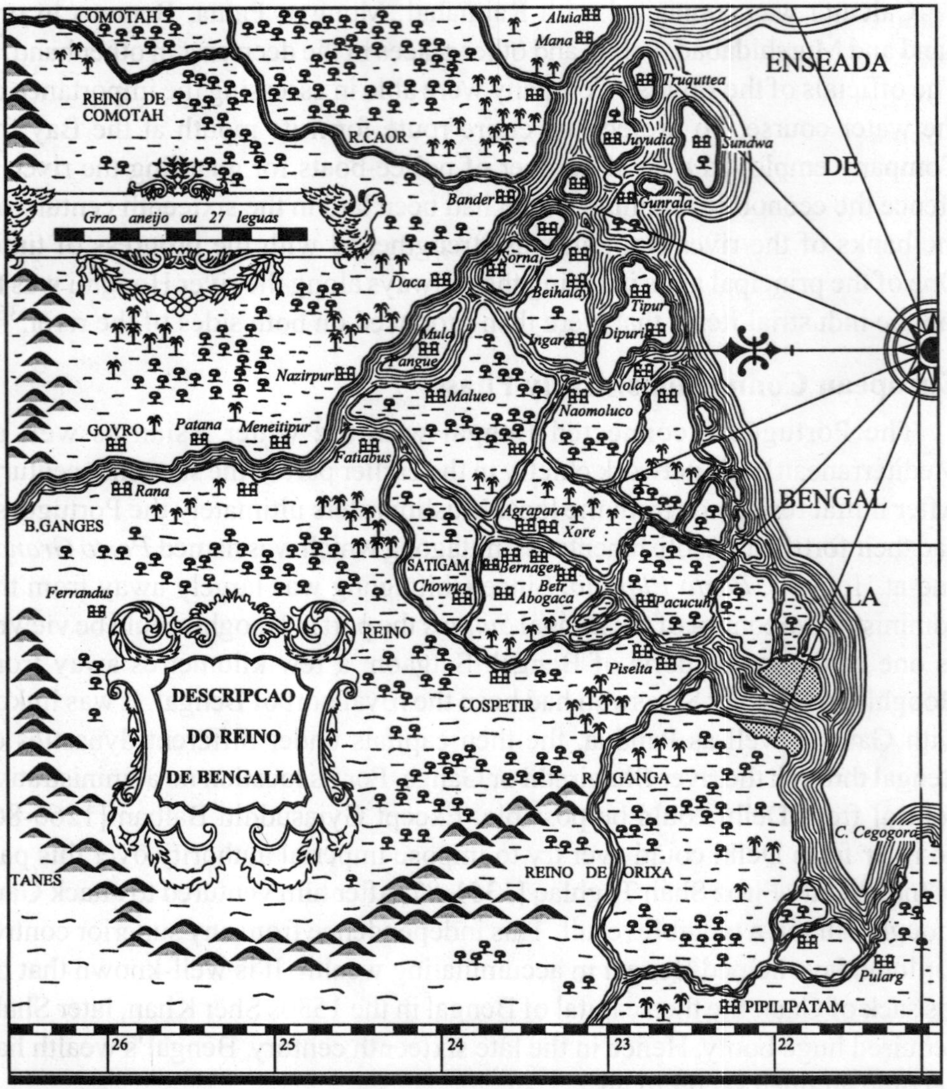

Detail Map of Bengal by Joao de Barros (c. 1559)

known as the famous commercial city of Hugli. By the end of the sixteenth century or the beginning of the seventeenth the Portuguese had managed to create a highly profitable commercial network centred on the river Hugli".[39] The trading activities of the place reached such a peak that, by 1588, Hooghli became a well established town and a "common emporium of Indian and inter-Asiatic trade". It was then the destiny of the rich people for their settlements.[40]

The Portuguese explored Bengal very soon after their arrival in the western coast of India. In 1518, Joao da Silveria with the help of a Bengali youth, tried to start the Portuguese trade. But he failed. This initial failure could not mar their future ventures.[41] By the 1540s, there were two regular carriers to Bengal, one each to Chittagong and Satgaon. Often this trade was directly patronised by the Portuguese monarch.[42] Initially Chittagong had certain degree of importance over the other one. But within a very short period the Hooghli waters started attracting the Portuguese in a bigger way. Writing in 1634, Peter Mundy recorded the presence of two ports—namely Satgaon and Hooghli—while Chittagong was still the only one in the eastern part. Probably bulk of the foreign trade by this time was centred on the Hooghli water. In Peter Helyn's Cosmography of 1568, one can find the following cities: Bangala [*situated on a branch of the Ganga*], Gaur, Tanda—very close to Gaur, Satgaon; [*on the bottom of the gulf of Bangala, a well—traded port*], *Porto Granade*, i.e.; Chittagong, and *Porto Piqueno*. Hence, in the pre-Mughal days, the trade and urban centres were chiefly concentrated along the course of the Bhagirathi-Hooghli.[43] Even shipbuilding activities were also noticed. A contemporary, Pyrard De Laval, found this industry located in Hooghli and Jessore [*now in Bangladesh*]

The Portuguese settlement at Hooghli caused the fissures. This was then the "only large navigable port in Bengal" which had "legendary wealth."[44] Bengal was then directly connected with the European ports thanks to the activities of the Portuguese. After visiting this part of Bengal Caesar Frediriki, the English factor in 1578, wrote "rice, cloth of Bombast of Diverse sorts, Lacca, great abundance of sugar, mirabolans, dried and preserved, long pepper, oyle of zerzeline, and many other sorts of merchandise" were regularly exported through the port of Satgaon.[45] As the trade with Europe expanded, it led to the growth of the settlements of both indigenous and foreigners of different origins. Particularly the weavers and other artisan communities populated this part. Streynsham Master's *Diaries* present a lot of information on the Portuguese trade from this place. "There live many weavers who weave cotton cloth, and cotton, and Tesser or herbal of Several sorts, and from the parts thereabout there is brought silk, sugar, opium, rice, Wheat, Oyle, Butter, course hempe, gunnyes, and many other Coomodityes."[46]

Bengal could taste a different type of livelihood, food habits and agricultural products. All these were absent in many parts of Bengal then. But the Portuguese were no less than a bunch of pirates and resorted to looting and arson against the merchant marines not related to them. They had acquired notoriety for their forcible capture of men and women whom they sold as slaves outside India. For their piracy the coastal habitation of Bengal faced insecurity for many years. But in 1632, under the orders from Shah Jahan, the then Mughal Emperor the imperial army ransacked the Portugese possessions and they were all driven out from Hooghli and their factory. They returned after a gap of few years but the history could not be repeated.

From the 1640s onwards Bengal became the destiny of many till the English East India Company wrote another history in 1757. During the heyday of the Mughals "The main north Indian water route was, of course, the Ganges, linking Allahabad to Rajmahal via Benares and Patna. Beyond Rajmahal, the trade goods moved to and from places like Malda, Hugli and Dacca along the numerous tributaries and distributaries of the same river."[47] Emergence of Dhaka as the provincial capital failed to rob Hooghli of its prime position in trade. Since the decline of Satgaon it witnessed an uninterrupted boom for nearly one hundred years.[48] Wealth was continuously poured into Bengal through this region. The Portuguese failed to keep hold over the river Hooghli for long and the Dutch and the English Companies came into their place. "In the 1720s and 1730s, so large was the annual turnover of the two Companies that the treasures imported by them gave an ever–increasing financial liquidity to the merchants and the political elite of Bengal."[49]

When the Europeans ventured into Bengal the others—whether Indians or other Asians, did not fail to assess its importance. "For centuries a large volume of trade had passed between Bengal and other parts of Asia, either by sea or overland along the river valleys. Groups of Asian merchants, such as the Gujaratis from western India, Marwaris from the north, or Armenians, had settled there. From the mid-seventeenth century The Dutch and English ships began to visit Bengal regularly. French and Danish ships followed at the end of the century, and in the eighteenth century… the Ostend or the Royal Prussian companies also appeared in Bengal."[50] Though the Portuguese had their factory at Chittagong, the centre of trade and foreign settlements were the Bhagirath-Hooghli region. As Satgaon till the end of the sixteenth century had been the royal port of Bengal, this region attracted many. Location as well as political environment also had their respective contributions.

Ralph Fitch, the English merchant, visited Bengal around 1586. He was surprised to observe the wealth and affluence of the town like Tanda [*presently within the district of Malda*] standing at a few miles distance from the river Ganga. Fitch noticed the movement of huge quantity of cotton cloth here. He "travelled from Agra to Satgaon 'in the company of one hundred-and-four score boats'".[51] Similar notes were left by Thomas Bowrey. He mentions about the "'patellas' plying between Patna and Hugli, each carrying 4,000 to 6,000 'Bengala maunds' (i.e. 130 to 200 tons)".[52] It has been computed that goods "from Malda by riverine routes is estimated at Rs 1.5 to 2.5 million and about

Rs.0.75 to 1.25 by land" were annually exported in the late seventeenth century.[53] Hence the Mughal rule unfurled with a legacy of prosperity. This wealth had led Abul Fazl to term Bengal the "paradise on the earth".

One must remember that to the Mughals then Bengal did not usually meant the eastern or southern parts of the province. To Abul Fazl, the regions below Nadia were nothing but *bhati* or low as well as marshy lands. The eastern Bengal was then hotbed of serious rebellions and an easy prey for the Portuguese as well as Arakanese pirates. To combat those menace Islam Khan, the Mughal governor, shifted the capital from Rajmahal [*presently within the province of Jharkhand–opposite to Malda on the Ganga*] to Dhaka in the heart of eastern Bengal. From 1604 to 1704 this city was the capital of the province. Again, Murshid Quli Khan transferred it to Murshidabad. After the acquisition of diwani by the English East India Company in 1765 the capital moved downward at Calcutta. Ultimately, Calcutta became the capital of whole of India and eventually the second capital of the mighty British empire after 1858. The well-known thesis of resultant decay for moribund nature of the Bhagirathi-Hooghli does not hold good if one goes through the history of such a stupendous growth in all fields in this region.

But the observations of Thomas Roe were confusing. He found Bengal a country of 'very poore Gentiles'. "He himself was also confused when he found the place so rich in many articles like wheat, rice, sugar, musk, fine cloth, civit, amber etc. and the people was poor.[54] The inventory of Roe speaks a lot. Some of the items like civit, musk and amber were not produced locally and these were certainly imported here. The Bengalee merchants probably regained some of their lost grounds in the seventeenth century. "With the weakening of Portuguese naval power in the first decades of the seventeenth century, it may be assumed that the indigenous merchants of Bengal grew out of the Portuguese protective umbrella and began trading independently to the major Asian ports".[55] Since Satgaon-Hooghli served as major ports it will not be improper to conclude that this portion of Bengal was the seat of a vibrant economy even after the reduction of the major flow of water in the Bhagirathi.

As Bengal was a rice surplus area its export trade assumed importance particularly, after 1650. Most probably this trade was concentrated in and around the present district of Hooghli. The Dutch first established their factory at Hooghli in 1635 only to be abandoned in the very next year. It was re-established sometimes between 1645 and 1647. Between 1645 and 1651 the Kasimbazar factory was opened. In 1656 the factory at Hooghli was recognized as the principal factory of the region and that status continued for next 150 years. They had other factories at Baranagar, Bazar Mirzapur and Malda, all situated in the Bhagirathi-Hooghli region. For economisation Malda factory had to be closed in 1687.[56] "It appears that some Bengal vessels were making a longer voyage to the Maldives where also they had a market for their rice."[57] In exchange of her produce Bengal used to receive cinnamon from Sri Lanka through the port of Hooghli.[58] This was the region which became most sought after not only by the imperial officials like Mir Jumla and Saiasta Khan but also by the various foreign trading companies. Towards the end of the seventeenth century the following places can be found in the contemporary work, namely, *Khulasatul-Tawarikh*: Akbarnagar or Rajmahal, Maqsudabad or Murshidabad, Mirdadpur [*not identified*], Khizrahati [*31 miles east of Murshidabad*] and Dhaka. Those places also found mention in Van den Broucke's map. In 1666, Tavernier who travelled down the Ganga mentioned having reached a great town called Donapour after having left Rajmahal. The same Donapour had its place both in Van den Broucke's map and in Rennell's. Among the large towns, which were visited by Tavernier, Malda, Murshidabad, Kasimbazar, Nadia or Navadwip and Hooghli were most noteworthy.[59] All these places were known either for their production of silk or for fine weaving.

It is commonly believed that the art of rearing silk cocoons and silk weaving were introduced in India from China through Assam and Bengal. Though this art was experimented in other parts of India none was able to match the products of Bengal. This particular product helped in generating various types of employments and in circulation of liquid money. The silk was the product of the Bhagirathi region. Starting from Malda down to Murshidabad production of this particular commodity involved a lot of persons, a large number of whom were the womenfolk.

The Lure of Silk

Demand for silk reached such a height that the factors of the English East India Company's Masulipattam factory in their letter dated 26 Feb. 1622 to their counterparts at Surat expressed their happiness after "further search—after Beng [ala] silk" which could be in "good quantities procurable in" Masulipattam.[60]

Since 1640, the Dutch East India Company started exporting raw silk from these regions to Japan. In 1641, the Japanese government imposed certain restrictions on the Chinese silk within Japan. As the Chinese variety was the chief competitor of the Bengal silk this decision helped the Bengal exports.[61]

After a few years Tavernier wrote that Kasimbazar alone could furnish about 22,000 bales of silk, which at his equation of a bale with 100 *livres* might mean 2.4 million English pounds.[62] Though sandbars had already affected the river Bhagirathi and Bernier could not sail down Rajmahal the importance of those oft-mentioned trading centres remained nearly the same. Manucci, a contemporary of Bernier, found in 1663 as many as three factories being run by the French, the Dutch and the English at Kasimbazar.[63] The Dutch were exempted from the payment of *radari* or transit duty in the province by the Emperor. The rate of custom duty payable at Hooghli was also reduced in 1679 or later. The said duty was further reduced in 1709.[64] Bowrey also found in Kasimbazar "Stately Factories" of the Dutch and the English.[65] The depth of the Ganga as understood by him always helped easy movements of boats in it. "Some of the barges on the Jamuna were of 100 tuns, while those on the Ganges ranged up to 400 or 500 tuns."[66]

The chief attraction of Bengal during those days was silk. "The silkworm was multivolatine with six crops in the year."[67] Quoting Tavernier, Moreland writes that there had been a huge local consumption of silk. If it was so then the financial capacity and taste of the people could easily be guessed.

"Apart from what was recognised as silk by travellers familiar with the material, Bengal produced at this period fabrics made of some fibres which they compared to silk."[68] Since the Bhagirathi-Hooghli watercourse was directly linked with as far a place as Lahore the trade along its course received uninterrupted boost. We have the record that Ralph Fitch travelled from Agra to Bengal with a fleet of 180 boats.[69] It was not an isolated case. Bengal's silk was then the prime attraction to the European companies. It has been argued that the "Bengal merchants were forced to reduce the volume of their trade with a number of Asian markets..... No doubt the initiative and drive of the Europeans—particularly the Dutch-opened up new markets for Bengal goods in Asia. Thus the Japanese market was opened up.... The level of production, employment and income in the economy must have consequently gone up."[70] The bulk of that trade was controlled by the foreigners. "It will be remembered that the active development of the Trade of Bengal began when the Dutch and English settled at" Hooghli in the 1650s.[71] The English, though not so mighty then, could raise a habitation in Hooghli town.[72] In 1670 the officials of the English East India Company made it clear that Hooghli would be their chief trading centre. Till that day Balasore held that position. Though the river posed as "the perils of navigation" the demand for trade made Hooghli so important.[73] The security umbrella provided by the Mughals helped the traders of all shades. Duties were levied only on the cargo boats and with the money respective *faujdars* used to deploy security personnel on the river to guard it.[74] Hooghli became the principal trading mart from where raw silk in a cheap rate, sugar, bee wax, long pepper, civet, rice, butter, oil, wheat and dried ginger brought from Patna were exported by foreigners. The goods were "all at about half the price of the other places."[75] No political upheaval like the decline of the Mughals, total disorder in the north and central India, the recurring incursions by the Maratha *bargirs* into western Bengal in the 1740s and passing of the state to a foreign trading company could alter the steady curve of such growth. Economic activities—notwithstanding natural calamities like famine, crop failures etc. remained vibrant. Provisions in Bengal was much cheaper then in any part of India, the fact which led the Court of Directors of the English East India Company to conclude that it was "perhaps the most plentiful country in the whole world."[76] Soon after the battle of Palasi, the strength of the English East India company rose sharply. Their object was to monopolise the silk trade. The first filature at Malda was started on the intiative of the Company's resident.[77]

The Company also encouraged privated Europeans in this trade. These people started their factories along the banks of Bhagirathi in the district of Mursidabad. Jangipur and Azimganj on the western bank of the Bhagirati were given importance. Once Jangipur was described as "the greatest station" of the Company.[78] By 1777-79, within India, by virtue of its status as the principal supplier of textiles and raw silk, Bengal completely dwarfed the other two well-known regions, namely Bombay and Madras.[79] The artisan produce and trade were not the monopoly of the foreign companys alone. The indigenous consuming class was no meagre. The *Imperial Gezetteer* compiled in 1909 presented the financial capacity of the population in the lower Bengal chiefly comprising the present district of Hooghli, Burdwan, Medinipur, Nadia, Howrah, the 24 Parganas and Calcutta and some south-western districs of present Bangladesh. Even after a long foreign rule the masses of these regions were termed "much better off."[80] This buoyancy was not a sudden phenomenon. Surely the foreign trading companies and particularly English had reaped the advantage of it.

Towards Colonistation

With the involvement of the Europeans, chiefly the French and the English the European method as filature silk overtook the native method of *khamru*. The volume of trade was such that in the late eighteenth or early nineteenth centuries "a turnover of Rs.10,000 on hat days is common."[81] Amaniganj on the Bhagirathi was an important mart. "the turnover on a single day in the busy season occasionally amounts to a lakh of rupees."[82] Both silk and cotton fabric constituted the artisan craft, one of the chief occupations in the region for long. No political revolution could destroy those. Even under the English the craft did not lose importance. The commercial residents in succession were stationed in Malda for conducting the business.[83] During those fateful years of the Maratha incursions the trade suffered a lot. The merchants had to bear the burden–they were robbed. The invaders ransacked their establishments and they were also squeezed by the administration for maintaining its army. The English factory at Kasimbazar was much worried. The raids had "in great measure prevent the currency of trade and occasioned scarcity of all sorts of grain, the country people flying from their habitations upon every trifling rumor."[84] There have been a lot of writings on the effects of those events over the indigenous trading communities. How far the effects of the Maratha raids could spoil the trading activities is still matter of debate. In the worst years of the raids the factory of the English Company at Kasimbazar were asked to procure one lac fifty thousand *sicca* rupees for investment from the house of *Jagat Seth* and from Hooghli in case of their inability.[85] Bengal's textile and silk constituted the bulk of imports into England till the middle of the eighteenth century. That position did not change during the following years of 1757.[86]

It has been shown that the *dadni* [or advance system] run by foreigners simply declined. But in a recent research it has been pointed out that the Dutch returned to the *dadni* in 1750. This could not have been possible without the economic strength available among the indigenous traders.[87] Traders as well as artisans, though they had to suffer from the disorders, were never pennyless. The instance of Kasimbazar, then the chief silk producing area can be cited. In the wake of the Maratha raids the merchants failed to procure their stipulated quantity and started demanding "extravagant" price as the French, Dutch and even Gujarati merchants had collected silk at the fancied prices.[88] Shortly after 1757 "the filature system was introduced by help of a Frenchman" and, in 1770, Mr. Henchman, an English, built the residency house at the English Bazar as manufactory of *sufeda*, or lace work on cloth. Mr. Henchman had to the credit for introduction of weaving of cloth from silk alone. Between 1760 and 1790, Bengal silk industry experienced a period of boom in its European market. The Asians were also involved.[89] Huge demand of raw silk created vast employment in the Bhagirathi region with the present district of Murshidabad, acquiring its prime position. Still the supply failed to meet the demand. Hence the English resorted to force. "In 1767..., a public announcement at Kasimbazar, accompanied by the beating of drums, ordered all silk reelers working for the Company not to accept work from anyone else." The target was the Dutch who are prevented from procuring silk and then transporting that to Hooghli[90] and the industrial revolution in Europe ultimately spoiled everything of Malda variety. Till that eventuality Malda had a proud presence in the field of artisan produce.The skill of weaving was also manifest in the production of gunny bags. The jute produced in and around these areas helped to develop the said industry. The gunny bags had a long-spread market. Even Sri Lanka required those regularly for use.[91]

Malda had its strong competitor in the shape of Murshidabad. The silk industry of this place was the principal non-agricultural industry since seventeenth century. "Tavernier obtained figures of the output in this region in the middle of the seventeenth century, when the Dutch had established themselves at Kasimbazar and had worked up a considerable export trade. At that period the total output was about $2\frac{1}{2}$ million pounds,.... The Dutch export was, of course, a new feature of the trade: their demand was unsatisfied, and it is probable that production had responded to it."[92] The growth "of a silk culture in Bengal in the 1630s" changed the axis of the trade in India, "Bengal's silk could be produced more cheaply than the Persian or Chinese; it was of equal or better quality than Persian silk."[93]

The volume of production and trade both grew sharply during the century. "The centre of the industry was Cossimbazar, where the [*East India*] Company started a factory at about 1658..... In 1670 a factor 'well skilled in silk' was sent out from England to Cossimbazar, and in 1681, when the Chief was Job Charnock...out of £230,000 sent out by the East India Company as 'investment' to Bengal, £140,000 was assigned to Kasimbazar. From this time forward the Company made unremitting efforts to foster sericulture and extend the trade in silk, until by 1776 Bengal silk, dorve all competitors, except Italian and China silk out of English market."[94] Probably the English themselves did not procure the China silk. Their procurement from Asia was entirely made in Bengal.[95] The production cost was always favourable. "Labour was not only abundant but cheap too."[96] Liquidity of cash and availability of foodstuffs as well as other necessaries helped to keep the wage level low.

With the arrival of Murshid Quli Khan and making of Murshidabad city the capital of Bengal in the first decade of eighteenth century, the trade received further boost.The silk of Kasimbazar was the prized possession of connoisseurs of Europe. The silk of Murshidabad occupied prime position in the trade of Bengal and India as well. "The value of trade...may be realised from the fact that, in the time of Alivardi Khan, raw silk to the value of $87\frac{1}{2}$ lakh was annually entered in the Custom House books at Murshidabad. This exclusive of the

European investments,....."[97] This is buoyancy continued some years after the passing of the *Diwani* to the Company's hand. In 1779, Major Rennell wrote that "Cossimbazar is the general market of Bengal silk, and a great quantity of silk and cotton stuffs are manufactureed here."[98] Probably the effects of the industrial revolution in England was yet to be felt. Hence in the closing decades of the eighteenth century the Company invested nearly twenty lakhs of rupees in the silk filatures and other machinery. The nearby township, Jangipur, ably supported the city of Murshidabad and Kasimbazar. In 1802, the place was viewed as "the greatest silk station of the East India Company with 600 furnaces and giving employment to 3,000 persons".[99] In a single year of 1809 there was an investment of at least 1,12,000 rupees in Kasimbazar and Jangipur.[100] In 1815, Jangipur received rupees 1,08,000 and Kasimbazar, rupees 1,00,000.[101]

But the English had already monopolized the trade. There was a report that the Dutch factory of Kalikapur in Kasimbazar was nearly ruined.[102] A plan was implemented for the settlement of silk-manufacturers along the eastern bank of the Ganga in Malda.[103] The entire region covering both the banks of the river Bhagirathi was then full of silk filatures and weaving systems. After the assumption of *Diwani* the scope and authority helped the English to enlarge their production as well as marketing of silk. "Better investments" were then regularly made for the said purpose.[104] The chosen places were Malda and Murshidabad. There was constant pressure to utilise the full capacity of the Malda filature.[105] These generated a variety of employments—both in the fields and in artisan manufactory. This also helped to generate liquid money and its regular circulation.

The rich tradition of artisan craft and trade continued for centuries. The moribund nature of the delta in this part of Bengal had no effect at all on its economic growth. All these areas became trade and manufacture centres. Since the Bay of Bengal was not so far, salt was being produced by using the saline seawater. The adjacent district, Medinipur, and the Sundarbans in the present district of the 24 Parganas, south and southern districts of Bangladesh were salt producing areas. We have a record that being driven out from Hooghli, Job Charnock, the then chief factor of the English East India Company on eleventh February 1687, took the Tanna fort and plundered several royal salt depots in the locality. But those plunders failed to stop the trade of salt. Similar incidence occurred again when the Maratha raiders overran the entire region in the 1740s.

The credit for the introduction of several types of new varieties—both in agriculture and in artisan craft—certainly goes to the Portuguese. After gaining mercy from the Mughals they had built their fort at Balagarh or Bandel or the strong house as the local people used to say at a place to the north of their former fort and factory at Hooghli. In 1646 they were allowed to possess 777 *bighas* of land free of rent with a limited version of magisterial power. They were also allowed to build their church there.[106] That was the beginning of a new culture in the history of Bengal, which ultimately paved they way for its subjugation to a foreign trading power. The Portuguese could change a lot of things: the crop variety, artisan products and social arrangements also. From Thomas Bowyer's descriptions written during 1669-79 some data can be collected: "They knit stockings of silk and cotton; they make bread... they make many sorts of sweetmeats."[107] The Portuguese were not the only race from Europe who settled here. The Dutch had their factory in the same area since 1634 and the English since 1651. By 1650 Hooghli became the imperial port of Bengal.

Location also played an important part. "Hugli having the advantage of Situation upon the bankes of the river Ganges,..., was in former times in the prosperity of the Portuguez when in their possession sailed to yearly from India and Malaya with 60: 80: to 100: vessels."[108] Chiefly the western bank of the river Hooghli on the north of Calcutta became the hub of the foreign companies in the seventeenth and eighteenth centuries. Hooghli town was the seat of the Portuguese, Chinsura—just adjacent south of Hooghli—was occupied by the Dutch; Chandannagar or Chandernagar, a few miles of south Chinsura was the seat of the French since 1673; Srirampur or Searampur at the south east of Chandannagar was the seat of the Danes since 1755 as their first factory at the Gondalpara in the south east of Chandannagar had to be closed for the alleged official tyranny. On the other side i.e., on the eastern bank the Dutch had their second factory at Baranagar-a few miles north of Calcutta and adjacent to Dakhineswar.

The production systems in the Dutch factory at Chinsura was modelled after the prevailing European factory system employing daily wage-earners on the basis of division of labour.[109] The volume of purchase from Bengal was such that, only in 1674, the Dutch in Chinsura brought 24 tons of gold with some other, metals like copper, tin etc. The imported item also included "Brimstone, Quicksilver, Vermilion and some cloth, which sell not soe well".[110] The quality of cloth was certainly not up to the expected standard the fact that amply proved the abundance of finer varieties available in this part of Bengal. The foreigners often used to receive favour from the administration. The rate of customs duty payable at Hooghli was reduced in 1679 to favour of the Dutch.[111]

Being encouraged by the success of the Dutch, the English East India Company lost no time in curving out their own trading fortunes. In late seventeenth century "the East India Company's factors and even some free merchants had begun to trade on their behalf from Hugli".[112] Apart from the Dutch who was then leading European trading people, a large number of Asians posed as threats to the trading interests of the English east India Company in the first half of the eighteenth century. The bulk of operation was conducted from Hooghli.[113] Since Bengal was "by far the largest Asian supplier of" silk and opium, "it should come as no surprise that goods produced in the region accounted for as much as 40 per cent of the total Asian cargo imported by the Dutch and the English East India Companies into Europe at the turn of the eighteenth century".[114]

All these companies played vital roles not only in the economic activities but also in the political activities. Ultimately, as the consequence of the conflicts between the French and English, Bengal had to witness the worst of events in its history. The wars staged in Europe cast their shadows over the affairs in Bengal. Robert Clive, the conqueror of Calcutta, frightened and then forced Sirajud daulah, the then Nawab to concur with his objectives of destroying Chandannagar in March 1757. Finally Clive could conquer Bengal. With the victory of English over the Nawab, the fortune of the French started declining. In 1823, Bishop Heber could not find a single French ship along its bank.[115] Hence, the allurements were tremendous. Circulation of the liquid money in the later part of the seventeenth century was such that in the whole north "copper becoming expensive over time, and with the increased import of silver into Bengal, silver prices fell, pushing up the general price-level in terms of the silver-based currency".[116]

Like those very well known European trading nations the merchants of Ostend, Antwerp, and other towns in Flanders and Brabant appeared for a very short period early in the eighteenth century. First in 1720, and again in 1721, they sent six ships of which one was consigned to Bengal. In 1722, the company was formed and in the very next year it obtained permission from the Nawab to build a factory at Bankibazar on the eastern bank. "The European nations faced their rivalry, for 'placing obliquely the cap of vanity on the head of pride, the bragged they would sell woollen stuffs, velvet, and silk-stuffs at the rate of gunny-cloth.'The other Europeans accordingly intrigued against them, and gained over the *Faujder* of Hooghli, got him to induce the Nawab to order the closure of the factory."[117]

The Prussian also tried for having their settlement on the bank of the river of Hooghli. Having gained possession of East Friesland in 1744, Frederick, the Great of Prussia tried to convert its capital, Embeden into a northern port. Hence in 1753, he founded the *Bengalische Handels-Gesellschaft* or the Bengal

Company of Embeden. But they had serious problem in Bengal. "If the Germans come here' the Nawab wrote to the English, it will be very bad for all Europeans, but for you worst of all, and you will afterwards repent it.... Therefore take care that these German ships do not come." Still in 1752-53, the Prussians established a factory a mile south of Chandannagar. But they could not survive.[118]

For the sake of trade, conflict among the European nations were then a very common picture. They usually tried to exhibit the same aggression against the local rulers as and when those suited their respective interests. The Portuguese had initiated the game of which we have mentioned a few. But the Dutch did never show such inclinations. They also gave settlement to the Armenians who had come in this part long ago and had their establishments mainly at Kasimbazar. In 1717, some leading Armenian merchants helped the English factory at Calcutta in obtaining the famous *farman* for nearly a duty-free trade in Bengal from the Emperor of Delhi. The political clout of the Armenians probably was the eye-opener to the English.

Presence of a large number of foreigners in the Bhagirathi-Hooghli region helped the trading activities in different parts of Bengal. It is true that prior to the rise of the European companies there had been traders of various types. But the Europeans were of different sorts. They came here as the employees of the companies, generally joint stock in character, who had a vast network spreading different parts of the globe. Hence the investment and procurements were usually huge in quantity. Moreover, there were fixed times for the arrivals and departures of the ships in and from India. These companies were also engaged in mutual competitions among themselves, which lead each of them to concentrate as deep as possible in procuring chosen articles in chosen price. For their trading ventures Bengal witnessed unique system. They employed a large number of brokers. "The European Companies' brokers were often considerable merchants with independent trading activities of their own." When working for the Europeans they usually charged commissions of 1 to 2 per cent according to the class of goods. There are references to *dalals* [or brokers] being "accustomed with and appointed by the Government to particular lines of business in different parts of Bengal."[119] Sometimes the foreigners tried to resolve their differences mutually so that the local agent could not ride upon them. The French governor of Chandannagar, Dupleix, once tried to do that in 1763 to fix the rate of saltpeter, which had then been in huge demand. Before the 1750s usually the Dutch scored over their English and French rivals.[120] But they could not continue with this dominance.

Then eighteenth century witnessed the metamorphosis. The 1750s was the decade which saw the rise of the English East India Company at the expense of other even the independent Nawab. During the century "Bengal occupied the central place among British interests in Asia"[121]. To procure the product of Bengal the foreign merchants used to bring species and pumped those into the Bengal economy.[122] Very soon the English understood the depth of Bengal's economy. The entire century saw the arrival of those people whether employees of the Company or as free merchants in increasing numbers. Making Calcutta their centre these people spread over the entire province. When the Company's only aim was to enlarge the volume of trade and to secure the funds for 'investments' the aim of the free merchants was to be rich.[123] The rising number of free English merchants in Bengal soon after the events of 1757 was such that their activities could threaten all the gains that the Company itself had calculated. Bulk of those traders operated from Calcutta as the company did not allow them to function freely in the districts. It was decided in 1764 that "Trade would in future be carried on solely through Indian *gumashtas*".[124] The very action of the Company created a bunch of Indian middlemen, some of whom were associated with the making of Calcutta into a modern city.

For the policy undertaken by the English after 1765 Bengal's pre-emptive position in the trading world suffered considerably. Its policy was to mop up gold as fast as possible. Before 1765 the Company had a large import trade, mostly bullion, varying in amount from 1,700,000 to £1 million. Others also brought bullion in similar fashion. Hence there had never been any currency shortage.[125] Notwithstanding the annual payment at the tune of more than one crore of rupees per annum in the first half of eighteenth century, Bengal was not a pauper—thanks to the regular inflow of bullion. After 1757, the said flow increasingly dried up and the demand on the resources of Bengal began to increase. Both the agrarian and artisan produce chiefly originating in the Bhagirathi-Hooghli region were still matters of envy. Even in the 1760s the English factors had to offer much higher prices for the silk to beat the other European companies and merchants.[126] There was still no demand of foreign made goods in spite of the best efforts made by the English. "...besides the large investments of the different European Nations—the Bengal Raw Silk, Cloths &c. to a vast amount were dispersed to the West and North Inland as far as Guzerat, Lahore, and even Ispahan." All the political changes had no effect on the production and marketing process. It was also claimed that the motto of the administration should be to maintain the said tradition, which had been built up during the rule of Alivardi Khan. During those days "nearly 70 lakhs were entered there only Raw Silk exclusive of the European investment" in the custom house at Murshidabad.[127] The sufferings caused by the famine of 1770 and then several experiments in relation to land revenues made havocs both in rural and urban economy. But the transactions of huge liquid money at the aftermath of the Permanent Settlement in 1793 prove the inner strength of the economy. It is a fact that by 1800, the availability of gold was nominal. Whatever was available, found their place into the Company's treasury. It was then official decision that nothing other than gold and silver could be accepted into the public treasuries. This forced the poor farmers to take help from the money-changers [called *shroffs*] by paying commission at higher rate.[128]

Those trading activities gave required boost to the indigenous industries. Though Dhaka achieved an international fame for its cotton *maslins* the regions along the Bhagirathi-Hooghli were the principal locations for weaving—whether silk or cotton. A lot of things have been written on the silk of Malda and Murshidabad-Kasimbazar. But cotton weaving could not be ignored. Santipur in Nadia[129]; different centres in Hooghli; parts of Howrah and the eastern bank were very known production areas. Kalna in the district of Burdwan on the opposite bank and also certain adjacent areas also flourished as weaving centers.[130] Tefenthaller writes that "Baranagar was famous for its *bafta* cloths, and Price in his, Observations, says the cloth factories there determined Charnock to choose Calcutta" as the English settlement.[131] Baranagar was the Dutch factory where it is said, 3,000 hogs were annually killed and were salted for export. In 1828, the English in lieu of further lands in Chinsura took this settlement from them.[132] Not only that, the foreign companies ran their respective business of cotton products. Some enterprising Indians were there not as the agents and petty traders but as serious competitors of the foreigners. One Bissumbhur Sen had his big chintz manufactory at Rishra a few kilometers south of Hooghli on the river. He with his family members used to run "the oldest and most profitable ...manufactories in the country." Later silk handkerchiefs in bulk numbers were printed here.[133]

Manufacture of cotton cloth in and around Santipur in the district of Nadia assumed a proverbial name even in the face of strong competition raised by the machine-made textiles imported from England in the wake of the industrial revolution. Probably trade and such manufacture helped the people to be rich. It "has a great number of brick houses; it is noted for ... tailors and weavers: fine clothes called *urini* are made".[134] Productions were "as fine as" and to procure those, suitable "investment" were suggested.[135] The procurements by the East India Company even higher from here than those from elsewhere in Bengal. The Company maintained its commercial residency till 1828; "clothes to value of 12 or 15 lakhs were purchased every year by the company from the weavers: the commercial resident had a salary of 42,351 Rupees annually".[136] Similar amounts were also invested for procuring silk as the place produced one of the very finer qualities of silk in the region.[137] Indigo factories also came up. The chief promoters were the Europeans and these people were largely patronised.[138] The volume of production was such that in 1822, the cloth manufactory of the Company alone could employ 5,000 persons.[139] Road communication with the district headquarter was also improved.

Traditional craftsmanship helped the other industries to grow. Use of glazed tiles on the style of the Chinese technology in some celebrated mosques at Gaur is an example of such fine craftsmanship.[140] Humayun is said to have been surprised after visiting the glazed floors in the houses at Gaur. The workmanship usually required a connoisseur's patronage and Bengal's artisans got that all along. No doubt, for many centuries till the rule of Murshid Quli Khan the aristocracy was mainly constituted of foreign elements. But these chosen people maintained and enriched the traditional artisan crafts in their several forms.

Besides silk there were other items too which were not related to agriculture. Ivory carving and bell-metal works were two such crafts. The Nawabs of Bengal had brought the first carvers from Delhi. With the passing of time this became a major industry chiefly in Khagra in Berhampur which place was the only one in the entire province. The same place along with Kandi, Baranagar and Jangipur were also renowned for its bell-metal works. The cotton weaving chiefly centred around Aurangabad, Khagra, Baluchar and Mirzapur.[141] Even in the first half of the nineteenth century the pressure of traffic on the river was such that the administration often failed to regulate those.[142] Change in the course of the main flow of the river still failed to deter the volume of trade and traffic as well as vitality in life.

Later certain other industries sprang up in the region. We have already noted about the cultivation and processing of indigo. Apart from that article cultivation of sugarcane became increasingly popular. Bengal was known for long for its sugar production. But the European method and processing system were introduced. Nadia was one such district, which witnessed such change. Santipur and its adjacent areas produced sugar in considerable quantity—thanks to the factory run by the Company. In 1792, "there were shipped for England from the Santipur factory 4,000 mds.[*around 370 quintals*] of sugar."[143]

Even Sutanuti, northern part of the city of Calcutta, was a strong cotton mart. The derivative meaning of the word Sutanuti clearly shows that this place was a centre of weaving. *Suta* meant cotton thread and *Nuti* meant a bunch of thread. For the growth of Calcutta the weaving community's contributions cannot be ignored.[144] Weaving assumed such importance that in 1758, the English company issued orders for settlements of weaving community in the present district of Howrah [*during Murshid Quli Khan's rule a strip of land on the west bank of the river from Hooghli down to Howrah was separated from Hooghli and raised into a distinct zamindari called Muhammad Aminpur. In 1787, this zamindari was transferred to Nadia and in 1795, the city of Howrah was formed which was ultimately given shape of a separate district.*] But weaving industry collapsed with the mass-scale import of cotton goods from Europe. Similarly, silk rearing in the same region also followed the fate of the weaving in the later half of the eighteenth century. Even after 1765 the commercial activities in that region remained as vibrant as before. In 1784, the officials were found unhappy with the rate of rents collected from the farmer of the *hat* at Muhammad Aminpur and resolved to lease out that on better terms.[145]

In 1774 a group of Company's servants financed for the raising of coal from the large seams in western Bengal. Similarly iron deposits from Birbhum in the heartland of the *Rarh* and copper from Bihar were tried for mining. But the lack of encouragement dampened their initiatives. "The Directors [*of the Company*] were hostile to any development of Bengal's mineral resources which might detract from British exports of metals."[146] All those were undertaken to suit the respective need of the traders. As the political authority was vested with the English East India Company its primary aim was to reap trading benefits as much as possible. No doubt the Mughal officials, were not any exceptions. Mir Jumla and Saista Khan during the reign of Aurangzeb [1658-1707] gained notoriety for resorting malpractices for their private trade. But the individuals like them could not damage the artisan craft and trade of Bengal. Now the English as a bunch of people jumped into the field to extract as much possible to aid the industrial revolution in England itself. As Calcutta was made the principal seat of the Company the entire Bhagirathi-Hooghli region was converted into a field of extraction and experiment too. From the 1770s some "attempts were made" by the Europeans "to diversify Bengal's products... Europeans tried to raise the quality of Bengal's raw silk, indigo, or sugar by introducing new machinery and new expertise".[147]

New ventures were initiated in various ways. The primary objective of the servants of the Company was to spread their activities from their seat at Calcutta. On the other side of the river, Howrah had a strong presence in the industrial map not only of Bengal but also, of the whole of India. In the earlier part of eighteenth century some Muslim families, though not along the bank of the river were engaged in making brown papers. They were called *kaghaji* [the persons engaged in producing *kaghaj* or paper]. Howrah had a tradition for making salt from the saline water of numerous watercourses in the area. That trade continued till the arrival of better quality salt from outside. Salkia was the centre of production, which provided employments to a considerable number of *molunghees*, or salt-manufacturer.[148] To get maximum benefit from the artisan products, the Company's government built an all-season road at Salkia.[149] Very soon a road up to Benares from Howrah was laid.[150] New industries began to flourish hitherto unknown in this region. In the 1840s, "very extensive sugar factories have been built" in and around Bali.[151]

The entire region got its momentum for Calcutta on the eastern bank of the Hooghli. "Neither did contemporaries grasp the importance from a strategic standpoint of Calcuttas' position as the European fort nearest the mouth of Hugli, though they realised the necessity of a European military presence".[152] The period between 1680 and 1740 witnessed a "a tremendous expansion in the value of the Indo-European trade" carried on by the English[153] in which Calcutta rose sharply.[154] The battle of Palasi and the rise of the English made Calcutta the most important urban centre in the whole of Asia. The policy of the Company soon after their victory over the Nawab was to get an enlarged settlement at Calcutta. It persuaded the new Nawab to grant the zamindary "of the grounds to the northward of Calcutta as high as Banquebazar" a few kilometres north of Barrackpur and also "A tract of land to the north east of Calcutta belonging to the *pergunnah* of Annerpoor has been, likewise, applied for in order to square the Companies boundaries."[155]

All the political as well as administrative changes transformed the economic activities along both banks of the river Hooghli when the Company acquired the *Diwani* or the right to collect tax and right of civil administration with judicature. In 1773, the British Parliament by an Act made Calcutta the supreme seat of authority in India. All those acted together in making Calcutta the seat of East-West trade too. The number of ships visiting Calcutta suddenly multiplied. The directors of the Company sitting in London could guess the importance of the changed scenario. They "were desirous of promoting the commerce of Bengal" and "recommended' the erection of a lighthouse at the Sagar Islands[156] in the Sundarbans on the junction of the Hooghli with the Bay. Ultimately all the "factories of the French, Dutch, and Portuguese at Chandernagore, Chinsura, and the town of Hooghli...remained small trading posts".[157]

Lord North's Regulating Act of 1773 made Calcutta supreme in the entire Indian affairs of the East India Company. Calcutta of today owed much to Warren Hastings, the governor of Fort William of Bengal since 1772. In 1774 he was made the Governor General with supervisory power over other two Presidencies—namely, Bombay and Madras—after the enactment of the said Regulating Act. Hence Calcutta was the focussed area in the trade as well as administration of the Company. With the liberation of the colonies in the North America in the 1780s India was viewed as the prospective empire. An increasing number of persons started arriving in Bengal and chiefly in Calcutta. All had a common notion that fortunes were to be made here. They not only started accumulating wealth but also became habituated with leading an extravagant life. "The expense of life for Europeans in Bengal became notorious."[158] Their numbers also rose which certainly put burden on the economy of Bengal. But Calcutta could withstand.[159] Apart from the servants of the Company there were a good number of free European merchants whom the Company's officials looked at askance. Still their arrivals could not be stalled and ultimately, in 1833, all the restrictions on their settlements and trade were to be removed. In this way the number of job-seekers rose.

As the money and finance were prime in the game, Calcutta assumed more importance in the field of international trade. England had been importing tea in exchange of silver from China. The main flow of silver in England was from the Spanish America. Between 1779 and 1785 as a result of Spain's involvement in the American war of independence the said supply dwindled. But England could not stop importing tea from China. Now it invented a new device. It started exporting cotton from western India to China. But that trade was never lucrative. Hence opium was tested and got better result. An increasing amount of opium was brought from Patna and was shipped through Calcutta.[160] Another reason was "to find new ways of transferring money to Britain".[161] Calcutta's trade arms reached as far as South East Asia. "Even Batavia, the capital of the Dutch Indies, was being drawn into Calcutta's orbit".[162]

For the increased handling of goods, employment opportunities were also higher. Increased maritime engagements created the demand for more ships. We have nearly no information regarding the history of shipbuilding in the Mughal era in Bengal. The merchants' vessels as described in the medieval Bengali literatures were nothing bigger than enlarged sloops. The foreign ships primarily ran the maritime trade. But the sudden enlargement of the volume and that too under the English created the demand for more ships of higher burthen. Now Calcutta entered into a new era in her life. "The demand for cheaper ships, however, usually compelled the Bengal builders to use teak only for the vital parts of the ship. The Nonesuch, one of the first large ships built on the Hugli by Colonel Watson in 1781, was constructed of teak planks and sisoo timbers. Henceforward, the Bengal yards developed rapidly with Colonel Watson and Captain Kyd."[163] "From 1781 till 1821 more than 230 ships were built at the Kidderpur Docks at a cost of more than two millions sterling".[164] In fact, starting from the initial decades of the nineteenth century till the partition of India [1947] this Kidderpur port and dock continued to maintain their prime positions in the Indian economy.

The 19th Century Experience

The first field for the deployment of European capital and technology for modern industries and infrastructures was the banks of the Hooghli. In the closing decades of the eighteenth century from Ghusuri to the city of Howrah extended a series of docks and ropeworks. In 1796, one Mr. Bacon opened a dockyard at Salkia, a frigate named the *Orpheus* being the first vessel hauled in for repairs. In 1800, James Mackenzie constructed another dock at Golabari and next year opened another. By this way Howrah got a new identity, till not known in Bengal. A very limited area facing the waterfront was the hub of docks and shipbuilding factories—the scene that surprised Bishop Heber in 1823.[165] Titagarh, a few kilometres north of Calcutta also attracted the attentions of the shipbuilders. Messrs. Hamilton and Aberdeen of Calcutta established a dock-yard here. In 1801, the largest merchantman ever built on the Hooghli, the *Countess of Sutherland*, of 1445 tons, was launched here[166]. Though it was not the motto of the company to help indigenous trade its own interest as well as private Europeans' trading interest were to be looked after. One of the major administrative measures included the abolition of innumerable custom houses kept in the *zamindaries*. By removing those the Company tried to give the trading vessels free movements.[167] Later the then Government of India purchased the Calcutta Docking Company at Kidderpur from the family of Col. Kyd at four lakhs of rupees in 1843.[168] Soon after, for better use of the dock a new one was constructed and the Tolley's Canal was widened for free movement of bigger vessels.[169] Since the surface transport system could not be built for the poor or rather non-availability of adequate number of roads as late as 1837 the river Ganga starting from its principal station at Calcutta up to the deep in the northern India was always busy with traffic.[170]

Howrah also witnessed the rise of the Indian entrepreneurs like Tarak Nath Pramanik who after taking the shipyard of Mr. Beanchemp, converted that into a dock in 1850. He was followed by Jay Gopal Mallik who, with a partnership with Mr. Reid, built the Hooghli Dockyard in Salkia; by

Pitambar Mukherji who with his English partners built the Albion Dock and by Ramkinu Sarkar, Jay Narain Santra and Kali Kumar Kundu. "In 1823, the opening out of the Strand Road in Calcutta....caused the breaking up of the docks, which had been established in Clive Street. Consequently the ship-builders came over to Howrah, and by degrees set up docks there."[171] Bishop Reginald Heber visited this place in the closing months of 1823 and noticed that the western side of the river was "covered with large ships and craft of all kind, and [*the*] suburb....of Howrah, chiefly inhabited by ship-builders"[172]. The first steam tug, the *Falcon* was launched from here in 1829.

In the nineteenth and earlier part of the twentieth century Howrah had an enviable record as the seat of innumerable iron and engineering works of different capacities. In 1811, the Albion Mills started a new era of industrialisation in this part of India. Kishori Lal Mukherji can be termed as the pioneer among the Indians who had ventured for modern iron works in Sibpur, which was later shifted to Salkia.[173] Howrah was chosen for raising the railway workshop in 1855.[174] The arrival of European technology in production on a huge scale brought the modern era of factory system. It was then the ultimate destiny of many entrepreneurs who helped to rewrite the industrial scenario of Bengal. It was the birthplace of many big industries including the Burn and Company, one of the biggest steel mills in the earlier decades of twentieth century.

With the coming of the engineering industry mechanised spinning mills also arrived. Probably in 1794, Mr. Samuel Clark first started cotton spinning for the East India Company itself. By 1822, the Bauria Cotton Mills—the oldest cotton mill in India, came into being. The Englishmen initially owned the majority of the mills. But there was at least one reference of the Rustam brothers- a family of the Parsies in this field. Cotton spinning and weaving were followed by jute industry. Jute as a cash crop became increasingly popular in the eastern Bengal. The crop achieved a global market for its long and fine golden fibers. But the majority of mills, which produced finished goods like gunny bags and hessians were concentrated along the river Hooghli. The jute mills in Howrah predominated as the principal industrial concerns on the European lines.

Along the line of jute mills a number of cotton spinning mills; mechanised bread manufactories; lime and paint works; printing presses; salt crushing mills; oil mills came up. The Europeans led the age of industrialisation on the western model. Some of the leading companies were M/s. Anstruther and Company, Collin Fielman and Company, Cowie and Company, Phoenix Steam Flour Mills under Jessop and Company, Ahmutty and Company, Balmer Lawrie and

Company, Kilburn and Company, Turner Morrison and Company. Besides producing the conventional consumer and capital goods some purely western products were manufacture in Howrah. Bakery was one such. But the presence of Europeans were felt when in 1767 a rum distillery after the western method was opened here. In the 1840s a German firm Putz and Company started operation of a large sugar-house with a rum distillery.[175] For the growth of a variety of industries the port of Calcutta and the water route towards the north had their respective roles. The number of ships visiting the port annually increased. Several regular steamer services between Calcutta and Kalna in Burdwan which were further extended up to Murshidabad helped immensely.[176] In 1842-43, the river carried as much as 120 lac *maunds* of goods and even so late as 1876 carried 40 lac *maunds*.[177] Though the railways after the 1850s had robbed a lot of traffic, the river route was not deserted.[178]

The railways changed a lot. All the major connections were designed to reach Calcutta. The principal aim was to open new and hitherto inaccessible areas for selling goods. The security and fastness provided by the railways were more lucrative than those available in the commonly used water-routes. For these it was commonplace observation that the value of lands along the railway tracks was enhanced.[179] But the officials were not so sure about the financial capabilities of the people, residing along those tracks. It was concluded that the railways would not render any support to them and, hence, the prime object was to multiply goods transport.[180] Moreover, a railway line between Calcutta and Mirzapur, in the district of Hooghli "would be highly beneficial in a military point of view". Still the trade and commerce were to be encouraged.[181] Now for the coming of this new mode of transport the commercial activities along the river got further momentum. The lines were laid along the river course to reap maximum advantage. The railways simply succeeded the transport route already laid down by the river Ganga. In this way after 1757 Calcutta became the "focus of transport and marketing networks, and therefore the base to which all north Indian traders looked and directed their efforts to control".[182] The port at Calcutta practically made the place the only metropolis of eastern, central and also of northern India. The position remained even for some years after the British left India. As large numbers of employments were generated here in the nineteenth century Calcutta became the biggest urban agglomeration in South Asia. A figure of 1905-06 proves the continual growth of the port at Calcutta. Nearly 87 per cent of Bengal's products were exported through it.[183]

In fact, the banks of the river Hooghli from Calcutta to Naihati on the north became gradually urbanised though it was often difficult to distinguish them from villages. Probably for the presence of a large number of modern industries certain municipal amenities were provided and in the Census Report of 1872 all of them were shown as towns.[184] By the turn of the century this part of the globe ultimately became the largest agglomeration of urban and industrial settlements.

NOTES

1 Ludovico di Varthema; *The Travels of Ludovico di Varthema in Egypt, Syria, Arabia Desert and Arabia Felix, in Persia, India and Ethiopia, A.D.1503-1508.* trns. John W. Jones; ed. by George P. Badger. (Hakluyt Society, London,1863), p. 212

2 Durate Barbosa; *The Book of Durate Barbosa.* trns. M.L. Dames (Hakluyt Society, London, reprint, 192 1) Vol. II., pp. 136-40

3 *Ibid*

4 G. E. Lambourn; *Bengal District Gazetteer, Malda.* (Calcutta, 1918), p. 20

5 *Gazetteer, Malda*, p. 53

6 *Gazetteer, Malda*, p. 59

7 *Gazetteer, Malda*, p. 63

8 W. H. Moreland; *India at the Death of Akbar.* (New Delhi reprint, 1990), p. 175

9 *P. W. Dept. Railways Progs.* 3 Sept., 1845

10 Moreland; *Agrarian System of Moslem India* (New Delhi reprint, 1990), pp. 68-9 and H. Nelson Wright; *The Coinage and Metrology of the Sultans of Delhi.* (New Delhi, 1974), p. 160

11 Mirza Nathan; *Baharistan I Ghybi.* Trns. M.I.Borah. (Gauhati, 1936) Vol.II., pp. 691-2

12 *Baharistan*... vol.I., p. 43

13 S. N. Sen ed; *Indian Travels of Thevenot and Careri.* (New Delhi, 1949), p. 52

14 Bipradass; *Manasamangala* in Bengali ed. Achintya Biswas. (Calcutta, 2002), pt.VIII canto, 19

15 *Manasamangala*, pt. IX. canto, 2

16 Moreland; *India from Akbar to Aurangjeb* (New Delhi reprint, 1990), p. 48

17 *The Diarie's of Streynsham Master* Vol.II., p. 83

17A Sanjay Subrahmanyam; *Improvising Empire: Portuguese Trade and Settlement in the Bay of Bengal, 1500-1700* (New Delhi, 1990), p. 120

18 Thomas Bowrey; *op.cit.*, p.166

19 Moreland; *India from Akbar* ..., p. 179

20 Sanjay Subrahmanyam; *op. cit.*, p. 125

20A "the balance of trade was against all nations in favour of Bengal; and it was the sink where gold and silver disappeared without the least prospect of return" Dow; *Hindostan.* Vol. I. p. iii. Quoted in S.Chaudhuri; *From Prosperity to Decline: 18th Century Bengal.* (New Delhi, 1999), p. 23

21 S.Arasaratnam; 'India and the Indian Ocean in the 17th century' in A.Das Gupta and M.N.Pearson eds.; *India and the Indian Ocean: 1500-1800.* (New Delhi, 1999), p. 122

22 Tapan Raychaudhuri; *Bengal under Akbar and Jahangir* (Delhi, 1969), p. 113

23 Bowrey; *op. cit.*, p.167

24 Irfan Habib; *Agrarian System of Mughal India.* (New Delhi, 1999), p. 78

25 Bowrey; *op. cit.*, p. 167

26 Om Prakash; *The Dutch Factories in India,* 1617-23. *A Coltection of Dutch East India Company's Documents pertaining to India.* (Delhi, 1984), p. 66

27 Moreland; *India from Akbar....*, p. 183

28 Moreland; *India from Akbar...*, p. 167

29 *Indian Travels of Thevenot...*, p. 275

30 Moreland; *India from Akbar...*, pp. 46-7

31 Moreland; *India at the Death of Akbar* p. 167

32 Marshmann; 'Notes on the Left or Calcutta Bank of the Hooghly' in the *Calcutta Review.* Vol. 3. No.VI

33 D.Kumar and M. Desai eds. *The Cambridge Economic History of India.* (New Delhi reprint,1984) vol.II. p. 257

34 *P.W. Dept. Railways Progs.*, 24 Sept., 1845

35 *Home Dept. Public Branch.* 6 April, 1821

36 *P.W. Dept. Railways Progs.*, 7 Aug., 1850

37 Mukundaram Chakraborty; *Chandimangala.* Sukumar Sen ed. (Sahitya Akademi, 1984) 7th day; no. 417

38 T. Raychaudhuri; *op. cit.*, pp. 94-5

39 K.N. Chaudhuri; *Trade and Civilization in Indian Ocean; An Economic History from the Rise of Islam to 1750* (New Delhi reprint, 1985) p. 74

40 T. Raychaudhuri; *op.cit.*, p. 95

41 Frederick C. Danvers; *The Portuguese in India* (London, 1894) vol.l., pp.340-41, 358

42 Om Prakash; *European Commercial Enterprises in pre-colonial India* (New Delhi, 2000), p. 53

43 R.K.Mukerjee; *op. cit.*, p. 178

44 K.N.Chaudhuri; *op. cit.*, p. 74

45 L.S.S. O' Malley and Manmohon Chakravarti; *Bengal District Gazetteer, Howrah.* (Calcutta, 1909), p. 20

46 *The Diaries of Streynsham Master.....* vol.II , p. 82

47 T.Raychaudhuri and I. Habib eds. *The Cambridge Economic History of India* (New Delhi, reprint,1984) vol.I, p. 337

48 S.Chaudhuri; 'Rise and Decline of Hooghli' in the *Bengal Past and Present*, Jan.-June, 1967

49 K.N.Chaudhuri; *The Trading World of Asia and the English East India Company, 1660-1760*. (Cambridge, 1978), p. 188

50 P.J.Marshall; *East Indian Fortunes: the British in Bengal in the 18th century.* (Oxford, 1976), p. 5

51 *The Cambridge Economic History.* Vol. I., p. 351

52 *Ibid.*

53 S. Chaudhuri; *From Prosperity...*, pp. 204-05

54 T. Raychaudhuri; *Bengal under Akbar...*, p. 99

55 S. Arasaratnam; 'India' in A.Das Gupta and M. N. Pearson eds.; *India and the Indian Ocean 1500-1800* and the Indian Ocean in the seventeenth century', p. 121

56 Om.Prakash; *European Commercial Enterprises....*, pp. 132-33

57 S. Arasaratnam; 'The Rice Trade in Eastern India, 1650-1740' in the *Modem Asian Studies.* Vol. 22. No.3

58 S. Arasaratnam; 'Ceylon in the Indian Ocean Trade: 1500-1800' in A. Das Gupta and M.N. Pearson eds.; *India and the Indian Ocean,* p. 229

59 R.K. Mukerjee; *op.cit.,* pp. 179-80

60 Foster ed.; *The English Factories in India, 1618-1621.* (Oxford, 1906), p. 45

61 Om.Prakash; *European Commercial Enterprises.....*, p.199

62 Jean Baptiste Tervernier; *Travels in india.* Trns. V. Ball (London 1889) Vol. ll., p. 2

63 R.K. Mukerjee; *op. cit.,* p. 181

64 Om Prakash; *European Commercial Enterprises ...* , p. 133

65 Bowrey; *op. cit.*, p. 213.

66 Moreland; *India at the Death of Akbar.* p. 175

67 Habib; *Agrarian System....*, p. 57

68 Moreland; *India at the Death of Akbar*, p. 175

69 Moreland; *India at the Death of Akbar*, p. 167

70 Om Prakash; 'The European Trading Companies....' in the *Indian Economic and Social History Review.* Vol.I. no. 3

71 Moreland; *India from Akbar.....* p. 179

72 *The Diaries of Streynsham Master....* Vol. II., p. 47

73 Sir Charles Faweett ed.; *The English Factories in India,1670-77.* (Oxford,1952) New series, vol. II., p. 325

74 *B.O.R. Sayer Progs*. 3 May, 1790

75 Foster ed.; *The English Factories in India, 1646-50.* (Oxford, 1914) pp. 337-8

76 S.Chaudhuri; *From Prosperity....*, p. 25

77 P.J.Marshall; ' Private British Investment in 18th century Bengal' in the *Bengal Past and Present.* Golden Jubilee vol., p. 50

78 K.M.Mohsin; *A Bengal District in Transition: Murshidabad,1765-1793.* (Dacca, 1973), p. 17

79 Om Prakash; *European Commercial Enterprises...*, p. 119

80 *Imperial Gazetteer of India,* 1909 vol.l:, p. 72

81 *Imperial Gazetteer...* Vol. I., p. 61

82 *Imperial Gazetteer....* Vol. I., p. 84

83 B.O.R.Misc.Progs. 17 March, 1789

84 *FWIH*. (Delhi,1958) vol.l A letter dated 24 Feb. 1747/8 to the Court. Para, 104

85 *FWIH* Vol. I. A letter dated 10 Jan.,1747/8 to the Court. Para, 173

86 for details, K.N.Chaudhri; *The Trading World....*, pp.540-45, 547-8

87 S.Chaudhuri; *From Prosperity* p.103

[88] FWIH. vol. I. A letter dated 20 Aug., 1757 to the Court. Para, 64

[89] S.Chaudhuri; From Prosperity, p. 64

[90] Om Prakash; *European Commercial Enterprises...*, pp. 279-80

[91] *B.O.R. Misc. Progs.* 1 July 1800

[92] Moreland; *India at the Death of Akbar* p. 173

[93] Holdlen Furber; *Rival Empires trade in the Orient, 1600-1800* (New Delhi, 1990) p. 245

[94] *Gazetteer, Murshidabad*, p. 126

[95] *Om Prakash; European Commercial Enterprises....*, p. 241

[96] S.Chaudhuri; From Prosperity, p. 25

[97] Gazetteer,Murshidabad, p.126

[98] Gazetteer,Murshidabad, pp.126-7

[99] *Ibid.*

[100] Ber. Coll. *Letters Received,* Assorted vol, 1809. a number of challans

[101] Ber. Coll. *Letters Received,* 1815 a number of challans

[102] Ber. Coll.; *Letters Received,* Assorted Vol., 1809. A letter dated 25 Jan. 1809 from the Rev. Board to the Collector

[103] *C.O.R. Progs.* 27 April, 1786, 3 July, 1786

[104] *B.O.R.Misc. Progs.*, 30 April 1804

[105] *Sudder B.O.R. Lower Provinces Progs.* 21 March, 1836

[106] *Gazetteer, Hooghly*, p. 52

[107] *Gazetteer, Hooghly,* p. 55

[108] *The Diaries of Streynsham Master.....* Vol.II., p. 79

[109] *The Diaries of Streynsham Master...* Vol.II., pp. 40-41

[110] *The Diaries of Streynsham Master...* Vol.II., p. 83

[111] Om Prakash; *European Commercial Enterprises....* p.133

[112] P.J.Marshall; 'Private British Trade in the Indian Ocean Before 1800' in A. Das Gupta and M.N.Pearson eds.; *India and the Indian Ocean* ..., p. 288

[113] Marshall; *East Indian Fortunes...*, p.78

[114] Om Prakash; *European Commercial Enterprises...*, p. 341

[115] M.A.Laird ed. *BishopHeber in Northern India: Selections from Heber's Journal.* (Cambridge, 1971), p. 53

[116] *Cambridge Economic History.* Vol. I., p. 335

[117] *Gazetteer, Hooghly,* pp. 88-9

[118] *Gazetteer, Hooghly,* p. 87

[119] *Cambridge Economic History.* Vol.I., p. 343

[120] Holden Furber; *op. cit.*, p. 257

[121] Marshall; *East Indian Fortunes....*, p. 1

[122] *FWIH.* Vol.I. A letter dated 10 Jan.,1747/48 to the Court. Para, 32

[123] Marshall; *East Indian Fortunes....*, p. 3

[124] Marshall; *East Indian Fortunes....*, pp. 129-30

[125] *Cambridge Economic History.* Vol. II., p. 814

[126] *FWIH*. Vol.V. (Delhi, 1949). A letter dated 17 March, 1769 from the Court. Para, 32

[127] *FWIH*. Vol. V..A letter dated 5 April 1769 to the Court. Para, 6

[128] *B.O.R.Misc Progs.* 17 June, 1840

[129] its reputation continued even in the beginning of the 19th century; for details, *Gazetteer, Nadia*, p. 92

[130] *Gazetteer, Burdwan*, p. 123

[131] *Gazetteer, the 24 Parganas*, p. 44

[132] *B.O.R. Misc. Progs.*, 24 Oct.,1828

[133] Marshmann; 'Notes on the Right Bank of the Hooghly' in the *Calcutta Review* vol. VI. No. 4

[134] James Long, 'The Banks of Bhagirathi' in the *Selected Papers* (Calcutta, 1968). p. 74

[135] *C.O.R. Progs.* 24 Sept., 1784

[136] Long; *op. cit.*, p.74

[137] *Home Dept. Public Branch* 12 Oct., 1821

[138] *B.O.R.Misc. Progs.* 23 April, 1789; 26 Jan., 1791

[139] Long; *op.cit.*, p.74

[140] M.Abid Ali Khan; *Memoirs of Gaur and Pandua*. Intro.A.Ray and C.Datta. (Calcutta,1986), pp. 31-5

[141] *Gazetteer, Murshidabad*. p. 140, 145

[142] Ber. Coll. *English Correspondence, Nizamat Dept.* Bound Vol. A letter dated 6 Aug. 1842 from the Superintendent, Khalsa Mahal to the Agent of the Governor General at Murshidabad.

[143] Long; *op .cit.*, p. 74

[144] Long; *Selections from Unpublished Records of Government.* M.P.Saha. ed. (Calcutta, 1973) No.170

[145] *C.O.R. Progs*. 25 Oct.,1784

[146] Marshall; 'Private British Investments..'in the *Bengal Past and Present*. Golden Jubilee Vol.pp. 62-3

[147] Marshall; *East Indian Fortunes ...*, p. 15

[148] *B.O.R. Misc. Progs*. 5 April, 1790

[149] *C.O.R. Progs.* 11 April, 1785

[150] *C.O.R. Progs.* 17 Jan.,1785

[151] Marshmann; 'Notes on the Right Bank of the Hoogly'.

[152] Furber; *op. cit.*, p. 131

[153] Om Prakash; *European Commercial Enterprises ...*, p.239

[154] Furber; *op. cit.* p. 131

[155] *FWIH.* Vol. II. (Delhi, 1957) A letter dated 31 Dec 1758 to the Court. Para, 72.

[156] *FWIH.* Vol.VI. (Delhi, 1960) A Public letter dated 25 March ,1772 from the Court. Para, 8

[157] Furber; *op. cit.*, p.131

[158] Marshall; *East Indian Fortunes...*, p. 14

[159] *Ibid.*

[160] *Cambridge Economic History* Vol. II.. p. 312

[161] Marshall; *East Indian Fortunes....* p. 97

[162] Marshall; *East Indian Fortunes....* p. 103.

[163] Furber; *op.cit..* p. 296

[164] A.K.Ray; *A Short History of Calcu'ta: Town and Suburb.* Intro.N.R.Ray. (Calcutta, 1982), p. 260.

[165] Quoted in *Gazetteer, Howrah,* p. 105

[166] Marshmann; 'Notes on the Left or Calcutta Bank of the Hooghly'.

[167] *Provincial Council of Rev. at Murshidabad.* 23 Dec., 1773

[168] *Marine Dept. Progs.* 10 May, 1843

[169] *Marine Dept. Progs.* 18 Sept., 1843

[170] *Cambridge Economic History* Vol. II., p. b258

[171] *Gazetteer, Howrah,* p. 106

[172] M.A.Laird ed.; *Bishop Heber in Northern India: Selections from Hebers Journal* p. 45

[173] *Gazetteer, Howrah,* pp. 108-9

[174] *B.O.R. Lower Provinces, Land Rev. Dept. Progs.,* 5 Jan.,1855

[175] *Gazetteer, Howrah,* pp. 111-14

[176] *Gazetteer, Nadia,* p. 98

[177] *Gazetteer, Burdwan,* p. 141

[178] *Gazetteer, Burdwan,* p. 126

[179] *P W Dept. Railways Progs.* 30 July, 1851

[180] *P W Dept. Railways Progs.* 3 Sept., 1845

[181] *Ibid.*

[182] *Cambridge Economic History.* Vol.II., p. 267

[183] *Cambridge Economic History.* Vol.II., p. 757

[184] H. Beverly; *Report on the Census of Bengal, 187,* (Calcutta, 1872), p. 99

4

SETTLEMENTS

The Gangetic delta had a long history of settlements. In Bengal the Aryan culture had first its roots along the western banks of the river Ganga. The growth of agriculture, trade and human habitation in this region was faster in comparison to the other parts of eastern India. The *Rarh* or chiefly the lands on the western bank of the river Bhagirathi had put its mark in the life of the people of Bengal. But the river Ganga suddenly shifted its principal course towards its channel in the east and assumed the name of Padma in the closing decades of the sixteenth century. Since the bifurcation which was affected in the present district of Murshidabad the western or the principal channel has been known as the Bhagirathi whose lower part is known as the Hooghli. Hence the principal flow of water found its way through the eastern channel. It was argued by some that for last couple of centuries prior to the nineteenth the delta-building activities by the river Bhaghirati-Hooghli had been stopped. The natural growth was severely affected. "Majoriy of population (about 60%) is concentrated within the Delta Proper having only two-fifths of area, whereas the two other units the *Rarh* Plain and the North Bengal Plain accommodated only about 26% and 16% of region's population with more than the 1/3rd and 1/14tharea, respectively."[1]

But the importance of the region along the banks of the Bhagirathi-Hooghli did never diminish. The capital of the independent *Sultans* of Bengal was Gaur, once situated on the bank of the Ganga. Lakshman Sena [1178-1205] the last Hindu king, from whom the Turkish invaders occupied the western part of Bengal, had his capital too on the same river. Though its actual location is still debateable, it is widely believed that in face of the sudden attack the old king fled his capital by boarding a boat on the river, which was then flowing behind his palace. The Mughals had their first capital too at Gaur from where it was shifted at Rajmahal on the opposite bank of the same river. Except for a hundred years, roughly corresponding to the sixteenth century, the capital of Bengal was on the banks of the Bhagirathi-Hooghli. Bengal's wealth and might–both were exhibited through this region. Certainly, the region had always been well settled; a majestic hub of several activities. The resources had assumed such a fame that a large number of foreign nationalities came here to settle permanently.

The Legends

In Bengal, the presence of a good number of towns and cities can be presented as proof. The river-route followed by the legendary Bengali merchant, Chand of a number of *Manasamangala* fame indicate the presence of a thick human settlement along the Bhagirathi-Hooghli. Chand's fleet passed Nadia i.e., Navadwip, Ambua or today's Katwa, Fulia on the other side of the river, Guptipara and Mirzapur and then reached Tribeni where Chand landed to have a look of Satgaon, the great emporium of Bengal. Bipradas writes that both Tribeni and Satgaon were full of fine buildings, huge granaries and fine temples. Every household had huge stock of "golden" crops. Both the Hindus and Muslims used to reside in large numbers.[2] "Hindus and Muhammadans lived in peace and enjoyed equally the prosperity of the city and its surrounding country ... The first place after passing Triveni, was Kumarhatta, an important Brahmanic settlement ... on the right he saw Hugli ... Then it mentions on the left Bhatpara, and on the right Boro Chinsura and Chandannagar are not mentioned at all". There has been confusion in identifying Boro. Probably it was a place within Chandannagar. On the opposite of it was Kankinara. "Then on the east are mentioned Mulajore and Garulia...and on the west Paikpara ... to the south of Telinipara, and Bhadreswar... Then on the two sides of the river are described two villages, viz., Champdani and Ichapur... Then on the Eastern side of the river is mentioned a place named Bankibazar... Beyond Bankibazar, but on the other side of the river, is mentioned the celebrated "Nimai Tirtha."[3] Shastri has indentified the places which are mentioned in the *Manasa* epic of Bipradas Pipilai. In this course Chand sailed through "Dviganga, a double river, because a branch of the Sarasvati fell here into the Ganges and is still known as the 'Baidyabatir Khal'… Then the merchant passes by Chanak... Here is mentioned the Burania country ... It may be the region of floods or it may [*be*]...inhabited by…the divers. On the other side of Chanok are... Ramnan, Akna and Mahesa, but Srirampur is not mentioned... Then on the Chanok side of the river is mentioned Khardaha. It is one of the oldest and most respectable settlements of the Rarhiya Brahmans... On the western bank are... Rishra, Konnagar and on the east Sukchar, Kotrung, Kamarhati, Ariadaha and Ghusuri...before the fleet reaches Chitpur... After passing Chitpur...mention is made of Calcutta... More prominent mention is …of...Betor."[4]

Though there are certain doubts as regards the authenticity of the original text as claimed to have been written by Bipradas[5] still one should not have any doubt regarding the presence of a good number of towns as referred to in Bipradas's composition.

The old Portuguese and Dutch maps give some names, e.g., Agrapara and Xore [i.e., *Agarpara and Dakshineswar, north of Calcutta*], on the other side of the Hooghli, Abegaca which is most probably Ambika or Kalna, Bernagar or Baranagar below Xore, Betor, Caatgam or Satgaon, Tripeni or Tribeni and Pandua[6]. Bengal under the rule of the Mughals attracted people from different parts of the world who came here and setteled permanently. Mukundaram's imaginary city of Gujarat was as magnificent as any affluent city could be.[7] Some of the places continued to have their original trading and professional classes even during the closing decade of the eighteenth century [*the traders of Sukhsagar in Nadia and of Hooghli used to pay police tax which were prevailing there for long years*].[8]

The settlements as drawn in the contemporary literary works had their presence in large extent in the contemporary history too. The large number of Vaisanava literatures on the life of Chaitanya present nearly the same pictures. Chaitanya was born [1485] in Navadwip in the later part of fufteenth century and spread his teachings starting from the region along the banks of the Bhagirathi. The entire region was then bustling in several activities.

Not only economy of the region but also, the intellectual environment of the contemporary Bengal took shape from this part along the river. Certainly the river acted as the principal source of communications. The high concentration of people of varied interest made the stretches along the rivers, hubs of many activities. Nadia had a relatively high rate of urban population. It also witnessed the spread of the Vaisnava movement. The river here had changed its course several times. Still those failed to diminish the importance of Navadwip which stood on the west bank of the Bhagirathi, opposite the confluence of the Jalangi with that river "Navadwip is a very ancient city, and is reputed to have been founded in 1063 A.D. by one of the Sena Kings of Bengal.... -on the east bank of the river, immediately opposite the present Nabadwip".[9] Very soon the place acquired its importance as a place of learning. The attraction of Navadwip to a huge number of Vaisnavas made the place populous. The 'city' Navadwip during the days of Chaitanya [1485-1533] was full of beautiful buildings made of bricks. The number of big assembly halls for worship was also note-worthy.[10] Since the river Bhagirathi was considered holiest of the rivers by the Hindus each one of them wished to have a residence along its course. Though the main flow shifted toward the east in the sixteenth century the people still considered the western course as the original. This popular belief contributed towards the increase in the number of population in the places along the course of the Bhagirathi-Hooghli. Brindavandas [1507-89], while writing the life-story of Chaitanya, noted the assemblage of men from various caste and professions in Navadwip. There were colonies of weavers, milkmen, dealers in spices and scents, garland-makers, betel-dealers, conch-shell dealers etc.[11] Moreover, Navadwip was well-known as a place for learning. The people from far and near like, Chittagong, Sylhet and Orissa used to come here for learning and then for permanent habitation.[12] Even in 1829, Professor H. H. Wilson "found between 500 and 600 pupils studying" at number of *tolls* or traditional Sanskrit schools.[13] Normally lakhs of persons used to take bath in the river daily.[14] The number of followers who accompanied Chaitanya in his pilgrimage to Puri in the standard of the day is astonishing. He used to halt at a number of places along the course of the river and in each such haltage the number increased.[15] Santipur, Khardaha, [*Kulinpara in the Chaitanyabhagbat where Kamdev Pandit, the most respected and learned man used to reside and where Nityananda, one of the Vaisnava saints, next only to Chaitanya, also stayed for few days*][16], Sukhchar [*in the south of Khardaha and one can find it getting a place in the map drawn by de Barros in 1516*] Panihati, Suksagar [*a well-populated settlement but, wiped out in the flood of 1842*][17] Baranagar were some of the places, all of which were termed as well-populated cities.[18] A well-paved road along the riverside helped in connecting these settlements. One of the legendary merchants, Dhanapati's, fleet of boats crossed a number of densely populated places in the middle of the sixteenth century.[19] The economic prosperity in those places can be guessed from the list of the trading articles, some of which were too costly and rare, like pearls.[20] A place called Chattrabhog in the Sundarbans [*presently nearly 4 miles south of Joynagar-Majilpur in the 24 Parganas,south*] and on the mouth of the river Hooghli also had a good number of Chaitanya's followers who extended him a warm reception.[21]

Under the Mughals

The arrival of the Mughals in the late sixteenth century gradually changed the scenario. Bengal was made a province of the empire and that was for the first time that Bengal lost its near independent identity. Arrival of a number of people from various parts of India and abroad ultimately changed the settlement pattern of the region. Though it has been argued that mass-scale peasentisation of the present Bangladesh, which was then the core area of the growing delta, was made possible under the Mughals, the economic activities were still concentrated around the Bhagirathi region.

The life-style and purchasing capacities of the new settlers chiefly from the north India and central Asia helped to create new types of industries. Bengal earned its fame, which ultimately brought a large number of foreign nationals who made their respective settlements along the banks of the Hooghli. The entire area became densely populous.

"Broadly, the rural settlements are: (a) compact, (b) semi-compact or hamleted clusters and (c) linear emerging as a result of the interplay of both physical and cultural factors." The west of the Bhagirathi had semi-compact villages for the undulating nature of soil. The entire zone, particularly on the west, was not so fertile like the eastern portions. The presence of good quality of lands on the close areas of the river channel contributed towards "a high degree of compactness and evenness of distribution of settlements."[22] During earlier decades of the seventeenth century the fine artisan crafts, cloths in particular, was the example of high-grade urban life and an affluent purchaser community. Probably the urban centres were developed by the Muslims who usually stayed in the army cantonments, most of which were transformed into towns. Shifting of the provincial capital to Dhaka in the beginning of the seventeenth century failed to rob the western part of its well-settled habitations.

Gaur and Pandua, the earlier seats of administration lost their political importance hitherto enjoyed. Yet, economy and urban culture of those regions remained nearly the same as they had been earlier. Mirza Nathan, one of the chosen generals of emperor Jahangir during the earlier years of Jahangir's reign [1605-27] still found Pandua a big trading mart where costly articles could be found. Actually, he purchased a piece of cloth at four hundred rupees.[23]

The thickly populated areas were a matter of surprise to many. The oldest European account of Bengal can be found from the writings of Durate Barbosa [*a Portuguese official in India between 1500 and 1516-17*]. He was surprised to find "the kingdom of Bengala wherein many towns, as wee inland as on the coast... The Moors dwell in the seaports where there is a great traffic in goods".[24] The large houses in which the "respectable Moors" used to live had "great tanks" within them.[25] Another such surprised person was Thomas Bowrey while visiting this part of India between the years 1669 and 1679—he found a good number of "faire villages" along the course of the river.[26] The same was the experience of Careri, a French traveller. He found the country "full of Castles and Towns" among which Satgaon and Kasimbazar were most important.[27] Since the agricultural productions were higher in comparison to the other parts of the Mughal empire[28] Bengal was very populous.[29]

This population were engaged in various works including artisan crafts even prior to the coming of the Mughals. During the rule of the *Sultans* of Gaur i.e.; in the thirteenth to sixteenth centuries, Bengal had been a place for envy. In the absence of sufficient records it is difficult to ascertain the actual picture and wealth of Bengal. But, it is a fact that when Babar encountered the Afghans in the eastern part of India in the earlier decades of the sixteenth century he had fixed his eyes on Bengal. In the war-torn India, Bengal still had vast resource.[30]

"The chief attracting forces for settlements in the region had been the high banks. In addition to the fertile land, the sanctity of the Bhagirathi water, the then main channel of the Ganga, attracted human settlements".[31] A good number of "faire villages" sprang up upon the banks of the river in the seventeenth century and the varieties in agricultural products and their flourishing trade were the reasons behind the growth of the settlements.[32]

Regional Variations

When Akbar started to enforce the Mughal rule a pestilence broke out in and around Gaur, which ultimately took away a large number of people. Casualties were so heavy that Gaur lost its pre-eminent position and the capital was shifted forever from this city. That was also the time when the river began to change its course from the city front. The erratic behaviour of the river was registered for the first time. For such changes a continuous line of islands and accretions formed in the bed of the river that were popularity known as the *Diara*. These *Diara* lands were extremely fertile and the climatic conditions were very much congenial for agriculture. Hence, from Sakrigali Ghat, the river started moving gently in a southerly direction having a congested habitation zone. Here the pattern of settlement also presented certain distinct features. Chiefly the Hindus inhabited the northern and western portions. Since majority of these people used to speak in local Hindi of the neighbouring Bihar[27] there is no doubt of their immigration. The Muslims occupied the southern part. These Muslims called themselves *Shershabadis* and used to claim a foreign origin. These people claimed that their ancestors followed Sher Shah when he occupied Gaur in the late 1530s and a large number of those warriors decided to settle here permanently. Interestingly enough, these people ultimately took agriculture as their principal occupation. But under the Mughals such immigration did never take place, as there had not been any reference of the Saiyids i.e.; traditional Mughal aristocrats having their origins abroad. The number of grants for revenue-free lands to such persons as *Syurghal* was simply negligible. On the other hand, such grants in the names of Hindu deities were not so nominal.[34] Hence with the arrival of the Mughals, immigration of people of foreign origins diminished considerably.

Moreover, the majority of the landholders of the region were the Hindus while the farmers and sharecroppers in general called themselves *Shekhs*.[35] It is difficult to find out the reasons. But the financial acumen of the Hindus and the new land settlement policies undertaken in the late eighteenth century helped to create such a pattern. Newly reclaimed lands were occupied in large by the people from Bihar who immigrated here. Even a section of the Muslims called themselves as the Darbhanga Shekhs of Darbhanga [in Bihar] origin. In the late eighteenth and in the nineteenth century this situation took its shape. Since Gaur had long been well-connected with the other parts of eastern India the process of immigration was easier. In the seventeenth century those arteries could be found in the map drawn by Van den Brouck.[36] Though this region failed to attract the Mughal aristocrats as the capital was transferred to Dhaka, agrarian affluence allured common people.

The river Ganga took a turn towards east at Suti in the district of Murshidabad and the bulk of water started flowing through that channel. From this point the river has been known as Bhagirathi, which flows from north to south through this district, dividing it into two parts. The tract west of it is known as *Rarh* and the east as *Bagri*. Murshidabad, "standing at the head of the Gangetic delta, affords a striking example of the grand operations of nature produced by fluvial action".[37] The region had a long tradition of early settlements. The *Rarh* is high and slightly undulating, "but is interspersed with numerous swamps and beds of old rivers". The lands "are liable to sudden freshets, but they never lay the country under water for any long space of time". For this the fields are not so fertile in comparison to the fields on the other side of the river.

The *Bagri* lies almost entirely between the Ganga, Bhagirathi and Jalangi rivers. "The whole area lies low, and is exposed to annual inundations...but usually do no more than deposit over the land a top dressing of almost inexhaustible fertility."[38] Such fertility in addition to the well-communicated river-routes helped this portion of the district to flourish. Time and again even in the 1660s, complaints against poor flow of water did not deter the people from coming here and settling permanently. The *Rarh* had a long and cherished history. Bengal's culture had a distinct variety, which had its origin at *Rarh*. No doubt the entire area had long been well populated. Both agriculture and artisan craft flourished they attracted the people from far and near to settle permanently. In the middle of the seventeenth century, when the Portuguese traders were driven out from Hooghli, Kasimbazar and Muksudabad assumed importance as the centres of trade and manufacture. The presence of high roads connecting Muksudabad with Patna through Suti, Rajmahal and Munger helped transporting merchandise.[39]

"There is a well-developed regional variation in the types of settlements. Distribution and setting of rural settlements in the *Rarh*, west of the Bhagirathi, are distinct from that of the *Bagri*, east of the Bhaghirati. The former is to be a great extent marked by closely clustered settlements situated about 2 km apart, while the latter is dominated by linear assemblage,...as most of the villages tend to merge here with each other so that it become difficult to recognize their singular entity."[40] The economic activities of the people residing in the delta region had made Bengal rich. "For centuries the immense wealth and resources of the delta were the lure of the foreign invaders. The Mughals described Bengal as, the Paradise of India, while Aurangzeb went further and termed it 'the paradise of nations".[41]

It is also a fact that after his short-time occupation of Gaur, the capital of the then Bengal, Sher Khan [*later Shah*] had shifted a huge amount of treasure to his strong fort at Rohtas in Bihar. Bengal's riches had become proverbial. The Portuguese traders—the first nation from Europe to arrive at this part of world—made Chittagong [*now in Bangladesh on the Bay of Bengal*] their first seat of establishment. But very soon they shifted to Hooghli on the Bhagirathi. Very close to Hooghli was Satgaon, the port of Gaur. Satgaon was on the river Saraswati. In 1569, the Venetian merchant, Caesar Frediricki, came to Satgaon and to him it "is a faire citie.. of the Moores, and very plentiful of all things".[42] A contemporary, Master Ralph Fitch, found "The country is very fruitful and populous".[43]

The Portuguese spread the information on Bengal to Europe. Within a very short span of time. Bengal attracted a large number of foreigners of different countries. All flocked here for her wealth. Bengal's wealth lay in her agriculture produce, and in her artisan craft. With those, commerce flourished. "Through the waterways of the Gangetic delta" Bengal was connected with her wider parts and with northern India as far as Agra.[44] For the regular inundations in the Ganga and its river system the fields along the course of those rivers and the agriculture productions were higher in comparison to the other parts of India.[45] There had not been any information regarding oppression of the people on the plea of higher rate of rents and revenue. During the *Sultanate* rule, "apart from Bengal the sources of silver supply in India were scanty".[46] Bengal's wealth was the result of the networks of the rivers of which the Bhagirathi-Hooghli system was the principal one.

But "degradation" in the Bhagirathi began in the earlier decades of the eighteenth century "when the Ganges marched on its way to the Meghna, and the rivers of the region, which were active offshoots from the Ganges began to be reduced to a network of moribund channels".[47] Hence, this part of Bengal which was situated along the course of the Bhagirathi-Hooghli suffered in many ways. It has been argued by some that "The silting up of the Saraswati and the Bhagirathi... the detour of the Damodar towards the west in 1770, the decline of the rivers of Nadia and Jessore since the beginning of the nineteenth century, and the interference of natural drainage by railway and river embankments, all have" contributed to the "decrease of cultivation and population".[48] Still the wealth of Bengal for which people from far and near arrived here was principally concentrated in the region along the course of the Bhagirathi-Hooghli channel.

The Mughal conquest of Bengal not only helped it to connect itself more deeply with northern India but also led people from various parts of the country to come and settle in Bengal. But how the process of that settlement was completed is very difficult to determine. The problems multiply for the absence of sufficient amount of data. Topographical analysis is very scanty and sometimes-defective. William and John Blave drew their maps of India based upon the Dutch and Portuguese sources of sixteenth and seventheenth centuries. As far as Bengal is concerned, they produced a reprint of the map drawn by De Barros at about 1540. "In point of accuracy it is much inferior to Van den Broucke's map of 1660 given in Francois Valentyn's 'Oud en Niew Oost Indien', Amsterdam, 1728. But none of these present a perfect picture"[49] The European cartographic analysis, which had been in vogue there since the sixteenth century were used in respect of Bengal. Some maps drawn in those days help to understand the physical geography of the then Bengal though none of those was accurate. As per those the *Diara* lands were extremely fertile and the climatic conditions were congenial. Probably reclamations here took place !ater in comparison to the *Rarh*. Caste compositions were unique. The pioneers among the Hindus were from the people of low origins viz.; the *Mahishya*, *Pod* and *Namasudras* and along with these were the Muslims. They spread into separate zones. The *Mahishyas* predominated in the southwestern portion of the delta, the *Pods* in the southern and the *Namasudras* in the southeastern. This region had a high concentration of Muslims too. The Muslims, by and large, were peasants and fishermen like the *Namasudras*.[50] The entire area is now in Bangladesh.

The Mughal conquest of Bengal expanded its trade and linked the province with the north. *Mahal* Mandalghat at the confluence of rivers Rupnarayan and the Hooghli was then the south-western frontier of the province while the northern outskirt of the Sundarbans from Hatiagarh, south of Diamond Harbour on the Hooghli to Bagerhat in southern Jessore was its southern frontier.[51]

The generation of resources by the Muslims from land was meager. The occupational sects of the Muslims prove the fact that they had little or no ownership of land apart from the peasantry. The majority of the *Jolas* (low–caste weavers), *Dhunias* (cotton carders), *Nalus* (seed-sellers) *Nikaries* (small fishermen) and *Kunjaras* (vegetable-sellers) belonged to the Muslim community.[52] Understandably, those people were of small or even of no fortune. Neither did they have resources to lead decent life nor they could own land. Most probably they could not shed their age-old professions that were ultimately synonymous to their caste or class.

Though the Hindus were well-off than their Muslim neighbours the number of high-caste Hindus was very nominal. "Most of the Bengali-speaking Hindu inhabitants profess Baisanabi doctrines"[53] which was an ample example of the spread of Vaisanvism since the days of Chaitanya. Since Chaitanya's preachings chiefly attracted the low-caste Hindus their large-scale presence in this part could not be denied. Once Chaitanya visited Ramkeli, a near-by place of Gaur. The individual profession was also linked with some castes of the Hindus. Sometimes change in professions effected change in caste-names too. "Castes peculiar to the district are Chasatis and Puros, agriculturists and silk-worm rearers, respectively. Castes mainly found in this district are Ganesh and Gangai, weavers and potters, though also agriculturists".[54] Inter-mixture of different castes here were effected due to the conditionality of the nature.

The river Ganga here, in keeping with its tradition, made havocs by flooding large areas too and often.The affected persons were offered help in many forms to restart their family lives. There had regularly been appeals made to the *zamindars* even in the 1780s to render assistance to the poor cultivators.[55] Sometimes the landholders had to bring people from outside for cultivation.[56] In majority of such cases the original holders used to leave old professions and adopted new. In these manners land-holding as well as settlement patterns changed. To keep the farmers tied with land, *raiyati* holdings were generally offered in lieu of comparatively low rate.[57] With the increased population the demand for land was also high. "Formerly large areas of inferior land were cultivated irregularly on the system of *hal hasli* tenure, by which a tenant paid rent only on the area which was found to be under cultivation...for that particular year."[58] This was an age-old system prevailing in northern India where incentives were offered for reclamation of land. This region was not an exception. But each year a large number of people used to lose their lands, even homestead, for the floods of the Ganga. By custom the *zamindars* used to offer lands in some other places to those people in concessional rates.[59] The islands created on the river were also occupied and those were very fertile. Large-scale habitations came up and often bloods were shed for enforcing control over those.[60] "When new land forms, the village takes settlement ...,and ploughs it jointly, the produce being divided according to the number of ploughs of each household, until the land has become reasonably permanent."[61]

Silkworm rearing and weaving had long been a major profession along with agriculture. The trade in silk attracted both monetary investments and settlements of professional class. But the Muslims did not use silk fabrics due to certain religious superstition. Hence, the culture of silk-manufacture was lost. With the desertion of Gaur in the 1570s this trade was revived. There is at least one reference of one Sheikh Bhik set sail for Russia with his *Maldahi* cloths in 1577.[62] With the coming of the foreigners in Bengal the trade in silk got momentum. That required a large number of artisans and professional men. In the seventeenth century the English East India Company established its factory at English Bazar, a few kilometres away from the present Malda town. In consequence to that a vast settlement of silkworm as well as cocoon rearers appeared in the vicinity of English Bazar and in some near by areas. Those people belonged to *Puro* caste of the Hindus.[63] In the decades between 1760 and 1790 Bengal witnessed a boom in silk trade. The filature system was introduced which employed a considerable number of persons. Naturally the growth of population was high. The river Ganga, sometimes unaffordable, was used as the major transport route. It was well connected with the Mahananda, Kalindri, Tangan and the Punarbhaba- all of which helped the people connected with the trade to reside along the river, Ganga. Not only human settlement but also trade-marts sprang up. Amaniganj was such an "important silk-mart on the Bhagirathi. There is no resident population".[64] Such was the importance of those areas for which the population pressure is too high even now.

Very soon Muksudabad assumed importance with the coming of Murshid Quli Khan as the *Diwan* of the province in 1703. Murshid Quli had a soured relation with prince Azim us Shan, the *Subedar* or the Mughal governor who had his office at Dhaka. Aurangzeb himself gave Murshid Quli extreme liberty in the revenue administration of the province. In consequence of such conflict Murshid Quli chose Muksudabad—a few hundred kilometres away from Dhaka. He christened the place after his own name i.e.; Murshidabad. In 1712, Murshid Quli was appointed as the *Subedar* in addition to his earlier post of the *Diwan*. This was a unique arrangement where both the posts were offered to a single official in contrary to the prevailing Mughal administrative norms. However, with Murshid Quli, the rule of the independent Nawabs began in Bengal. Till 1774, Murshidabad was the official capital of Bengal though the province was already under the control of the English East India Company. But Murshidabad could effectively command importance in the field of commerce for some decades after those fateful years.

Both political and commercial importance helped Murshidabad and all the near-by areas to flourish. The settlements along the course of the river Bhagirathi were of very ancient roots. Rangamati on the western bank was connected with the legendary Chandsawdagar merchant, of the *Mansamangala* epic as Henry Beveridge makes us to believe. It also found a place in Van den Broucke's Dutch map of about 1660 and it was "the only town which appears there in the west part of Murshidabad".[65] A large number of settlements are marked in Broucke's map and all were on the eastern side of the river. Among them important were Palasi, Daudpur [*spelt Danepoer*], Barwa Serai, Saiyidabad [*part of Berhampur*], Kasimbazar and Muxudabad. Beveridge understands that the western part of the Bhagirathi was not well-known during Brouke's time. Tavernier in the 1660s found Muksudabad and Nadia or Navadwip very large towns.[66] This part of territory was later used for mulberry cultivation and silk-production and it extended up to the confluence of the Ajay and the Bhagirathi. This area was a part of *Sarkar Tanda* under the Mughal administration. Bhagabangola, 19 miles [31 km] N. E. of Berhampur and 12 miles [20 km] from Murshidabad, situated on the Padma and had long been used as the port of Murshidabad.[67]

With the shifting of the capital here a large number of high officials started arriving, some of whom stayed permanently. The places became well-populated. For making the places habitable the official patronage was never lacking. A large number of *lakheraj* or revenue-free grants had been made.[68] The Europeans, visiting Murshidabad city and Kasimbazar, were amazed by innumerable big structures in those two places. Murshid Quli himself established a big market complex or *katra* and attached a mosque to it. Though the market could not be completed the vastness of the ruins of the *Katra* mosque is a proof of the huge number of *namazies* for whom the said mosque was built. From it the number of people residing in the city of Murshidabad during the first quarter of the eighteenth century can easily be imagined.

These construction works continued generation after generation. Nawab Sarafraj Khan [1739-40], during his short tenure as the Nawab also established Shereef Ganj or Berhampur of later date for his son Shereef Ali.[69] Siraj Udaulah made Heera Jheel, on the other side of the river, his place of residence and Mir Jafar at Jaffarganj on the northern end of the city of Murshidabad. Both the places were increasingly populous.[70] Riches of those places became proverbial. Murshidabad and Kasimbazar attracted people of many walks. The city of Murshidabad in 1759, "are said to have been five miles along the Bhagirathi in length, and two and a half miles in breadth on each bank of the river". Even Robert Clive, the conqueror at Palasi, was surprised to see the wealth of the residents of the city.[71] Since Murshid Quli reorganized the revenue administration he had ousted all the old and traditional bureaucrats, and replaced them with the local people. In this way a good number of Hindu families got eminence. This was completely a new phenomenon. In the administrative structure of the previous regimes the Hindus of Bengal had a very nominal role. The new gentry along with the trading communities took their new shelter at those places under the patronage of the rulers. Murshidabad was a new addition to the urban history and culture of Bengal. Similar though not of that same nature was Kasimbazar.

Both agriculture and artisan craft were responsible for the growth. The land, encircled by the rivers, produced ample agricultural products having good varieties. Murshidabad as well as Kasimbazar produced both raw silk and products made of silk. The silk had international demand and for this commodity the Europeans came here. Apart from this, certain other industries like ivory-products, bell metal etc. also came up. Chiefly, the aristocrat families and rich men whose numbers were not so meagre, were the patronizers. Hence, the present district of Murshidabad and particularly, the areas along the course of the river Bhaghirati became the seats of habitations. A bulk of the settlers were not Bengali-speaking people. They constituted the initial gentry of the society for their high official positions and also for their high connections. Like these people a good number of traders and bankers from different parts of India also came here for permanent residence. Majority of them were from Rajasthan and Gujarat and were Jains by faith.[72] The *Jagat Seths* belonged to one of such communities. Their chief concentrations were Jiaganj and Azimganj on the banks of the Bhagirathi. During the eighteenth century the regions along the course of the river witnessed a tremendous growth in every field.

Chiefly for the trade in silk and availability of expert artisans a large number of people from far and near arrived in these places. The Armenians, Dutch, French as well as the English merchants assembled in these places for trade. Father Joseph Tieffenthaler speaks of the vast and magnificent buildings of the Dutch in Kalkapur at Kasimbazar.[73] Despite the fall [1757] of the Nawabi rule in the middle of that century Murshidabad was able to maintain its earlier position for some decades. It was officially admitted in 1789 that all the places between Beernagar and Jiaganj were too populous. Jiaganj was a vast settlement of the north-Indian Jain trading families. The bazaars here were "being of greater magnitude than any" in the whole of Bengal[74]. The thickness of habitation acquired such magnitude that a new hospital had to be built by removing habitation at Shereef Ganj in Berhampur in 1790.[75] Since 1765 Murshidabad and its adjacent areas lost their political as well as administrative importance. But those failed to reduce the population pressure for which a better police arrangement for the city of Murshidabad had to be made in 1793.[76]

The Maratha *bargirs* or cavalrymen had earlier looted the resources of this part of Bengal. By a treaty the Mughal emperor had surrendered a right to Sahu, the Maratha King, to collect *Chauth* or one-fourth of the produce of Bengal, Bihar and Orissa. In pretext of that treaty the cavalrymen of Raghuji Bhonsle, the head of the Nagpur family, started plundering the entire region west of the river Bhagirathi. Once they even succeeded in attacking the city of Murshidabad. To prevent them from invading Bengal Alivardi Khan, the then Nawab of Bengal, pursued a vigorous course. But he failed and ultimately had to buy peace by surrendering Orissa to Bhonsle. Prior to the conclusion of this arrangement, the Marathas simply had devastated the western Bengal and Bihar. A contemporary author, Gangaram's descriptions provide vast information about the persons affected by the Maratha invasions. The regions were then inhabited by the Brahmins, goldsmiths as well as dealers of gold; dealers of spices; bell-metal workers; blacksmiths; potters; conch-shell dealers; doctors, official clerks etc.; apart from many others.[77]

Surprisingly, those fierce devastations, which continued for years together, failed to make those people poor. After 1765, when the English Company introduced new revenue demands all the parts of these regions had to abide by those. Most probably, majority of the landholders were the Hindus. This was the result of the arrangements made by Murshid Quli Khan. In the first decade of the nineteenth century; the over-whelming majority of the Muslims were agriculturists who were commonly known as the *Shekhs*. They were distinctly different from the Mughals, Pathans and above all from the *Sayids* or high-class Muslims, having foreign origins.[78] Other than the *Shekhs* there were *Jolahs* or *Kulus* i.e.; weavers by caste.

Majority among the Hindus were from *Chasi Kaibartta* or *Mahishya, Sadgop, Bagdi, Chains* the milkmen community and from the Brahmins. The *Kaibartta* is fisherman but those who had left their original profession and adopted farming of lands were called the *Chasi Kaibartta*. Similarly, the milkmen when left their original profession and adopted farming were called the *Sadgop*. Entire Bengal was full of such communities who adopted land farming and agriculture since this profession stood at higher level from their original castes. Some castes had their origins outside of Bengal. One of such castes was the *Chains* who constituted a bulk of agriculturists in the districts of Malda and Murshidabad. "The *Chains* have a limited geographical distribution, the only other place where they are numerous being Malda.....and Bihar. They are a low-caste [*among the Hindus*], whose occupations are mainly cultivation and labour."[79] Most probably these people had migrated here from Bihar. Similar were the *Puros* and *Chasatis*. Like Murshidabad, they could be found in Malda too. The *Puros* were agriculturists, vegetable-growers and silk-worm reares. They were thought to be an offshoot of the *Pod* caste. Both the *Pods* of the 24 Parganas and the *Puros* of Murshidabad are said to "exhibit in physical appearance a approach to the aboriginal type". From the very nomenclature the *Chasati* it is distinct that the people, belonging to this caste adopted agriculture as their profession. Since the lands adjacent to the Bhagirathi were well-cultivated, the concentration of people belonging to these castes was considerable. But the *Bagri* had a higher concentration of Muslims. This trend continued roughly in the neighoubering district of Nadia.

Composition of population in some other places was such that religion and caste played important role. In the western part of the river Hooghli is the district of Burdwan, one of the most affluent regions in terms of agricultural produce. Here the flow of water during the summer was too meagre.[80] Still, population pressure in these places proves the richness of soil. It was the "part of great Gangetic delta and here, in land under rice cultivation, are found the usual marsh weeds of the Gangetic plain and many sedges".[81] As a result the growth of settlement was steady. The original inhabitants were mainly the *Bagdis*, a low caste Hindu who constituted the bulk of population.[82] But Burdwan was the heart of the *Gopbhum* or the kingdom ruled by the *Sadgope* caste whose principal profession was agriculture. They were energetic and hard-working as well. Burdwan's affluence was primarily the handiwork of such castes. This-district had a particular caste, which could not be found anywhere in Bengal. Those people not only took landholding as their primary profession but also acquired education. "The line of marshes which lies south of Katwa to the west of the Bhagirathi is still held by this caste [*Aguri*]. . .The *Aguris*, by their own admission, are the product of unions between the *Khatries* of the house of Burdwan [the *zamindars* had their origin in northern India and they claimed themselves *Khatries* or of warrior caste] and the *Sadgops* of the Gopbhum and the caste arose within the last two hundred years [*or since eighteenth century*][83] The Maratha raids in the 1740s too failed to make those areas poor.

Patronage

Frequently homesteads as well as agricultural lands in new areas were allotted by the *zamindars*. The chief aim was to raise rent. This was an age-old practice in India. Often under the leadership of a person his fellow caste-men raised settlements for which they used to receive lands free of rent. In every village one or more families could be usually found whose ancestors had received lands for many reasons. These were nothing but extension of patronage. The vast majority of such recipients were the Brahmins of the Hindu society. But in many cases Muslims were also bestowed with such favour. A Hindu *zamindar* granted *cheragy* [*i.e.; rent free land to those who used to lit lamp in the Muslim shrines and graves*] lands for rendering religious services.[84] Similarly, often the Muslim *zamindars* used to allot the Hindu Brahmins *Berhmotter* lands[85]. Through such grants a large number of people—chiefly of professional class or caste raised their own colonies. The grantees were free to transfer their respective grants at their free will. Raja Krishnachandra of Nadia was a well-known benefactor. From his *zamindari* that spread from Nadia down to the deep of the present south 24 Pargans district along the bank of the river Hooghli, Krishnachandra generously granted lands to the Brahmins. Sometimes those grants amounted hundreds of *bighas* of lands.[86] It is no wrong if one concludes that the habitations at Chanok or a part of present Barrackpur, Ariadaha near Dakshineswar and Palasi in Nadia increased due to such benevolence. On the other hand Kidderpur, where a modern dockyard was constructed, was populated largely with the initiative taken by the family of Gocul Ghoshal[87]. Huge amount of land was allotted to different Brahmins in *Paican* Boro i.e.; present day Howrah and Bally.[88]

But in Malda some lands were allotted to the farmers in particular areas of Ratua and Kaliachak for mulberry plantation only.[89] Often lands were made suitable by way of several improvements to facilitate its cultivation. Since highlands were required for the plantation those were made as per desire by cutting ditches around that particular piece of land. In this way those became tablelands. Particularly in Malda a good number of people immigrated in such areas where the mulberry cultivations were very popular.

The foreign trading companies who had taken lands from the imperial and local authorities also followed the same practice. The Dutch East India Company used to grant lands on easy terms to a large number of persons in and around Chinsura where their seat was established.[90] In fact, a well-settled urban population grew up there for their activities. The officials of the English East India Company did not require much time to realise the importance of those grants. Though their primary objective was to enhance the productivity of the factories and the rents from those lands, the foreigners also knew that by granting a few bighas of land to a person they could attract a good number of people from nearby areas. Since the initial years of the eighteenth century the Company—as the *zamindar* of Calcutta and adjacent villages started distributing lands in favourable considerations to several persons. The leading families involved in the process included the Setts and Basaks, the early developers of the town.[91] Lands were distributed even for raising infrastructures like drainage etc., to private persons.

After 1757, the English Company as the ruler of Bengal implemented this system vigorously. Whenever required the Company followed the Indian traditions. As a principle the company did not favour in allotting lands free of anything. Still there were a number of records, which prove that its intention was to raise settlements in unsettled lands and that too in lieu of nothing. In 1764, R. Marriot as the Collector granted rent-free lands to one Brahmin, named, Ramkant Bhattacharjee in Pargana Ambika [*present day Kalna in Burdwan*] in a farther corner of the village.[92] The Brahmins of the Hindu community were largely benefitted in the villages like Khardaha, Kamarhati, Havelishahar, Bhatpara—all of which are situated on the river bank.[93] Similarly, Mr Middleton as the Collector of the 24 Parganas, allotted substantial amount of rent and revenue-free lands to several Brahmins in Chitpur, on the northern outskirt of Calcutta in 1763.[94] The continual patronisation certainly helped the settlers in many ways.

This patronisation had been heavily extended to the Sundarbans, i.e., the mangrove forests on the sea—extending from a part of Medinipur in the west to Khulna in the east. We are told that once under the rule of Pratapaditya, the *zamindar* of Jessore and also one of the 12 *bhuians* of Bengal who challenged the Mughals, the greater part of the northern portions of the Sundarbans facing the rivers Meghna, now in Bangladesh and the Hooghli had been a modern settlement in the standard of those days.[95] In the 1560s i.e.; prior to the Mughal conquest the area had been considered to be one of the most populous places. This observation can be questioned but one cannot ignore the fact that Pratapaditya's achievements were remarkable. He employed the Portuguese army men and used their advanced technologies in manufactures. With the defeat of Pratapaditya all of his deeds vanished within a very short span of time.

But the drastic change in the scenario was not for political reasons only. Here the changes in the course of the river Hooghli also created havoc. The present channel of the river is very different from the bed that river had formerly followed below Calcutta. The original channel was identical with Tolley's Nullah or canal from Kidderpur, in the south west of Calcutta to Garia, which is eight miles [13 km] south of Calcutta. Tradition has it that it had emerged out of the Sundarbans at Kakdwip, and then passed along the present Muriganga or Baratala river, after which it found a passage along the creek between Dhoblat and Monsardwip and proceeded first in a westerly and then a southerly direction until it fell into the Bay at Ganga Sagar.[96] The legendary merchant Dhanapati of the *Chandimangala* fame while following this river route interacted with the locals in many places. Not only the legends or literary works, the history also proves the presence of a well-settled habitation in those places. The history also has its records. When Chaitanya on his way to Puri on a boat through the river Hooghli reached at Ambulingaghat in the Sundarbans, his large number of followers there lavishly greeted him.[97] The place was then called Chhatrabhog. As noted in the lexicon prepared for the *Chaitanyabhagbat* the place was identified with the region situated roughly four miles [6 km] south of Joynagar in the present, district of the south 24 Parganas.[98] Chaitanya's experience as noted in the contemporary chronicles proved the presence of good number of villages along the river route.

But all those habitations were wiped out due to sudden natural changes. For the tectonic movements the deltaic rivers also changed their course affecting land formations too.[99] The political scenes also changed. Bengal was subjected to the Mughal rule in the closing decades of the sixteenth century. The Mughal never ventured to proceed towards the deep south and all lands below Nadia. The patronages hitherto enjoyed by the people residing in those places were withdrawn. All the protective embankments had been damaged and remained unattended. Very soon the vast tract of land was covered with forests and became the happy habitations of wild animals.

The topography and the settlement patterns in the Sundarbans present certain unique features, which could not be found elsewhere in Bengal. Probably the composition of settlers differed widely between the western and eastern halves. The people in the eastern part had "their Malay-like character" and they acquired a serious infamy for notoriety.[100] Undoubtedly, wild nature had forced those people to adopt such mode of livelihood.

It was widely believed that due to the blessings of some holy men or their spirits the people could stay peacefully side by side with the wilds. Here the role played by the religious personalities assumed much importance than the administrative or political actions. It is a fact that the *Sufi* saints came here with a mission to convert the local people and to spread their fields of influence. With the peasentisation of the eastern part of the delta their activities intensified. During the reign of independent *Sultan* Nasiruddin Mahmud [1442-59] the official patronisation to the Muslim holy men started.[101] The role of such persons is highlighted in the folk literatures and is still being read by the people of the region.[102] Here the Muslim saints outnumbered their Hindu counterparts. It is said that not only human beings but the wild animals also used to pay their obeisance to them. In such way the patronisation assumed an interesting character. Chiefly the European travellers visiting this part of Bengal used to spread the myths surrounding those holy men and their spirits. In 1670, John Marshall, an English traveller, visited the forest and recorded his experience. He had seen "That every Thursday at night a tiger comes out and Salams to a fukeers tomb".[103] In a similar fashion, James Wise, another Englishman, wrote of Zindah Gazi in 1898. Gazi was regarded as the legendery protector of woodcutters and boatmen. He was "believed to reside deep in the Jungle, to ride on tigers, and to keep them so subservient to his will that they does not touch a human being without his express commands".[104] Wise also writes of one Mubarra Gazi, another *pir* who " is said to have been a faqir who claimed the Jungle traits along the left bank of the river Hooghli, and each village has an alter dedicated to him". Their names are closely connected with the reclamation of the forestlands and extension of cultivation. These "faqirs residing in these pestilential forests, claiming to be lineally descended from the Gazi, indicate with pieces of wood, called Sang, the exact limits within which the forest is to be cut".[105]

The myths run in many shades and shapes—all of which speak aloud for the miracles performed by those holy men and their disciples. Often there were serious strives for gaining territorial controls. The *Rayamangala* of Krishnaram Das, composed around 1686, relates the story of a serious conflict between Dakshin Ray or the lord of the south and *Bara* Gazi Khan.[106] Dakshin Ray is still worshipped as the tiger-god who once used to rule alone over the entire south of the delta, which had then been sparsely populated where the penetration of the Muslims was personified with the cult of Gazi Khan. *Bara* means elder and *Gazi* means the warrior in the crusade. After a long battle a compromise was reached. Both would be revered. The mythological narrations reflect the actual composition of the population in the region. James Wise has a strong thesis towards a mass conversion that was responsible for the presence of huge Muslim population in these regions.[107] Though currently Wise is being challenged[108] the myth in relation with the settlement pattern, to a some extent, reflects his conclusions. When the people failed to procure any administrative favour their faith was bestowed upon certain saints and spirits and their strength was derived from those.

Hence the Muslims constituted majority in the eastern half of the Sundarbans for the works done by the Muslim holy men. The *Bonobibir Jahuranama [first published from Calcutta in 1877-78]* by Munshi Bainuddin is the story of human penetration and a mass-scale conversion in those regions. The myth here also involves the same Dakshin Ray. There is little doubt that the Muslim population increased at the expense of the Hindus. The history of settlements in the Sundarbans in the late medieval and early modern periods is the history of the increase of Muslim population. The independent *Sultans* directly or indirectly patronised the Muslims. The legacy continued for the following centuries till the beginning of the East India Company's rule that developed agriculture and other occupations in different manners.

Artisans

Agriculture in all respects did not create jobs everywhere. For more then 500 years silk created a lot of jobs. For the growth of silk industry mulberry cultivation also assumed importance that, in turn, employed a bigger number of different types of artisans and labourers. Between the seventeenth and early nineteenth centuries this particular artisan craft helped to develop a good number of settlements. Since the womenfolk of the agrarian community, in general, was employed in rearing silkworm the scope of employment was wider. Silkworm rearing required skill of a particular kind. Malda also had a good record as a producer of silk but Murshidabad was the centre of fabrics. Hence, concentration of artisans was higher at Murshidabad city as well as at Kasimbazar—the two major centres. Father Joseph Tieffenthaler speaks of the vast and magnificent buildings of the Dutch in Kalkapur at Kasimbazar.[109] In 1663, Manucci found three factories of the French, English and Dutch.[110] There had been some very prominent structures to protect the towns of Kasimbazar and Sydabad from the inundation. After the political upheavals in 1757, all these places gradually lost their previous importance. The artisan craft suffered. Still the high concentration of population remained as before. When the Company's government initiated a new police administration it was found that both sides of the "Cossimbazar River" were well-settled. In the western side there were 17 Police thanas while on the eastern the number was 11.[111] The growing trade certainly attracted a vast number of people from various parts of the country. The presence of Armenians and other up-countrymen apart from the merchants of different European races prove the vastness of population, which had a cosmopolitan nature in Murshidabad city. Murshid Quli's Katra mosque was an example of patronage extended to the merchants. Probably Murshidabad had become a populous place even before the Maratha raids commenced. Siraj had his palace on the opposite side of the river at Hira Jheel and Mir Jafar, at a place called Jaffarganj at the northern end of the old city, which caused its extension. An all-weather road was maintained which was further developed during the rule of the Company.[112]

The district is favourably situated for trade, being served by the two first deltaic off-shoots of the Ganges, viz., the Bhagirathi, and Jalangi and the entire riverine region "from time immemorial, been the seat of large commercial towns. The principal seats ... are Azimganj, Jangipur, Jiaganj, Khagra and Dhulian on the Bhagirathi". Apart from those, there were a number of small and medium size settlements along the course of the river. Jiaganj on the eastern bank and Azimganj on the western bank were developed as twin towns chiefly by the up-country trading communities.[113] The Jain merchants who had arrived from as far as Rajasthan, were one of the richest trading communities in India.[114] In 1679, Streynsham Master found rich "Guzzeratt Merchants" in a "towne" called Puttalee.[115] The later-day Company's administration also appreciated the importance of these places. While introducing its administration the police "Thanadari" or surveillance was made extensive.[116] The entire riverbank of Murshidabad was the government property in the days of the *Nawabi* rule and nearly all the lands fetched substantial revenue.[117] Even the havoc damage caused by the floods of 1798-99 failed to break the morale of the residents here. As soon as the floodwater withdrew the people came and rebuilt their damaged shelters.[118]

During the first half of the nineteenth century indigo was introduced as an agricultural product. Murshidabad, particularly the eastern half, was the principal indigo-producing area. Here, both the fields of crop and indigo factories were located. But indigo production had a unique feature of its own. The Europeans were the principal players who took lands under lease from the local *zamindars* and started cultivation by offering suitable advances [*commonly called and later hated, Dadan*]. However, the factories had generated different types of employments including clerical.

Leaving Murshidabad the Bhagirathi entered into the district of Nadia and then flowed downward. The river impinges upon this district near Palasi. Here it takes the name of the river Hooghli from its junction with the Jalangi opposite Navadwip town. Nadia has the district of Burdwan on its west, in between them flows the river. Nadia is criss-crossed by a number of rivers, majority of whom are the branches or tributaries of the Hooghli. For such presence of several watercourses the rate of fertility here was very good. "The soil is agriculturally classed as high land, and bears cold weather crops as well as rice".[119] Since the later half of the eighteenth century the rivers were treated as offshoots of the Padma for the major flow of the Ganga took this course. The Mathabhanga or Hauli river leaves the Padma about ten miles below the place where the Jalangi diverges from it. All those rivers were jointly called the Nadia Rivers in the official circle. Though, the rivers, including the Hooghli, were found not navigable by Major Rennell during his survey in 1781, the pressure of population was not negligible.[120] The rivers were used for both irrigation and communication. These advantages helped to grow settlements along their courses. The country was flat and appeared to be a vast alluvial plain dotted with innumerable number of villages. In the west of the district "is the Kalantar, a low-lying tract of black clay soil which stretches from the Murshidabad district through the gap in the north-western boundary between the Jalangi and Bhagirathi down into the Kaliganj and Tehatta thanas". Though this tract was severely flood-prone the high-yielding varieties of crops, when reaped provided employments and livelihood as well. When the Bhagirathi had suffered for the poor flow of water others also shared its fate. Early in the ninetheenth century, the Mathabhanga appear to have been more easily navigable. But this trend continued only till 1818.[122] Then the Company's government upon the urgent petition from the merchants of Calcutta took certain measure for augmentation of water flow in those Nadia rivers. The principal purpose was to make the Bhagirathi-Hooghli navigable for the purpose of trade. Subsequently, the upper channel of the Mathabhanga was deepened by means of *bandhals*, "constructed as followes: At the shoals, to be operated on, a line of bamboo stakes is run out from each bank of the river. These stakes gradually converge so as to force and concentrate the current into a narrow channel. They are well-driven into the bed of the river, supported by struts, and fastened at the top by longitudinal ties. Large mat screens (*jhamps*) are then let down as far as possible, and well secured to the bamboo frame-work".[123] The mechanism of those *bandhals* was a skilled craftsmanship and some people were trained to raise those generation after generation. Those people were not usually connected to agriculture.[124] They made the adjacent areas their permanent homes and settled in colonies.

Those *bandhals* were maintained as well as possible. The officials of the East India Company did not waste any time in appreciating their value. But the decaying flow in the rivers could not be augmented as desired. In 1823, dredging machines were also introduced. But the flow of water was still very unsatisfactory. In 1831-32, after a heavy flood in the Bhagirathi, the channel was cleared for the movements of boats of small size. In 1835, the establishment for dredging was closed. But as many as 359 *bandhals* were constructed in all the rivers passing through this district. Collection of tolls from the boats used to yield an annual surplus over the amount spent for dredging and other costs.[125] The deep interest shown by the government was the proof of the importance of the waterways. It was the avowed policy of the Company's government to protect the embankments of the Hooghli to provide better opportunities of harvesting to the residents settled along its course.[126]

As the behaviour of the rivers and prospective availability of water in each one of them in Nadia were unpredictable the agrarian production was never up to any expectation. But for the comparative insecurity of land the relative rate of urban population was much higher.[127] At the end of the eighteenth century a number of artisan craft and their trade started flourishing. Santipur led the weaving industry in this part of Bengal. Its fortune declined when the machine-made clothes from England invaded India in the beginning of the nineteenth century. Same thing happened to Chakdaha, another weaving centre on the river-bank. In the beginning of the century a new type of cultivation and trade were initiated through indigo. But indigo was a synonym of oppression by the selected band of local *zamindars* and the European planters. Still indigo brought new types of manufacture and generated several types of employments.

Nadia got the advantage of river transport and also the railway communication. Hoare Miller and Company ran a daily service between Calcutta and Kalna in Burdwan, calling at Santipur. The same company ran another service between Calcutta and Murshidabad, calling at Navadwip on every alternate day chiefly during the rainy season on the Hooghli.[128]

"The fine strategical position of Katwa at the confluence of the Ajay and the Bhagirathi was soon recognized by the Muhammadan invaders, and in the time of the Nawabs this town was one of the most importent places of Bengal and was regarded as the key of Murshidabad." Katwa and its neighbouring place, Kalna assumed importance for the trade using the river as the route of transport.[129] The Muslims were "found in greatest strength in the thanas lying along Bhagirati. The Muhammadan invaders who followed Bakhtyar Khilji soon spread over Burdwan". Very soon Kalna and Katwa became Muslim settlements.[130] There was some concerted move on the part of the administration. The numerous *aimma* estates or rent-free holdings prove the liberal grants of land were the prime attraction to the new settlers, majority of whom were the Muslims. Often those grants were also used for a speedy conversion.[131]

The Mughals at least inherited such a scenario. The entire province was newly assessed in the 1580s and administration took charge of the minutes. It can be said that from the vast landmass running down from the southern parts of the then Bihar down to the south of Bengal was quickly occupied by them."The southern frontier of Muhammadan Bengal was the northern outskirt of the Sundarban...from Hatiagarh, south of Diamond Harbour on the Hooghli, to Bagherhat in southern Jessore."[132] Still Abul FazI does not provide details of Bengal. There are only a few references from which it can be understood that Bengal was "densely cultivated" province.[133] But which portions Abul Fazl makes us to believe is still not very clear.

It has been agreed that between 1595 and *c*.1910 the rate of increase in cultivation in both the Gangetic basin and delta was considerable.[134] From Abul Fazl it can be found that the places down to Satgaon were well-cultivated which produced regular rents. The "sarkar, or revenue division, of Satgaon, which extended from near Sagar island on the south to a little above Plassey on the north, and from the Kabdak river on the east to beyond Hooghli on the west."[135] The Mughals could extend their authority primarily on the lands which were away from the domains of the local chieftains, popularly called the *bhuians*. These chiefs had a sway over the lands in the eastern and southern Bengal. Besides them, the Mughals had to encounter the Portuguese pirates who had settled in the deep of the Sundarbans and from there they used to ransack the villages. To stop the menace the capital of the province was shifted to Dhaka in1603-04 and for next one hundred years the political and administrative activities were conducted from that city.

All the *Bhati* lands down to present day Nadia did not attract the Mughals. All those places had a scanty population. Land in the eastern part of the delta was only reclaimed during Akbar's reign.[136] For this, possible migration of people from the Bhagirathi-Hooghli region could not be ruled out.

The European Colonies

After travelling from Agra to Satgaon in the closing decade of the sixteenth century the English merchant Master Ralph Fitch commented, Bengal was "very fruitful and populous."[137] This Bengal as referred to most fairly was western part of Bengal. Fitch also described Satgaon as "a faire citie for a citie of the Moores".[138] There is no doubt that the number of Muslim urban population was much higher in comparison to the Hindus in the medieval period in Bengal.

But Satgaon lost its place of eminence for the shifting of the course of the Damodar. Apart from this the river Saraswati also lost vitality. Still Hooghli commanded importance as a populous town for long. After visiting the place in 1676, Streynsham Master observed "Hooghli having the advantage of Situation upon the banks of the river Ganges...was in former times in the prosperity of the Portuguez when in the possesion sailed to yearly from India and Malaya with 60: 80: to 100: vessels".[139] Same was the observation of Thomas Bowrey around the same period. He found the "great towne of Hooghli" "is a famous and Sumptuous place, adorned with many fine Structures and very populous" with a "very large Bazar."[140] Both Hooghli and the Dutch factory at nearby Chinsura were designed to raise a modern urban settlement. Visiting these places in 1676, Streynsham Master reported that the Dutch factory "is very large and well built, with two Quadrangles. The Director showed us the new built warehouses, which are three very large". Apart from those there were other structures well built and also well maintained.[141] Similarly, "There being houses standing to and fro in the Hooghli, which are inhabited by Englishmen some in the Companyes service, and some freemen".[142] Both sides of the river Hooghli were well-cultivated. Agriculture helped artisan craft to grow. The economic activities were furthered by the presence of the foreign trading companies.

The Portuguese were the first to arrive here and founded the *Porto Piqueno* or the small heaven at Satgaon while Chittagong was the *Porto Grande* or the great heaven. In 1568 Caesar Frediricki, the Venetian merchant, noticed the port hubbing in activities. But the Portuguese earned a very bad name for their piracy. In the name of trade they started looting the properties of the local people. The account by Shihab ud din Talish, roughly at the end of the seventheenth century, "would seem to show that Hooghli could not have escaped the raids of the Magh and Firinghi pirates".[143] Being annoyed by their conduct Shah Jahan ordered the demolition of the Portuguese factory in 1632. Later however, they were restored to their places and were allowed to build a town to the north of the former fort, still known by the Europeans as Bandel and by the local people as "Balaghar"[*strong house*]. The land thus assigned [777 *bighas*] was given free of rent, and the friars were declared exempted from the authority of the *subahdars, faujdars* and other officers of state. No doubt, the

Portuguese had a very dubious distinction of being a race of pirates and whenever possible they started looting.

"Except for such raids, the internal peace of the district was only twice disturbed. The first occasion was in 1686-89, when war broke out between the British and the Mughals...Ten years later a serious rebellion broke out. Subha Singh, a zamindar of parganas Chitwa and Barda in the Ghatal sub-division of the Midnapore district, becoming dissatisfied with the government, joined hands with Rahim Khan, an Afghan chief of Orissa." They slew Raja Krishna Ram of Burdwan in a battle and took Hooghli. Then they spread over Murshidabad Kasimbazar, Malda as well as Rajmahal.[144]

The relatively calm atmosphere helped agriculture and trade in many ways that ultimately helped to spread human settlements in the entire region. Irrespective of the changes made in the course of the river the growth of habitation did not suffer. The northeastern portion of the river Hooghli was more affected. Here a number of *chars* [*or sandy landmass over and above the water level*] were formed and the river had shifted eastwards. The map of Stavorinus drawn in 1769 "showed Guptipara to the east of the Ganges whereas it now lies west of the main channel".[145] "If not swept away in a year or two, the *chars*, when sufficiently raised above flood-level are eagerly sought after by the ryots" for the high degree of fertility.[146]

The entire area was full of activities during the Mughal rule. Thomas Bowrey noted that, roughly in 1623 both the English and the Dutch merchants arrived here. But Bowrey had been challenged by Henry Yule who thinks that the English started their factory at Hooghli after 1651 and according to the English records, the Dutch trade from Chinsura and adjoining place of the town of Hooghli, commenced only in 1634. Bowrey observed that nearly one thousand "Frangues" i.e., Europeans used to live along the river Hooghli in the 1670s.[147] Roughly during the same period Hooghli had become the imperial port of Bengal. "For centuries the immense wealth and resources of the delta were the lure of the foreign invaders. The Mughals described Bengal as the 'Paradise of nations.[148] "The Country is full of Castles and Towns".[149]

The Dutch settlement at Chinsura was about a mile [1.6 km] long, and about the same breadth. Apart from the Dutch the town was well populated by the Armenians and local people. The Dutch had another settlement at Baranagar on the eastern bank of the river in the district of 24 Parganas. To reap "the magnificent possibilities of Eastern commerce" the English East India Company made Hooghli their permanent centre. But they were unable to hold on due to a serious conflict with the local officials and, ultimately reached Calcutta on the other side of the river and made the place the second capital of the mighty British empire.

From the life history and the route of pilgrimage of Chaitanya a rough picture of settlements along the river Hooghli can be gathered. Chaitanya visited a number of places on his way to Puri. The important places were Agradwip in the district of Burdwan, Mahesh in the district of Hooghli and near Srirampur in the western bank. The well-populated places in the eastern bank included Kanchrapara near Jagaddal where once Pratapaditya is said to have his fort; the foremost Khardah and Kulinpara which was once the seat of famous savant Kamadev Pandit and, later, a place of residence of Nityananda—disciple of Chaitanya.; Kumarhatta or Halisahar; Sukhsagar [*which was wiped out in a flood in 1842*]; Sukhchar etc.[150] The presence of urban and semi-urban places obviously attracted the Europeans in this area.

The first settlement of the French at Bengal was at Hooghli in 1673. Under the permission of the Mughal Emperor in 1688, they built the Fort Orleans at Chandannagar. In 1731, Joseph Francoix Dupleix was appointed *Intendant* at Chandannagar and this place reached height of glory during the ten years of his tenure.

The Danes set up their factory at Gondalpara in the southeast of Chandannagar, the French settlement. In 1714, they had to leave in face of strong opposition from the local officials only to return on 8th October 1755 at Srirampur, a few miles downwards with the permission from Alivardi Khan. It grew rapidly, Srirampur had significant contributions towards the spread of education and culture for which nineteenth century Bengal acquired a very important name in history. Even in the late eighteenth century, Srirampur had urban facilities nearly of prevailing European standard. On 13th October 1799, four Baptist Missionaries arrived at Calcutta and found no place to reside. Then they proceeded to Srirampur and took lodging at the hotel, "which was then in a very flourishing state."[151] However, by a treaty of 22 February 1845, the King of Denmark transferred Srirampur to the English for 12 and 1/2 lacs of rupees.[152]

The Prussians had their settlement in the same region. In 1753, the Prussian King Frederick the Great founded the *Bengalische Handels-Gesellschaft* [or The Bengal Company of Embden, the then capital of Prussia]. Probably their presence was not to the liking of the then Nawab. He warned the English of the troublesome future in case the Germans did actually arrive. Still the Germans established a factory at a place, a mile [1.6 km] south of the Fort Orleans in the earlier years of the 1750s. But they worked only for a few years.[153] The Flemish also, for a short time carried on trade. The merchants of Ostend, Antwerp, and other towns in Flanders and Brabant appear to have endeavoured to get some share in the trade in India early in the eighteenth century. They also chose Hooghli as their seat of operation. In 1722, they arrived at Hooghli but in the very next year lost that. They obtained permission from the Nawab and built a factory at Bankibazar on the eastern side of the river at the north of Ichhapur. But here too the Ostends faced hostilities. All the other. European companies unitedly opposed them and routed them from their establishment in 1727. In this way both the banks of the river Hooghli were thickly populated by the Europeans and the habitation extended far especially, in the western bank.[154]

Expanding trade with Europe helped the settlements to grow chiefly along the western bank of the river Hooghli. Apart from this, the decay in the river Saraswati also contributed to this process. Some trading families—led by the Setts and Basaks, both of the weaving communities—came down along the bank of the Hooghli and raised their new settlements at Betore in the present district of Howrah. Betore very soon earned its reputation as a trading settlement. "Every year at Buttor [Betore] they make and unmake a Village, with houses and shoppes made of strawe, and with all things necessarie to their uses, and this village standeth as long as the ships ride there, and till they depart for the Indies, and when they are departed, every man goeth to his plot of houses, and setteth fire on them."[155]

There is little doubt about the fact that the settlements spread too far towards the mouth of the river Hooghli in the closing period of the Mughal rule though it was a popular belief that population declined in these regions for the siltation in the Saraswati and the Bhagirathi and then for epidemics consequent to the laying of the railways in the middle of the nineteenth century.[156] Hence the decline of the population here had started in the seventeenth century. But the same authority put a different story in the same book. "Towards the end of the seventeenth century we find the following important places on the Ganges mentioned in the *Khulasatul- Tawarikh*: Akbarnagar [*Rajmahal*], Maqsudabad [*Murshidabad*], Mirdadpur [*not identified*], Khizarhati [*31 miles east of Murshidabad*]". All those places were undoubtedly populous. "Mierdapur, Mexudabath and Hasierhati are to be found in Van den Broucke's map. Mierdapur is Mayrdadpur [*Thana Lalgola*] and Hasierhati is Haziragati. In 1666 Tavernier who travelled down the Ganges mentioned having reached a great town called Donapour...Donapour is also indicated in Van den Broucke's map as well as in Moll's and Rennell's... Travernier also visited Malda,

Murshidabad, Cossimbazar, Nadia and Hooghli, all of which were large towns."[157] All such places flourished for the arrival of the Europeans too.

Hence, down to Navadwip, both the banks of the river Hooghli had been well settled during the Mughal rule. Some such places had also acquired homogeneity. Baidyabati in the present district of Hooghli had long been a place for residence of the traditional mediciners while majority of places like Santipur and Navadwip were full of Vaisanavas. These places maintained their respective characters even in the face of the foreign challenge.

Expansion of the European trade changed the character of some places. Starting from the Portuguese all the European nationals were too overzealous. They always tried to build their own fortified factories and to defy the local authority. But "As European trade ... expanded, it led to an extension of cultivation and to the settlement of weavers and other artisans along the river bank, so much so that after the capture of Hooghli from the Portuguese, a *Faujdar* had to be specially posted to Hooghli to control the growing trade along the river." AII those happened in the middle of the seventheenth century. Moreover, for the safety in the trade route and for the protection of the residence along the same a fort was to be built at Tanna on the western side of the river Hooghli in the present district of Howrah in 1666.[158] Being surprised by the vibrant nature of this region Job Charnock even recommended Uluberia on the river Rupnarayan near its confluence with the river Hooghli as the ideal place for having a factory.[159] However, the proposal did not materialise. During the rule of Murshid Quli Khan a strip of land adjacent to the river Hooghli was separated and was raised into a distinct *zamindari* called Muhammad Aminpur which was ultimately the nucleus of the district of Howrah. This *zamindari* had a good revenue record.[160] The action taken by Murshid Quli was ample proof of the growing character of the region.

Most probably the well-settled artisan communities and their trade acted behind such growth in which the association with the Europeans was an important incident. This place already had a good settlement of the weavers for which the arrival of the Setts and Basaks was possible. The presence of this community could be traced in the records of 1580.[161] But they were not the only community. Congregation of the Brahmins and also the Kayasthas, the two high caste Hindus, in Bally and Howrah city proved the presence of professional castes and their patrons. They were encouraged by way of presentation of rent-free lands, during the Mughal rule. Certainly, the Europeans reaped a good harvest by employing such persons. In 1758, the East India Company issued orders that the weavers should be encouraged to settle here.[162]

Now one can find there the Tantis and Jugis of the Hindu community and the Jolahs of the Muslim community. All such sects were by birth weaver. The presence of the *Tutia Kaibartta* caste proves the rearing of silk which provided substantial occupations to a lot of people.[163] This growth continued under the rule of the Company too. One of the surprising additions was the presence of the north Indian *Ahir* or milkman community in the region.[164] Hence, the Europeans also encouraged the chain of migration.

Calcutta and New Agglomeration

From the later part of the eighteenth century Calcutta grew up as the future metropolis of India and this prospect generated varieties of employments. Hence number of people gathering in Calcutta and its near-by places also grew. With the passage of time and with the introduction of mechanised factories along the course of the river Hooghli the rate of immigration in this region took a turn towards a higher rate. Then came the railways in the mid-nineteenth century, which accelerated the process of urbanization. "The urban tract consists of the narrow riparian strip between the Hooghli on the east and the railway on the west "By the end of the nineteenth century all the towns namely. Tribeni, Bansberia, Hugli, Chinsura, Bhadreswar, Baidyabati, Srirampur, Kotrong, Uttarpara were here. With them was also Chandannagar, one of the best towns in Bengal".[165]

All these places presented certain unique features. The number of Brahmins was higher. Probably for the presence of the holy river and for employment opportunities in and around Calcutta since the second half of the eighteenth century the Brahmins used to reside in these places. Initially Calcutta failed to attract high-caste Hindus. The execution of Maharaja Nandakumar, an aristocratic Brahmin, in 1775 might have been the principal cause for the absence of his fellow-caste in Calcutta. In 1848, the District Magistrate remarked that, "he had not met with any single patch of uncultivated land, and added that the number of brick buildings in every village, the comfortable appearance of the dwellings, and the many articles of foreign manufacture which the inhabitants possessed".[166] The density of population was mainly caused by the availability of several types of occupations. Apart from agriculture, weaving and fishing were two major occupations. Though weaving industry faced serious competition due to the sharp inroads made by the machine-made cloths from England, the weaver community did not vanish at all. The presence of number of members of the lower castes—especially *Bagdis*. Kaibarttas and *Tiyars*[167] all of whom were engaged in fishing traditionally—proved the importance of fishing as a major occupation.

After taking the reins of administration the East India Company pursued the policy of raising revenues vigorously. Their other and major interest, however, was trade. To achieve both the targets the Company seriously kept its eyes on the better infrastructure so that communications did never falter. On 9th May 1800, all the district magistrates were asked by the Governor General in Council to adopt "every practical means" for "extending the agriculture and commerce of the country' and for "facilitating the communication between the principal Cities and Towns throughout the different Districts" .Not only road communications but also other necessities were looked after. Jungles were cut down. Embankments were maintained and roads were properly laid out."[168] The Company's officials' principal aim was to maintain law and order so that their trading as well as administrative interests did not face any trouble. For easy transactions at the towns and markets at various levels the Company's administration introduced a new set of police. On 20th October 1792, the Governor General in Council decided that the expenses of the police offices should be borne by the "merchants, Traders and Shopkeepers residing in the Towns, Bazars and Gunges". At the same time all the prevailing *Sayer* duties were abolished.[169] For providing "essentially necessary" a better sense of security among the inhabitants the Magistrates were also asked to divide their respective districts into suitable number of police jurisdictions.[170] No doubt that under the rule of the English the artisan crafts as well as number of urban settlements shrank.

With the increased trade and political influence Calcutta and those places around it got increased attention as well. Moreover, the gradual decline of Bengal's traditional artisan craft ruined a large number of urban and semi-urban settlements. The number of villages became higher and it acquired an all-India phenomenon.[171] All the wealth, all employment opportunities, all educational institutions and all industries were centred in Calcutta. In this way, the settlement along the river of Hooghli gathered fresh life. In the first few decades of the nineteenth century those traditional settlements like, Hooghli, Chinsura, Srirampur, Howrah on the western side and Naihati, Barrackpur, Titagarh, Khardah, Panihati, Baranagar, Chitpur, Kashipur, Garden Reach on the eastern side became more populous. As Lord Wellesley built a garden house at Barrackpur for weekly sojourn of the Governor General there and as one of the earliest army cantonments was stationed there since 1772 the road communication was also very good. Extensive civil constructions apart from the cantonment were undertaken.[172]

Rapidly Barrackpur acquired a new look, very distinct from the neighbouring places."It was originally the intention of Lord Wellesley to have brought all the public offices up from Calcutta" but, the Directors of the Company had prevented him from doing so.[173] Still a new urban character was imposed in the entire region. A variety of new employments emerged. The markets in the surroundings became increasingly busy.[174]

Warren Hastings first initiated a programme of raising a number of establishments on the eastern side of the river. In 1777, he had resolved to start a mint for coinage of money and five years after one Mr. John Princep was entrusted to have the project completed at Palta, a few miles above Barrackpur. However, the said mint could not work and had to be closed in 1784. But a powder works came up at Ichhapur at farther north of Palta. A little beyond Ichhapur, once stood Bankibazar. All these places had a cherished history of urban settlements. It is also believed that Pratapaditya of Jessore once had his fort and army establishment at Jagaddal—not very far from Bankibazar. A little beyond Bankibazar was a place called Samookgarh. The Raja of Burdwan who had taken a temporary refuge here fortified this during the Maratha inroads. A large quantity of land was allotted revenue-free to different persons in these areas during the Mughal rule. It became one of the major policies of the Company's government to resume as many such land as possible.[175] It was widely held in the Company's quarter that the lands along the riverside in the northern part of Calcutta were very populous and hence could produce hefty returns.[176] For the powder works at Ichhapur the surrounding areas got a boost in employment opportunities and prices of land rose. On the basis of the new valuations the Company's government resolved to assess the lands up to Bhatpara in the north of Ichhapur.[177]

Similar was the conditions of the western bank. The nineteenth century witnessed remarkable industrial activities in these places. The coming of the railways accelerated the process of urbanisation. The jute mills, spinning mills and varieties of manufacturing units transformed the nature of settlements there. Konnagar was one such populous and wealthy place. The residents of this place and also its nearby places used to amass huge fortune at Calcutta and invested money in constructing magnificent houses and other beautiful structures.[178] Very close to Konnagar was Rishra. " Perhaps no place presents more of the appearance of an English country seat than this mansion [*i.e; The Rishra House*]... The tradition ran that the trees were planted by Mrs Hastings, when she and Warren Hastings made this villa their temporary residencc... A little higher up is the village of Muhesh... There is evidence that it was in existence three centuries ago, and that it stood, where it now does." It was simply surprising that nearly all the villages and towns on the vicinity of the riverbank "stand precisely where it stood three centuries ago, on the immediate bank of the river. This leads us to the conclusion that there has been scarcely any material change in its current within these limits during this long period".[179]

All the adjoining places had a long history of settled village and towns. Champdani, Giretty, Bhadreswar, all belonged to a chain of well-settled urban areas. For the presence of the royal port of Satgaon in the vicinity these places seemed to be well-populated even during the days of the independent *Sultans* of Bengal. The settlement pattern assumed a new shape with the victory of the English in Palasi. In 1690 Job Charnock finally came down to Calcutta and established a new factory for the East India Company. For long the Company's aim had been to have a permanent establishment, and that too in a congenial atmosphere. Sir Joshia Child in the 1660s first expressed the wish. But the Company had many problems. However, after a serious conflict with the Mughal officials at Hooghli ultimately Charnock chose this place. His choice proved right. Then the Company purchased the *talookdari* rights of the three villages namely, Sutanuti, Gobindapur and Kalikata or Calcutta from the family of Savarna Chaudhury. Since the factory of the Company was within the village of Kalikata or Calcutta the entire place ultimately was known by its name.

All those places produced annual rents and if it is judged in the standard of those days the amount was not so meagre. It is believed that mainly some enterprising weavers' family who originally hailed from Satgaon had arrived in the northern portion of the city and formed their settlement. Since the principal occupation was weaving and trade in cotton yarn as well as cloth the place was known as *Sutanuti.* Another story runs in this manner that those people established their settlement at Gobindapur after the name of *Lord Gobinda* or Krishna, their family deity. Whatever may be the reason for the early settlement, the growth was certainly not very negligible. The Company expressed interest involving their new settlement and they succeeded in procuring permission from the Mughal Emperor for purchase of 38 villages around those three villages in 1717. From the list of those 38 villages it can be found that villages even on the western bank of the river were also included in it. But the Company failed to buy any of them due to strong opposition from the successive Nawabs of the province.

Just like Howrah, the 24 Parganas—in which the city of Calcutta was originally placed—was similarly well populated. From the revenue record as appeared in the *Ain-i-Akbari* it can be found that this portion formed a part of the *sarkar* or the revenue division of Satgaon which extended from near Sagar Island on the south to a little above Palasi on the north. Both sides of the river were assessed in the single revenue division.

The events of 1757 removed all the obstacles. The first achievement was the acquisition of the *zamindary* of neighbouring 24 Parganas from Mir Jafar, the new Nawab. A mere cluster of three villages became the biggest urban agglomeration in Asia. The transfer of all the administrative authority from Murshidabad to Calcutta transformed the latter's fortune. Then, after the passing of Lord North's Acts by the Parliament in England, the prestige of Calcutta was enhanced further. First it was the capital city of one of the most wealthy provinces of the decaying Mughal empire, then it was the headquarter of the flourishing East India Company in the whole of Asia. All the job opportunities were gradually being concentrated in increasing number in Calcutta. The pressure on land was increasing and the same heat spread around the adjacent places.

The Company started building the Fort William in 1758 by removing the entire village of Gobindapur. The people so removed got their new shelter chiefly within Sutanuti.[180] By then the land prices in that place had reached at a higher scale and infrastructure, however nominal, was raised. Those were principally raised by the settlers

Calcutta presented a city that was basically divided into two parts-one housed the colonial masters and the men of the breed and the other housed the locals. Calcutta was divided into 'white town' populated by the Europeans and the 'black town', populated by the Indians.

Calcutta's urbanisation presents a unique history. The Company refrained from investing any amount from its coffer though the said coffer was built-up with the money collected here by various means. Even prior to 1757, in face of the Maratha raids in the 1740s the Company had mobilized the residents within its area to contribute towards digging the Maratha Ditch [*present Upper and Lower Circular Roads*]. This was the single defence barrier of its kind in the entire province. Ultimately this protective arrangement helped to build up confidence within the minds of the people. Very soon Calcutta became the destiny of many. Flow of money was also considerable and the residents were provided with certain legal umbrella, which was framed after the prevailing legal system of England.[181] The settlers knew that the securities of their persons and also their properties could not be injured without due process of law. The judges appointed in the then Supreme Court, constituted after the enactment of Lord North's Act, always looked the executive authority at askance and considered themselves as the guardian of law. Hence judicial activism helped in many ways.

All these in combination inspired the people in buying lands. Since each of the holdings produced rent, the Company could achieve two aims very comfortably. First, the settlements spread, number of rent-paying population increased, and, secondly, the quantity of rent also increased. In this way a number of new localities took their shapes. Rich and influential people started arriving some of whose names are synonymous with the early stage of urbanisation. Raja Nabakrishna, Dewan Ganga Gobinda Singha, Baranasi Ghosh, Kasinnath Babu and Madan Datta are a few among the long list. They invested money, brought people for new settlements, reclaimed lands, sold and purchased suitable properties and fought with each other for having better fortunes. It was these people who curved the future of Calcutta's real estates in the late eighteenth and early nineteenth centuries.

The Company's government usually refrained from investing any fund for raising urban structure. Their only investment in the late eighteenth century was for the Fort William. But that too took a very long time to be completed.[182] Hence the Company's contribution towards the creation of job opportunities, however unskilled, was nothing but nominal. But the Company's only major contribution was in the field of law. It allowed the settlers the right of pre-emption and the right of easement over the adjoining properties. Both of these were suitably exploited by the settlers.[183]

The bazaars were the most lucrative investments that produced regular rents. Calcutta in the late eighteenth century roughly grew up surrounding a number of such bazaars, some of which still exist in the same places as they did more than two hundred years ago. But the Indians considered the lands along the riverfront a prize-possession. The rate of rent was also higher in this area in comparison with the lands on the east of Chitpur Road-the principal road running between north and south in the northern portion of the city.[184] Apart from the presence of the river availability of better infrastructure probably contributed towards enhanced prices.[185]

The Company initiated a policy for regular survey of the entire city once in ten years. After every survey the holders of land were required to collect fresh *patta* or deed for which they had to pay a stipulated fee. The amount of fees generally surpassed the cost of the survey.[186] That the prices of lands were increasing could be proved from the official records prepared after such measurements. The importance of Calcutta attracted people from various parts of India for various types of occupation. It was not only the destiny of the people from neighbouring provinces but also from faraway places like Rajasthan. The Marwaries from Marwar in the desert were one such group who made Calcutta their second home.[187] Apart from them the people from far like Central Asia and even China also made Calcutta their permanent place of residence. Atchew, a Chinese was granted substantial quantity of land in the south of Calcutta for settling a Chinese colony. Often there were complaints of forcible occupation against those Chinese.[188]

In the nineteenth century, "the advantages of the Calcutta neighbourhood were many: the sea-entry to the areas of the greatest population and [*at least the rise of Punjab and Deccan cotton*] of highest agricultural productivity-including that of the great early staple exports, opium, tea, indigo; a monopoly of world jute supply at its doors; the only well-developed network of internal navigation in India; the region where British territorial power on any large scale was oldest; the seat of government, and, above all, of a forceful, not to say ruthless, dominant minority of British business men. Calcutta soon outstripped Madras and was not seriously challenged by Bombay until the cotton boom of the American Civil War and the opening of the Suez Canal".[189]

Calcutta's growth was unimaginable. Though full of bushes "pent narrowly between the river and the Salt Water Lakes..., there rose a 'city of palaces'—and a far larger city of hovels."[190] Calcutta—like the other towns on the banks of the river Hooghli was mostly an over-grown village retaining its rural character in some form or other. Certainly Calcutta and the adjoining places were able to reap the fruits of the earlier settlements that had sprung up mainly on the western bank of the river. In the nineteenth century, "the modern industrial landscape was appeared to this basin which was accelerated by the British policy to undermine the handicraft exports, aiming at the succeeding in destroying the indigenous art and craftsmanship of the country as a whole and in this region in particular. By the time the new transport arteries, the railways and modern road-nets, could develop this river frontage has acquired as much potentiality as to compel these arteries to pass through this urbanised belt, occupying the levees of the oscillating Hooghli channel, along whatever narrow high belts were available".[191] The importance of the river could be understood by the presence, a good number of *Ghats* i.e; landing place, namely, Old Fort Ghat, Clive Street Ghat, Jackson's Ghat, Armenian Ghat, Raja Daby Singh's, Rammohan Mullick's, Rooplall Baboo's, Cossinath Baboo's, Meerbahar Ghat, Nawab's Ghat, Seebtala Ghat, Puttorah Ghat, Jagannath Ghat, Neemtala Ghat etc.[192] All those *Ghats* were situated in the northern part of the city and were the main centre of trade and commerce. Land on the river bank was also leased out to the owners of the lands on the opposite side of the road at "so high a rate" as six rupees per cottah per month.[193] But the demand of land was so high that encroachments were rampant. This congestion posed serious difficulties to the moorings of the ships.[194]

Increasingly Calcutta became a "populous city" and the rulers began to think schemes for better living. Though complaints for unhealthiness regularly poured into the official quarters nothing was done to make the environment congenial for better living. The rate of mortality was too high[195] among the Europeans. For the absence of proper information it is not possible to assess the condition of the local population. However, a Native Hospital was opened in 1792, which failed to cater to the needs. Since there had never been any systematic arrangement for cleaning the city the places like Bara Bazar remained congested.[196] By the turn of the nineteenth century, Calcutta, particularly the Native Calcutta "is a dense mass of Native houses and huts" and another hospital was conceived in 1837.[197] That was known as the Fever Hospital whose governing body consisted better known "Natives" like, Dwarkanath Tagore and his brother Ramanath etc.

Meanwhile communication network around Calcutta had been improved. The "system of channels was devised..., in order to allow country boats to pass from the eastern districts to Calcutta by a direct inland route, and the problem has been to keep the natural cross-channels clear of silt, and to connect them with each other and with Calcutta by a system of artificial canals".[198] Major Tolley had canalised the old bed of the river Ganga that was popularly known as *Adi Ganga* in the 1770s.[199] For his efforts the distance between Barisal, a rice-producing district in eastern Bengal and the river Hooghli was shorten considerably. This helped in transporting goods from the eastern part to Calcutta, and *vice versa*. In 1810, a further step was taken to improve the approaches to Calcutta, and old channel through the Salt water Lake "what is now known as the Baliaghata Canal. Between 1826 and 1831 a new route was opened between Calcutta and the Jamuna river, following the same direct easterly course as the present Bhangar Canal."[200] This network was further extended when the Circular Canal was dug in 1831. In 1859, the New Cut was opened which led southeast from Ultadanga, on the Circular Canal, 3 miles [5 km] east of Chitpur to Dhapa on the Baliaghata Canal. Since the pressure on the port at Calcutta was sharply increasing a new dock for the Calcutta Docking Company was sanctioned at Kidderpur on the bank of the Tolley's Canal.[201]

Similarly, the railway network was developed as soon as that mechanical wonder arrived in India. When the rest of India was connected from Howrah through the railways the parts of Bengal were connected with Calcutta from a terminal at Sealdah on the eastern fringe of the then city. The works started from Sealdah in 1859 and the line was opened as far as Ranaghat in 1862. Another line in the southern direction up to Port Canning was opened. This line helped easy communication to and from the Sundarbans. Chitpur was chosen as the terminal of goods traffic.

The effects of the industrial revolution were felt here very widely. A dockyard, a number of ship-repairing workshops, mechanised mills and then the introduction of the railways transformed the character of both Calcutta and Howrah. Calcutta could not be directly connected with the rest of India by the railways. Principal barrier was the river itself. But Raniganj and the entire coal belt were to be connected with Calcutta. Hence, the railway tracks were laid from Howrah. By the last quarter of the nineteenth century Howrah was connected with as far as Lahore in the north west of India. This opened the floodgates of immigration in this region. The immigrants got easy jobs in the growing factories of various types. "Howrah, which Bishop Heber described in 1823 as a place 'Chiefly inhabited by the shipbuilders,'and which in 1848 was referred to as 'the wapping of Calcutta inhabited chiefly by persons connected with docks and shipping began to expand rapidly'" in many directions.[202]

Daily Calcutta became populated and the settlements spread without any prior programme. The Company had invented a unique scheme by which it could lay new road, clear jungles and develop new homestead lands without spending any amount from its coffer. In this way the Lottery Committee was born in 1793. Tickets for lottery were sold and with the sale proceeds a fund was created after allotting the prizes. The prizes were allotment of lands in chosen localities. With the profits of the lottery some notable structures were however, built. The Town Hall was the best example. In 1805, under the immediate patronage of the Governor General, the Lottery Committee was properly organised. In that year the lottery was advertised for five lacs of rupees in 5,000 tickets of Rs. 1,000 each. This was so popular that on 20 January 1809, the government formed an official organisation consisting of six commissioners for the conduct of lotteries for the improvement of the city.[203] But that was not the proper answer to the various problems which a budding urban centre used to face. It was feared that "without the aid of Government, this city will experience the gradual effects of neglect".[204] In general the poor men found their shelter in the tenements, which were commonly called *Bustees*. The rich people usually owned those *Bustees,* which were established by them to house their own men.[205] In the beginning of the nineteenth century the importance for development of those *Bustees* was felt. But the government refrained from bearing any responsibility on the arguments that those were owned privately. Since the municipal administration was yet to take shape the goverment felt that it was the duty of the respective owners to look after the *Bustees*. When the municipality was formed one of its basic duties was to frame rules for the betterment of the *Bustees*. Hence came the rules which guided the construction and maintenance of the *Bustees*.[206]

With the coming of modern industries the inflow of labours—chiefly from northern India—gave a new shape to the *Bustees*. The pattern of population mix-up also changed. The railways made the movements easier hitherto not possible. A large number of industrial colonies grew up, majority of which were filled up by the non-Bengali speaking populace. Their lifestyle also differed from the local people. Since industrialisation in eastern India took off at the places along the banks of the Hooghli the pattern of settlements had also undergone serious changes.

NOTES

1 R. L, Singh ed.; *India: A Regional Geography*, p. 226

2 Bipradass Pipilai *Manasamangala.* Canto IX. pt. 3

3 Haraprasad Shastri; "Notes on the Banks of the Hugli in 1495" in the *Proceedings of the Asiatic Society, Bengal,* 1892

4 Haraprasad Shastri; *op. cit*

5 Asit Bandopadhyay; *Bangla Sahityer Sampurina Itibritta* in Bengali, (Calcutta,Magh, 1384 B.S.) p. 75; here the authenticity of the text is challenged.

6 H. Blochinann; *op. cit.*, p. 25

7 Mukundaram Chakroborty *Chandimangala.* No. 130

8 *B.O.R. Police Circular Progs.* Vol. 3. A letter dated 30 June 1793 from the Magistrate of Nadia to the Sub Secretary of the Revenue Dept.

9 *Gazetteer, Nadia*, p. 180

10 Jayananda, *Chaitanyamangala. Nadiakhanda*; Nadia—3.

11 Brindaban Das, *Chaitanyabhagvat, Adikhanda*, pp. 46-7

12 *Chaitanyabhagvat, Adikhanda*, pt. II., pp. 5-6

13 *Gazetteer, Nadia*, p. 182

14 *Ibid.*

15 *Chaitanyabhagvat,* p. 246

16 Haridass Dass; *Gaudya Vaisnava Abhidan* in Bengali (Navadwip, 1956) Vol. IV. p. 1846

17 Haridass Dass; *op. cit.* p. 1976

18 *Gazetteer, Nadia.* p. 249, p. 258

19 *Chandimangala.* Nos. 347-48, 414 15,417-18, 514

20 *Chandimangala.* Nos. 406, 440.

21 Haridass Dass; *op. cit.*, pp. 1870-71

22 R. L. Singh; *op. cit.*, pp. 274-6

23 Mirza Nathan; *Baharistan-i Ghayabi.* tr. M.I. Borah. (Gauhati, 1936) Vol. I., p. 43

24 *The Book of Durate Barbosa*. Translation from Portuguese text; first published in 1812 by Mansel Longworth Dames. (London, 1921) Vol. II., p. 136

25 *The....Barbosa.* p. 147

26 Thomas Bowrey; *op. cit* 1905, p. 132

27 *Indian Travels of Thevenot and Careri ...*, p. 96

28 Moreland; *India at the Death of Akbar,* p. 123

29 *India at the Death of Akbar.* P. 10; p.13

30 Satish Chandra; *Medieval India.* (New Delhi, 1999) Vol. II., p. 38

31 R.L. Singh; *op. cit.*, p. 272

32 Bowrey; *op. cit.*, pp.132-33

33 *Gazetteer, Malda.* p. 27

34 Malda Dist. Collectorate, *Malda; Books of Patta.* (Bound Vol) No 1

35 *Gazetteer, Malda,* p. 27

36 Blochmann; op. cit., p.13

37 *Gazeteer, Murshidabad,* p. 9

38 *Gazetteer, Murshidabad,* p. 3.

39 Blochmann; *op. cit.*

40 R.L.Singh; *op. cit.,* p. 274

41 R.K.Mukerjee; *op. cit.,* p. 33

42 *The Voyages of Caesar Frediricki...*, p. 483.

43 *The Voyages of Caesar Frediricki...*, p. 476

44 Moreland; *India at the Death of Akbar,* P. 212.

45 Moreland; *India at the Death of Akbar,* P. 123.

46 H. Nelson Wright; *The Coinage and Metrology of the Sultans of Delhi.* New Delhi, 1974, p.160

47 R.K. Mukerjee; *op. cit.*, p. 74

48 R.K. Mukerjee; *op. cit.,* pp. 76-77

49 Blochmann; *op. cit.*, p. 35

50 Ralph A. Nicholas; 'Vaisanavism and Islam in Rural Bengal" in David Kopf ed. *Bengal: Region Identity.* (Michigan, 1969)

51 Blochmann; *op. cit.*, p. 35

52 *Gazetteer, Malda,* p. 27

53 *Gazetteer, Malda*, p. 29

54 *Gazetteer, Malda*, p. 27

55 *B.O.R. Misc. Progs.*, 17 Oct., 1789

56 *B.O.R. Misc. Progs.*, 21 Feb., 1832

57 *Gazetteer, Malda,* p. 53

[58] *Gazetteer, Malda,* p. 54

[59] *Gazetteer, Malda,* p. 55

[60] *B.O.R. Misc. Progs.,* 4 Sept., 1793

[61] *Gazetteer, Malda,* p. 55

[62] *Gazetteer, Malda,* p. 59

[63] *Gazetteer, Malda,* p. 61

[64] *Gazetteer, Malda,* p. 84

[65] Beveridge; 'Old Places of Murshidabad'. pt.1 in the *Calcutta Review.* April, 1892

[66] Jean Baptiste Tavernier; *Travels in India.* Trns.V. Bell. (Oxford, 1925) Vol. I., p. 108

[67] Beveridge; 'Old Places of Murshidabad.' pt.11. in the *Calcutta Review.* October, 1892

[68] *B.O.R. Lower Provinces, Land Rev. Progs.,* 27 Sept., 1850.

[69] *B.O.R. Misc. Progs.,* 10 March, 1789

[70] Beveridge; ...*Old Places* etc., pt. 1.

[71] W.W. Hunter; *A Statistical Account of Bengal* (London, 1876. N. Delhi reprint, 1984.) Vol. IX., p. 64

[72] S. C. Nandy; *Bandar Kasimbazar* (in Bengali) (Calcutta,1978) pp. 31

[73] Beveridge; old Places ...etc., pt. 1

[74] *B.O.R. Misc. Progs.,* 7 April, 1789

[75] *B.O.R. Misc. Progs.,* 11 Jan., 1790

[76] *B.O.R.Police Circular Progs.*Vol.2 A letter dated 12 July, 1793 from the Magistrate of Murshidabad to the Governor General in Council

[77] for details see *Maharashtrapurana* published in major part in the *Jhar.* September 2004

[78] *Gazetteer, Murshidabad,* p. 76

[79] *Ibid.*

[80] *Gazetteer, Burdwan,* p. 5

[81] *Gazetteer, Burdwan,* p. 14

[82] *Gazetteer, Burdwan,* p.18

[83] *Gazetteer, Burdwan,* p. 22

[84] *Surathals in the Bazee Zamin Daftar...for the month of July, 1791.* List no.35

[85] *Sunnuds entered in the Bazee Zamin Daftar...for the month of Feb., 1784* List no. 113.

[86] *Sunnuds...for the month of April 1789.* List no. 98

[87] *Sunnuds...for the month of Feb. 1789.* List no. 106

[88] *Sunnuds...for the month of June,* 1784. List no.108

[89] Malda Collectorate *Old Pattas* in bound vol. no. 3

[90] Govt. of Bengal; *Home Dept.Records Branch, Collection of Pattas.* in Bengali and Dutch languages Bundle no.1

91 for details see Soumitra Sreemani; *Anatomy of a Colonial Town: Calcutta, 1756-1794* (Calcutta, 1994)...,.pp. 3-4

92 *Sunnuds...for the month of Jan., 1783.* List no. 23

93 *Sunnuds...for the month of July, 1784.* List no. 46

94 *Sunnuds...for the month of May, 1783.* List no. 48

95 Satish Chandra Mitra; *Jessore Khulnar Itihaas* (in Bengali) Shib Sankar Mitra ed. (Calcutta, 1963) Vol. I., pp. 68-9

96 *Gazetteer, 24 Parganas,* p. 9

97 *Chaitanyabhagvat,* p. 220

98 Haridass Das; *op. cit.,* Vol. IV., pp.1870-71

99 'Report on the Hooghly River and its Headwaters' in the *Rivers of Bengal.* (Calcutta, 2002) Vol.II., pp. 4-5

100 W.W. Hunter, *A Statistical Account of Bengal: Sundarbans.* (reprint, Calcutta,) p. 101

101 *Gazetteer, the 24 Parganas.* B. De. ed. (Calcutta, 1994), p. 71

102 R.M. Eaton; *op. cit.,* pp. 209-12

103 *John Marshall in India,* p. 62

104 James Wise; 'Muhammadans of Eastern Bengal' *in the Journal of the Asiatic Society of Bengal* Vol. 63

105 *Ibid.*

106 B.D. ed. *Gazetteer, the 24 Parganas,* p. 451

107 James Wise; *op. cit.*

108 R.M. Eaton; *op. cit.,* chiefly the ch. 5

109 Beveridge; Old Places...pt. 1

110 R.K. Mukerjee; *op. cit.,* p. 181

111 *B.O.R. Police Circular Progs.* Vol. 3. A letter dated 2 May 1793 from the Magistrate of Murshidabad to the Governor General in Council

112 *Sudder B.O.R. Lower Provinces Progs.* 25 Aug., 1841

113 Hunter; *A Statistical Account...*Vol. IX., pp. 83-4

114 *Gazetteer, Murshidabad,* p. 49

115 *The Diaries of Streynsham Master....* pp.321-22. Ed.'s note, *Puttolee in Rennell's Atlas-is and between Bickeyhaut and Nuddeah i.e., Navadwip.*

116 *B.O.R.of Lower Provinces, Land Revenue.* 13 July, 1852

117 *B.O.R. Misc. Progs.,* 17 Jan., 1800

118 *B.O.R. Misc. Progs.,* 7 March, 1800

119 *Gazetteer, Nadia,* p. 4

120 *B.O.R. Misc. Progs.,* 2 April, 1794

121 *Gazetteer, Nadia,* p. 4

122 *Gazetteer, Nadia,* p. 6

123 *Gazetteer, Nadia,* p. 7

124 *B.O.R. Misc. Progs.,* 8 Sept., 1794

125 *Gazetteer, Nadia,* p. 12

126 *B.O.R. Misc. Progs.* 23 Sept., 1814

127 *Gazetteer, Nadia,* p. 67

128 *Gazetteer, Nadia,* p. 98

129 *Gazetteer, Burdwan,* p. 44

130 *Gazetteer, Burdwan,* p. 49

131 *Ibid.*

132 Blochmann: *op. cit.,* p.18

133 Irfan Habib; *Agrarian System of Mughal India.* (New Delhi, Reprint 2000), p.58

134 Habib;*op. cit.,* pp. 21-2

135 L.S.S. O'Malley; *Gazetteer, the 24 Parganas,* pp. 33-4

136 Habib; *op. cit.,* p.10

137 *The Voyages of Caesar Frediricki...,* p. 476

138 *The Voyages of Caesar Frediricki...* p. 483

139 *The Diaries of Streynsham Master...,* pp. 40-41

140 Bowrey; *op. cit.,* pp.132-133

141 *The Diaries of Streynsham Master...,* pp. 40-41

142 *The Diaries of Streynsham Master...,* p. 47

143 *Gazetteer, Hooghly,* p. 32

144 *Gazetteer, Hooghly,* p. 33-4

145 *Gazetteer, Hooghly,* p. 12

146 *Gazetteer, Hooghly,* p. 135

147 Bowrey; *op. cit.,* p. 195

148 R.K. Mukerjee; *op. cit.,* p. 33

149 *Indian Travels of Thevanot and Careri...,* p. 96

150 Haridass Dass; *op. cit.* Vol. IV, p.1825 and p.1981

151 Marshmann; 'Notes on the Right Bank of the Hooghly' in the *Calcutta Review.* No.VI Vol. 4 (1845)

152 *Gazetteer, Hooghly,* pp. 76-79

153 *Gazetteer, Hooghly,* p. 87

154 *Gazetteer, Hooghly,* p. 94

155 *The Voyages of Caesar Fredericki,* p. 486

156 R.K. Mukerjee; *op. cit.,* pp. 76-77

157 R.K. Mukerjee; *op. cit.,* pp. 179-180

[158] *Gazetteer, Howrah,* p. 20

[159] *Gazetteer, Howrah,* p. 21

[160] *B.O.R. Misc. Progs.* 12 Sept., 1794

[161] *Gazettee r, Howrah,* p. 97

[162] *Ibid.*

[163] *Gazetteer, Howrah,* pp. 98-99

[164] *Gazetteer, Howrah,* pp. 40-41

[165] *Gazetteer, Hooghly,* p. 95

[166] *Gazetteer, Hooghly,* p. 172

[167] *Gazetteer, Hooghly,* p. 173 and p. 176

[168] *B. O.R. Misc. Progs.,* 9 May, 1800

[169] *B.O.R. Police Circular Progs.,* Vol. I. A Circular dated 7 Dec.1792 from the Sub. Secretary to the Magistrates. Para 3

[170] *Ibid.* para 15

[171] *The Cambridge Economic History of India.* Vol. I, p. 7

[172] *C.O.R. Progs.* 12 Feb. 1784; 24 April 1784; 19 July, 1784

[173] Marshmann; 'Notes on the Left or Calcutta Bank of the Hooghly' in the *Calcutta Review.* No.VI. Vol. 3 (1845)

[174] *B.O.R. Misc. Progs.* 1 Oct. 1789; 10 Dec. 1789, here the improvements of the bazaars in Palta were the points of issue

[175] *C.O.R. Progs.* 16 Aug., 1784

[176] *C.O.R. Progs.*15 April, 1784; 5 July, 1784; 25 Oct., l784

[177] *B.O.R. Misc. Progs.*,18 May, 1792

[178] Marshmann; 'Notes on the Right Bank of the Hooghly'

[179] *Ibid.*

[180] Sreemani; *op. cit.,* p. 45

[181] Sreemani; *op. cit.,* pp. 7-14

[182] Sreemani; *op. cit.,* pp.15-16, pp. 23-24

[183] Sreemani; *op. cit.,* pp. 20-21

[184] *B.O.R. Misc. Progs.* 29 April, 1789

[185] *Home Dept. Public Branch.* 11 July, 1786

[186] *Rev. Board consisting of Whole Council Progs.* 23 July, 1773

[187] T.A.Timberg; 'A Note on the arrival of the Calcutta's Marwaries' in the *Bengal Past and Present* Vol. XC. pt. 1. No. 169

[188] *C.O.R. Progs.* 23 April, 1781 and 20 June, 1781

[189] Spate and Learmonth; *op. cit.,* p. 594

[190] Spate and Learmonth; *op. cit.,* p. 593

191 R.L. Singh; *op. cit.*, p. 281

192 *Judicial Dept, Judicial Branch.* 7 Nov., 1849

193 *Marine Dept. Progs.*, 2 March, 1842

194 *Marine Dept. Progs.*, 1 April, 1842

195 *Fever Hospital Progs.*, Vol. I., pp.

196 *Fever Hospital Progs.*, Vol. I., pp. 15-16

197 *Fever Hospital Progs.*, Vol. I., pp. 3-6, pp. 11-12

198 *Gazetteer, the 24 Parganas*, p. 205

199 Sreemani; *op. cit.*, pp. 204-206

200 L.S.S.O' Malley, *Gazetteer, the 24 Parganas* pp. 205-206

201 *Marine Dept. Progs.*, 18 Sept., 1843

202 *Gazetteer, Howrah*, p. 166

203 *Census of India;* 1901. Vol.VI. pt .3., p. 14.

204 *Fever Hospital Progs.*, Vol. I., pp., 13-18

205 Sreemani; "Sampattir Adhikar O Nagarayan, Astadash Shataker Sheserdhe Kolkata" in *Aitihasik*. September, 1998

206 *Municipal Dept, Municipal Branch Progs.*, Sept., 1875. File No. 99; Serial No. 7/9 'B', 68-71

5

CULTURAL LIFE

The history of Bengal presents unique facades. Since ancient days the geographical boundaries were distinctly defined in such names like, *Rarh, Barendra, Banga* etc. The western portion of the river Bhagirathi was and also is identified as *Rarh.* The landscape, the agrarian product varieties, social manners and customs and also language differed from those on the eastern portion. The settlement pattern also reflected those differences. Bengal's antiquity can be traced in history that is chiefly the history of mostly western, northern and north-western Bengal. Since the lower Bengal was the creation of the rivers Ganga, Padma and Madhumati and it was much young than its other parts the settlement pattern in this region differed from those regions. The culture of Bengal in the ancient and early medieval periods was chiefly shaped by Gaur-the region, which also witnessed the first arrival of the Muslims in Bengal. Quoting from the *Kamasutra* written by Vatsayana in the third or fourth century Dr. Nihar Ranjan Ray proves that the people of Gaur had a very high quality of urban life. He also quoted the findings of Huen Tsang [*in the seventh century*] who was all praise for the academic pursuits of the people. For gaining better education the students often went as far a place as Kashmir[1].

These cultural milieus had shaped the life of the people of Bengal. Bengal's riches in one hand and its improved life-style in other had gained fame for it. Even Marco Polo was aware of the place. Chaitanya's preaching and the rise of the *Vaisanava* movements in the sixteenth century brought a metamorphosis in the daily life of Bengal. Already the Hindu society had undergone a sea change for the arrival of the Muslims in the earlier decades of the sixteenth century. Tom Pires after visiting Bengal remarked that the king was a Muslim and all the kings for last three centuries prior to his arrival were also Muslims. But Pires had never mentioned about the religion of the masses.[2] Since the rate of conversion was not so heavy in the Bhagirathi-Hooghli region the co-habitation between the two communities helped in the creation of an atmosphere for mutual respect and understanding. The bulk of the elite during the *Sultanate* rule came from the Muslims, both nobles and traders.[3] The social status and privileges enjoyed by the trading community was a unique feature in the social life of Bengal. The Muslims were predominantly an urban population. But all of them were not aristocrats, commonly called *ashraf*. There were artisans and service people too. They were the urban proletariats.[4] These people could hardly be distinguished from their Hindu counterparts. Their professional connections helped them to build up a common livelihood. Finally they got a messiah in Chaitanya.

The Bhakti movement had a strong influence on the cultural life, which taught the people tolerance. Hence religion was dominant. But no orthodox leanings were ever dominant to kill the sense of tolerance among the common people.[5] The bulk of the literature produced during those days was simply religious where the life and activities of Chaitanya formed the majority. "Of the architecture of the period, the only notable survivals are mosques and temples. Forts and other secular buildings that have survived the ravages of time are not merely much fewer in number, but perhaps also architecturally less significant."[6] This environment did never support any type of hatred on the basis of creed. Chaitanya presented a new doctrine, a total devotion to the god. All the ideas that Chaitanya spread had their strong roots along the banks of the Bhagirathi-Hooghli. A good number of hagiographic works came up within a few decades of his death. From those one can get the glimpse of the life and society of the then Bengal.

Mukundaram Chakraborty in his well-known composition of *Chandimangala* drew a picture of the then economic as well as social lives. Dhanapati, his merchant-hero used to travel up to Sri Lanka with all the merchandise on various numbers of boats. The route was nothing but the watercourse of the river Bhagirathi-Hooghli. The banks were full with a number of rich habitations including well-built towns. His "poem can thus be read as a grand epic dramatizing the process of civilization-building in the Bengal delta".[7] But it is difficult to accept the theory that the story was nothing more than a "push of agrarian civilization into formerly forested lands."[8] Prior to the birth of the poet [*i.e.; in the earlier decades of the sixteenth century*] the hinterlands of his story were all well-settled. Hence the cultural setting of the story was predominantly urban in character. For this the towns as described by Mukundaram did not present any rural flavour. His "account of the various jatis coming to settle in the city of Gujarat begins with the, description of the Muslims".[9] There had never been any problem in accommodating various people from various communities and castes in the settlements. The settlements bore this legacy for many centuries.

The Bhakti movement initiated by Chaitanya helped to maintain a social order, which had not been known in other parts of India. "Later preachers freely 'saved' Muslims and Chandalas and the later authors asserted openly that a devotee of Krishna automatically ceased to be a Sudra".[10] Bengal from the present day Malda [*since Chaitanya himself had visited Ramkeli, so close to Gaur and both Rup and Sanatan Goswami started their religious lives from the area*] down to its southern portions in present day the south 24 Parganas were swayed by the followers of Chaitanya. In fact, prior to the beginning of the Mughal rule the Bhagirati-Hooghli region had already witnessed the vertical movement of the low caste people of the Hindu society.

Similarly, the Muslim society had also undergone changes for "conversions to the idolatrous faith." The *Vaisanavas* took the lead in doing so.[11]

The Mughal Rule

But it will be wrong to conclude that only religion shaped the cultural and intellectual lives of the people. The Mughal rule in Bengal created a new cultural environment. The Mughal officials sent from the centre were averse in mingling with the local people. "For Muslims in the imperial elite, their religion and their family and political contacts with North India served, in their own minds at least, to distinguish them from the delta's indigenous peoples."[12] It has been claimed that the Mughals—vast majority of whom were either military commanders or bureaucrats—did never forge any social relationship with the native population.[13] Probably this helped the Bengalis to maintain their identity very strongly. There had not been any crisis for the invading alien culture. Certainly the *Vaisanava* movement had a major contribution. "Faith in the unity of the Deity, tolerance and respect for Islam and an open challenge to the caste system were the most important of such features."[14] Strong devotion buttressed with learning—the twin legacy was the gift of Chaitanya. Hence, Bengal presented a very meager number of holy places in contrary to the numbers in many parts of the whole of India. Bengal's pride was rooted into the practice of studies of the various branches of knowledge.

The cities like Navadwip during the lifetime of Chaitanya and also Krishnanagar and Bhatpara acquired places of eminence in the field of learning. Navadwip could attract students from far and near Some came from Chittagong, some from Srihatta or Sylhet and even from Orissa.[15] Presence of so large a number of people of different language and varied taste helped to create a composite culture. The trend continued for centuries. What Navadwip had offered in the sixteenth or seventeenth centuries Calcutta offered that in the nineteenth century.

The culture of Bengal assumed a new dimension when Murshidabad was made the capital city in the first decade of the eighteenth century. With the emergence of a high class and efficient administrative system a high standard of livelihood also started to take place. The system "which appears to have grown stronger, not weaker, after the death of Aurangzeb, and where an elite ruling group which was representative of the political realities of the day".[16] Bengal was nearly independent though it regularly sent its dues to the centre. That was the only link with the decaying Mughal imperial authority. Hence the imperial officials sent from the centre lost their effective presence. The new administration paved the way for the growth of the big landed houses that had their roots in Bengal. Similarly, the growing trade and commerce helped the mercantile community to claim a bigger share in the state affairs. Bengal witnessed the beginning of a new social as well as cultural milieu. Moreover, the presence of the Europeans, chiefly on the western bank of the river Hooghli, had created an environment in which both the Indians and Europeans had their respective contributions. The principal effects were felt in the language.

Bengali is the language of the Gangetic Delta, and of the country immediately to its north and east. But the language varied so widely that the accent of the people in the deep of Medinipur district differed from those in the Dhaka area. But the literary language did not represent the language spoken by the people. "In no other speech of India is the literary tongue so widely divorced from that of ordinary conversation as in Bengali".[17].Primarily the language could be divided into two major divisions. The banks of the Bhagirathi-Hooghli witnessed this divide."The lines of perpendicular cleavage affect only the colloquial form of Bengali......We may, however, recognise two main branches, a Western and an Eastern. The Western includes the standard dialect spoken round Calcutta and Hooghli", while the Eastern branch was chiefly all over the eastern half of the Gangetic Delta having Dhaka as its principal seat.[18]

During the nineteenth century Bengali as a language for expression of one's own thinking took off. "The book language is quite unintelligible to uneducated masses, and as, apart from it, there is no generally recognised standard, the variations in the spoken language are very great."[19]

The most curious thing was the difference of vocabulary from district to district. The settlements on the banks of the Hooghli were the usual meeting points for various cultures—indigenous as well as foreign. In the late 1580s the town of Hooghli was viewed as a Portuguese country while Satgaon, only "a league" away was "a faire citie...of the Moors."[20] This cohabitation continued at least for next hundred years.[21] There is little doubt that by living side by side for many years the people of these places were able to imitate each other and by this could develop a novel culture. This was the best gift to the people of Bengal from this region. Frequent assemblage of a number of people having different cultures helped to maintain an environment of tolerance. The tradition started taking shape in the late sixteenth century when the Portuguese had rooted strongly their base at Hooghli and remained vibrant in the nineteenth. Even after the introduction of the railways the river could "rank as one of the most-frequented waterways in the world."[22] The position, which once was held by Hooghli, was occupied by Calcutta in the nineteenth century.

The town of Hooghli added certain features in the social and political lives of the region hitherto unknown. In the seventeenth century it gathered importance and dignity due to the growth of population and all-round prosperity. For better management in the prevailing administration the king of Spain and Portugal nominated "a *Captain Convidor*, as a sort of Mayor with four assistants, yearly elected by the citizens".[23] This added a new dimension to the social life of the people. Though the Mayor and his electors were all Portuguese the system left a long shadow. The Portuguese in many ways used the Indians but they did not constitute any part of the civil society of the town. Some of them were converted[24] as fallout of the global policy of Portugal in spreading the Christianity. In this way the Hooghli region could taste a lot of alien things.

Probably for its foremost position in the fields of economy and culture the region around the river could also spread its hegemony on the language spoken by the so-called educated and urban population. The Bengali language varied while spoken from place to place. "The well-known adage that the dialect changes every twelve *kos* [1 *kos* = roughly 2 miles = 3.2 km.] applies probably with greater force to Bengali than to any other languages in India".[25] To Dr Grierson, the language can be divided broadly into two parts—the eastern spoken by the people on the east of the 24 Parganas and Nadia—which was roughly the active delta. The language of the Bhagirathi-Hooghli region can be divided broadly into two parts: the central Bengali, spoken in the 24 Parganas, Nadia, Murshidabad, Medinipur, Hooghli and Howrah and, *Rarhi* or the language of the *Rarh,* Burdwan, Birbhoom, Bankura.[26] But the language of the book differed widely. Ultimately, the vocabulary of the central Bengal usurped the prime position by dislodging the others.

Surprisingly enough that western and central Bengal was chiefly peopled by no, so called high caste Hindus. Similarly, the number of highly placed *ashraf* Muslims was not so significant. But majority of the medieval Bengali literary works originated here. Whether it was Chandidas at Birbhoom or

Krittibas Ojha [1398-?], Kashiram Das [seventeenth century] or Mukundaram Chakraborty [1547-?]—all were the sons of these regions. The medieval Bengali literature bore the distinct marks of the languages of the said areas. This was the culture, which was carried through some generations. The *Vaisanava* literary works got a boost after the birth of Chaitanya in the late sixteenth century. Navadwip, the birthplace of Chaitanya, was a revered place for devotional Bhakti and for learning.

The Company Rule: A New Urban Milieu

The defeat of Siraj ud daulah in the battle of Palasi ushered in a new era in the life of Bengal. It was the period when Calcutta grew up as an urban centre hitherto unknown. Already a new set of bureaucracy and aristocracy had sprung up—thanks to the efforts of Murshid Quli Khan. Still this aristocracy had been constituted chiefly by the foreign elements. The Company in its initial days as administrator tried to gain the confidence of the local population. The Hindus took the maximum advantage. Calcutta's setting was completely new. By imposing the English legal concepts in Calcutta the Company attracted a large number of people from far and near.[27] These people tried to imitate their foreign masters in every sphere of life. The gradual spread of the Company's political as well as administrative influence all over India made Calcutta the most important city in India. The defeat and death of Tipu Sultan of Mysore in 1799 and then the virtual subjugation of the *Peshwa* to the Company in 1818 brought the vast part of the sub-continent under the English Company's rule. Even the neighbouring states like Burma and Nepal were also brought under the Company's hegemony. The vastness of the area and the diversity of each part required a great administrative genius and acumen. It was really enviable. Calcutta, being the principal seat of administration, gathered similar enviable position.

Calcutta already had certain advantages. Before the mid-eighteenth century Calcutta did not possess any urban milieu. Simply three tiny villages jumped into a new cultural life within a very short span of time. The Europeans started arriving in increasing number and all of them were not traders or the employees of the Company.A large number of them were fortune-seekers and certainly a good number were professionals. These professionals started practicing in the then Supreme Court where a good mixture of indigenous and English laws and conventions were successfully done.[28]

With the arrival of Lord Wellesley the proud sense of empire spread its wings. A new palace for the Governor General, which is presently the official residence of the state Governor, was constructed. By the turn of the century Calcutta had silently entered into a new urban life. Roads were built and fine mansions came up. These outer changes brought the other changes, which shaped the cultural mind of the Bengali population. The nineteenth century ushered in a metamorphosis, which acquired a proud place in the history of the contemporary world. Bengal renaissance, as it was popularly known, shaped the modern mind not only of the Bengalis but also the entire sub-continent. It was entirely a new phase in the history of India. Belying the common belief of decaying nature of the deltaic West Bengal the nineteenth century produced a vibrant culture, which made Bengal a role model to many. This was the result of introduction of the western education and the English language. Through Calcutta the whole of the south Asia became acquainted with the modern science and logic of the west.

New Society and New Intellect

In 1800, Lord Wellesley instituted the Fort William College at Calcutta much against the will of the Directors of the Company, for training up young 'writers' [clerks] as efficient civilians. The study of Bengali, Hindustani or Hindi, Persian and other 'native' languages was started. The College set a new trend though it was not for the Indians. In the same year, the Baptist Mission was founded in Srirampur in the district of Hooghli, and the Mission Press started printing works in Bengali and other provincial languages. "'From this time forward writing Bengali correctly may be said to have begun in Calcutta.'"[29] Assimilation of Eastern and Western cultures was speeded up after the foundation of the Hindu College at Calcutta in 1817.

Concentration of three high-castes in Calcutta and its sufurbs "shows how the opportunities offered by the metropolis attracted the high castes from east and west alike, and how far they now made it their city.[30] The company's insistence on following the Hindu as well as Islamic laws and scriptures in the family matters helped Calcutta in building itself a nub of the *Pandits* and *Ulema*. "Judge-pandits and experts in Islamic law therefore had to be appointed to assist Englishmen in the civil courts of the Company." This practice continued till 1830s. Ultimately, the oriental scholarship took its roots in innumerable 'tols' and in the Calcutta Madrassa.[31]

It was the result of continuous presentations and agitation by Rammohan Roy [1772-1833] and some men like him. Rammohan had also a role in guiding the British Parliament when it asked the Directors of the East India Company to spend money for the social and intellectual upliftment of their subjects in

India. That was the beginning. Now the English—educated Indians, chiefly from Calcutta and its nearest hinterland were allowed to high official posts under the Company's government.[32] These officials posted at far and near places spread the cultural ethos of the then metropolitan Calcutta.

This move of the indigenous people sparkled. Now some enthusiastic English women understood the need for female education. In 1819, they formed the Female Juvenile Society. The centuries-old custom in confining women within the four walls was removed silently but significantly. Raja Radhakanta Deb of the Sovabazar Raj family extended his co-operation. He also wrote a book, *Stree Seksha Vidhayaka*. In 1821, Miss Cooke arrived in Calcutta under the auspice of the British and Foreign School Society. Her endeavur resulted in the formation of ten girls' schools.[33] Following Calcutta's foot steps girls, schools were opened along the Bhagirathi channel. Srirampur, Kalna, Katwa, Burdwan, Krishnanager and Mursidabad were a prominent few.[34] Radhakanta himself led the School Society in imparting education to the women. But the Society's programme for opening women co-educational schools invited public ire.

In the nineteenth century, Calcutta and the places like Srirampur, Hooghli. Krishnanagar and Murshidabad assumed the role of a sheet-anchor for this cultural and social rejuvenation in India. No doubt, some Europeans also had their contributions. Men like John Palmer who was commonly called as the richest East India merchant at Calcutta took the responsibility of rousing public opinion in various issues. In 1818, he started his *The Calcutta Journal* on the line of Hickey's. This *Journal* did never spare the government for any of its faulty policies. Similarly, James Silk Buckingham, the radical advocate of free trade made a strident attack against the Company's monopoly in China trade. Now Bengal witnessed a new era where freedom of expression was viewed in the light of the west. Those invited official reactions very soon when John Adam, the temporary Governor General issued an order of prior censorship.[35] That censorship was also a cause for Rammohan to close down his Persian newspaper, the only and first of its kind in the subcontinent. To a some extent Rammohan's action began the process of constitutional agitation in India.

The Bengali language was struggling to break away from its traditional metrical bondage to become a suitable vehicle for modern thoughts and ideas, problems and complexities of life, till a regular periodical could be brought out in 1818.1t was the credit again to the Srirampur Missionaries who brought the monthly *Digdurshan* in Bengali and devoted to subjects of historical, geographical and commercial interest. It was followed by another Bengali weekly, *Samachar Darpan* in the same year and by the same Missionaries. In this way Bengali language entered into a new field–the journalistic mode of writing. The growth of the vernacular press was one of the most important developments in the field of culture and education. From these activities the Indian nationalism got its root. It was a surprising experience that Calcutta which had emerged just as an agglomeration of three tiny villages without having any cultural background in the mid-eighteenth century could transform itself into such a place which could occupy a substantial position in history. This was possible chiefly due to the growth of a urban middle class, a professional class who had a very workable understanding with their foreign masters. The English helped to build up a democratic set-up. The people in Calcutta increasingly became conscious of many things including their own benefits. They started ventilating their grievances and demands through their newspapers and journals. In 1826, only 8,000 copies were sold. The said number rose to three lacs in 1853 and to six lacs in 1857, the year of the Mutiny.[36] With the help of a growing trade and with the assemblage of a good number of landholder families Calcutta had money and other resources, which were deployed in many development works. The majority of the patrons and proprietors belonged to those families. All these made the English press annoyed and one of them, the *Asiatic Journal* openly advocated for a press censorship. The censorship was nothing new though Lord Hastings withdrew it in 1818. But the censorship was re-imposed in 1823 against which Rammohun Roy made his famous protest by closing his Persian newspaper.

The urban mind was then taking shape. Foundation of the *Atmiya Sabha* by Rammohan in 1815 in Calcutta can be termed as a watershed. His primary objective was social as well as religious reforms. He started publishing a number of newspapers in several languages. These broke the indifference of people and they were roused from their mental slumber. Opinions began to circulate, and ideas, strange and new, got wings. To counteract the liberal and radical views the *Samachar Chandrika*, a conservative Bengali periodical, also appeared. All these had no precedence at all.

Bengal's another fine achievement was the introduction of western education. Inspired by the Fort' William College the enterprising Bengalis started their own institution, the Hindu College in Calcutta to impart western education through the English language. The name of Henry Louis Vivian Derozio [1809-31] was closely related with this College. The young Derozio was appointed as a teacher. But the governors of the College, the majority of whom held conservative ideas, resented his radical views. Derozio was driven out and soon after died. But he left his mark. The students of the Hindu College took pride in calling themselves as Derozians whose principal aim was to remove all the prejudices. Through the eyes of Derozio the "young" Bengalis started looking at everything in new perspectives.

When the students of the Hindu College were engaged in removing the social taboos, Rammohan initiated his reform movements. Whether it was against the cruel practice of *Sati* or the burning of widows on the funeral pyres of their dead husbands or against the religious prejudices Rammohan's efforts were tireless. His *Brahmo Sabha* was re-shaped into *Brahmo Samaj* under the guidance of Devendra Nath Tagore, Keshab Chandra Sen, Sivnath Shastri and a lot like them. This period was popularly known as the age of Brahmo movement. A new generation of Bengali intellectuals emerged with vigour. The *Society for the Acquisition of General Knowledge* [started on 16 May 1838] and the *Tattwabodhini Sabha* [started on 6 October 1839], both were organised by the new generation. It may be said that Bengal was gradually emerging as a place for modern thinking and Calcutta was the only leader then.

The spread of western education helped the Bengalis to acquire knowledge and information of contemporary Europe. Emergence of western-educated *bhadrolok* or gentleman class ushered in a new era hitherto unknown. The vast majority of these people were the permanent residents of Calcutta though some had their roots in the villages. In fact, Bengal witnessed the emergence of a urban middle class in true sense of the term. Some of them stood firmly behind Rammohun Roy and Iswar Chandra Vidyasagar [1820-91] in their respective revolts against the social taboos and prejudices. Those who were opposed to their reform movements also belonged to the same *bhadralok* community. Opinions were sharply divided. The long verbal as well as cerebral battle between the reformers and the orthodox old elements is a well-known history.[37]

"The colonial middle class, particularly in Bengal, would be characterized not really by any association with capitalistic enterprise..., but by education" which was primarily then available in Calcutta.[38]

No doubt, Calcutta led a new and modern urban living standard which spread its wings in other parts of India. Since the city was the destination of various persons from different parts of India and abroad, Calcutta could experience inter-mixture of cultures. Moreover, its dominant position as the second capital of the British empire also helped it in acquiring good statues as a living place among the rich and mighty. Palatial buildings, out houses, gardens decorated with several art works – even brought from Italy and France, fountains and choicest plants were common feature in Calcutta's life. The European lifestyle slowly but was deeply imitated by the Indians. George W. Johnson in his *The Stranger in India* presented a vivid description of lifestyle being followed in the 1840s. Leading Indians of Calcutta like, Dwarkanath Tagore, Rustamji Cawasji and Prince Gulam Muhammad, the grandson of Tipu Sultan acquired legendary fame for themselves. They shaped the Indian aristocracy not only in Calcutta but also in the whole of eastern India.

Similar was the position in the European society. "Even the young, recently arrived East India Company writer, cadet or junior military officer would stretch his meagere resources to participate in Calcutta society."[39]

Shaping of modern Indian mind started during the governor generalship of Lord Bentinck [1827-35]. His successors, Metcalfe and Auckland simply followed him and continued official patronage to the liberal Indians like Dwarkanath Tagore and others. Their admiration of the western learning and culture created a deep sense of nationalism and of liberal democratic set-up in course of time. Their love for western education ultimately helped the Indians to assess the role of their foreign masters. Hence the journal, *Bangadoot* in its 13th June 1829 edition strongly advocated the benefits arising out of the presence of the *madhyabitta* [*middle class*] which would bring "freedom".

Similarly, a new arrival of north Indian court culture and aristocracy not only helped the spread of Arabic and Persian learning but also helped to set a new architectural pattern. The Mughal influence in the making of Dhaka in the seventeenth and of Murshidabad in the early eighteenth century failed to keep a permanent mark. But nineteenth century Calcutta witnessed a different scenario when the exiled ruler of Awadh, *Nawab* Wajed Ali Shah was allotted a four square miles of land in the Garden Reach–some few miles away from the Fort William. The *Nawab* was stripped of his kingdom and of many other privileges. But he along with his courtiers built up a new urban habitation which was literally and physically imported from Lucknow–the former capital and the centre of eastern royal culture of the *Nawab*. The *Nawab* was a connoisseur of art, architecture, dance and music. Moreover, he was a great animal lover too. His activity ushered in a new culture and sense of livelihood first in Calcutta and then in many parts of Bengal. Chiefly the Bengal *zamindars* and landowners came forward to patronise those which could not be found elsewhere.[41] The Garden Reach or *Matia burz* was transformed into *Bas-i Iram* [*a heaven on the earth*].

Like Wajed Ali the offsprings of the late Tipu Sultan were allotted lands in Tollygung, a southern suburb of Calcutta. The royal families of the former kingdoms, Awadh and Mysore were the chief patrons of Arabic and Persian learnings which were then facing serious challenge under the onslaught of foreign rule. They regularly organized literary conferences on grand style – hitherto unknown in this part of the land.

Calcutta was able to present a new atmosphere through which political consciousness could be generated. The preservation and protection of class interest became a prime motive. Calcutta saw the establishment of the *Landholders' Society* in 1837. The landholders of the post-Permanent Settlement [1793] era were the supporters of the foreign masters. But they too thought it better to look at their class interest in their own viewpoints. Their activities generated a modern political world. It was a new type of politics devoid of court intrigues and certain aristocratic whims. The newly educated people were talking in increasing number in the language of the Westminster. They were reading Thomas Hobbes, John Lock and even Rousseau. On the footsteps of Rammohun these people established the *Bengal British Indian Society* in April 1843. This was amalgamated with the Landholders' Society and the *British Indian Association* was born in October 1851.The principal task of the Association was to seek certain privileges from the British government when the Charter to rule India for another twenty years was to be granted to the East India Company in 1853. They put their "memorial" before the British Parliament in 1852. This can be termed a strong political document. The urge for western education was high. That was not expected but could not be prevented. The *Samachar Chandrika* in an editorial dated 12th May 1831 had regretted that the English-educated young Indians knew more about the West than about their motherland.[42]

But this political consciousness failed to enthuse the intelligentsia to share the cause of the revolting sepoys who, according to the historians, raised the banner of the 'First Indian War of Independence' against the foreign rule. The revolt broke out in 1857, the year that witnessed the foundation of the university at Calcutta. The Western-educated Bengalis saw one of their long-cherished dreams to materialise. This atmosphere led to a sense of globalisation which became manifest in the cultural and political activities of the people of Calcutta in the twentieth century.

Bengal's—or in the broader sense India's modernisation took its shape through the initiatives of Rammohun Roy.[43] The people in Calcutta in the initial phase chiefly covering the first half of the nineteenth century started talking in new voice, thinking in new methods. All were the results of the spread of the western education. The university at Calcutta was a great success in the process.

Similar was the success achieved by the Srirampur missionaries and their brethrens in Calcutta. The *Calcutta Diocesan Committee*, the *Church Missionary Association* etc. also rendered useful service.[44] This period witnessed a new scene—a long debate between the Orientalists and the Anglesites, mainly comprising the English officials and learned men. The crux of the problem lay in the official decisions. Some wanted to patronise the Oriental learning while the others wanted just the opposite. Whatever be the problems Bengal had already entered into a new world. It was exposed to the West and the learned few were too eager to acquire the fruits of the western culture. They were ready to sacrifice their own identity. Never before the same could be imagined.

The sense of nationalism began to develop under such an atmosphere in Calcutta whose foundation had been laid by Derozio and Rammohun. In the 1860s the *Hindu Mela* under the steward ship of Nabagopal Mitra ushered in a new era. Political, social as well as cultural atmosphere experienced morel ideas which helped the zeal of nationalism in the entire sub-continent. "Calcutta has the reputation," the Director of Public instruction reported in 1872, "of giving the best education, not only in law but also generally and clever boys are sent there from all parts of the country."[45]

Hence "The metropolis of Calcutta was the most constricuous centre of their [*Bengali*] civilisation, and the city was at once the educational and cultural headquaters of the Presidency as a whole".[46]

Centring Calcutta a new urban intellect who tried to grab the every opportunity available to them for the steady amelioration of their lot emerged. Rammohun's *Atmiya Sabha* led the way. *Bengal Landholders' Society*, the *British Indian Association*, the *India League,* the *Indian Associations* and such like other minors helped to generate a mind which could assesrs the colonial rule from a political angel. "When the Association had been founded, a patriarchal system was then best for its welfare".[47] gathered momentum. This was a novel trend which ultimately shaped the nationalist feelings of the masses. Calcutta led Bengal and in turn, Bengal led the whole of India.

NOTES

[1] Nihar Ranjan Ray; *op. cit.,* pp. 136-137

[2] Quoted from *Suma Oriental* in R.M. Eaton; *op. cit.,* p. 131

[3] Eaton; *op. cit.*, p. 99

[4] Eaton; *op. cit.,* p. 101

[5] T. Raychaudhuri; *op. cit.*, p. 131

[6] Raychaudhuri; *op. cit.*, p. 145

[7] Eaton; *op. cit.*, p. 214

[8] *Ibid.*

[9] Raychaudhuri; *op. cit.*, p. 27

[10] Raychaudhuri; *op. cit.*, p. 151

[11] Raychaudhuri; *op. cit.*, p. 177

[12] Eaton; *op. cit.*, pp. 178-179

[13] Eaton; *op. cit.*, p. 171

[14] Raychaudhuri; *op. cit.*, p. 131

[15] *Chaitanyabhagbad. Adikhanda.* Ch. 2

[16] P.B. Calkins, "The formation of a regionally oriented Ruling group in Bengal, 1700-1790" in the *Journal of Asian studies.* No. 4.

[17] Grieirson; *Linguistic Survey of India*...(Calcutta, 1927) Vol. I., pt.1., p.152

[18] Grieirson; *op. cit.*, p. 153

[19] *Census of India. 1901.* Vo. VI. pt. 1., p. 136

[20] Sir William Foster ed.; *Early Travels*…, pp. 25-26

[21] Shafat Ahmad Khan; *John Marshall in India*..., p. 65

[22] *Imperial Gazetteer of India*, *1909* Vol. I., p. 209

[23] Sir J.N.Sarkar ed. *History of Bengal.* (Dhaka, 1972) Vol. II. p. 321

[24] *Ibid.*

[25] *Census of India, 1901.* Vol.Vl., pt. I., p. 316

[26] *Census of India, 1901.*Vol. V1 ... pt., I. p. 317

[27] Sreemani; *Anatomy*..., pp. 12-13

[28] for details see Sreemani; *Anatomy*…, pp. 29-34

[29] Quoted from Ramcomul Sen; *A Dictionary in English and Bengali. in History of Bengal, 1757-1908.* N.K. Sinha ed. (Calcutta), p. 218.

[30] Anil Seal; *The Emergence of Indian Nationalism (Competition and Collaboration in the later 19th century)* (Cambridge, 1968) Seal computed on the basis of 1881 census, the total Hindu population of Calcutta during those days was 278,762 out of which the Brahmins constituted 38,868, Kayasthas 37,570 and Baidyas 2684. For details, p. 43

[31] Sumit Sarker; *Writing Social History* (New Delhi, 2009), p. 225

[32] Sivnath Shastri; *Ramtanu lahiri O Tatkalin Banga Samaj* (Calcutta, 1977), p. 107

[33] Sivnath Shastri; *op. cit.*, p. 171

[34] Sivnath Shastri; *op. cit.*, p. 172

[35] Anthony Webster; *the Richest East India Merchant: The Life and Business of John Palmer of Calcutta, 1767-1836* (New Delhi, 2009), pp. 33-34

[36] *History of Bengal, 1757-1908*, p. 226

[37] On *"daladali"* or group-fighting see S.N. Mukerjee; *Calcutta, Myth and History* (Calcutta, 1968)

[38] Sumit Sarkar, *op. cit.*, p. 169

[39] Webster, *op. cit.*, p. 1

[40] Sumit Sarkar; *op. cit.*, p. 169

[41] Abdul Halim Sharar; *Purano Lucknow,* Bengali tr. Munira Khaton and Gurudas Bhattacharyya (Calcutta, 1972), pp. 71-78

[42] Amitabha Mukherjee; *Reforms and Regeneration in Bengal* (Calcutta, 1968), p.121

[43] For details see Rabindra Nath Tagore's essay; "Rammohan" in Bengali collection of three essays in his *Charitrapuja* in Bengali, published in the Centenary year collections Vol.XI (Calcutta)

[44] N. S. Bose; *Indian Awakening and Bengal.* (Calcutta, 1 976), p. 108

[45] Seal; *op. cit.*, p. 59

[46] Seal, *op. cit.*, p. 48

[47] Seal; *op. cit.*, p. 218

CONCLUSION

No doubt Bengal had experienced a metamorphosis during those three hundred years between the seventeenth and nineteenth centuries. The change in the principal course of the river Ganga, here the Bhagirathi certainly had serious reactions. The western part of Bengal along the river Bhagirathi-Hooghli lost its prime position in terms of agriculture and peasentisation. But the scope of those was limited in the part in comparison to the eastern. During the sixteenth century Murshidabad and Nadia had already become a dead delta zone[1], which led to the process of decline in all respect, including falling physique of the people residing there. Hence the upward movement of progress and prosperity in the old delta, as it has been called, was stalled by the changes made in the river.

But the presence of the European trading companies along the river Hooghli in increasing number present a different story. From the middle of the seventeenth century the volume of revenue regularly exacted from Bengal started increasing.[2] When the peasantisation in the eastern part had just taken a faster pace the bulk of that revenue must come from the other part. This trend continued for next two centuries. Whether it was in Burdwan or in the Sundarbans especially, along the Hooghli river zone the growth in crop production and their varieties were remarkable. Not only food grains, varieties of cash crops were also reaped. Bengal earned an international fame for its silk goods. This silk was the produce of the Bhagirathi region. When machines came under the colonial masters a new variety of fibre was also introduced. Though the eastern Bengal produced good quality jute in huge quantities the factories for finished products were all located along the Hooghli.

Changes in the course of the Bhagirathi-Hooghli certainly affected the topography of the region. But the economic ambience did not lose its vitality. The ransacks of the Maratha *bargirs,* the systematic loot by the English East India Company and innumerable private European fortune-seekers failed to make the source of income defunct. Clive, after his victory at Palasi, was astonished to find the treasure hidden in this land. To him, still Bengal meant the Bhagirathi-Hooghli region as the English then had little knowledge about the east.

From the late eighteenth century Calcutta grew up as the biggest urban centre in India. Ultimately it was viewed as the second capital of the sprawling British empire. Europe's modernity made a strong impact on the lives and lifestyles of the people residing in and around Calcutta. Not only in intellectual life but also in agricultural production, in railway communication and in industrial developments the banks of the Bhagirathi-Hooghli made their importance felt world-wide.

The nineteenth century witnessed a new urban milieu hitherto unknown. By 1891 Calcutta proper—covering an area of 20.9 sq. miles had a population of 681,560. Not less than 1,95,985 person were engaged in various professions which are not at all linked with agriculture or farm. Even common people were employed in the tram company, the newly imported mechanised transport system[3]. The population of Calcutta including its adjacent suburbs like Maniktala, South Suburban etc. stood at 844,884 and the number was growing.[4] Calcutta led the way for a new urban settlement, which was absent in the other parts of Bengal. In 1891, the major seven districts like, Rajshahi, Rangpur, Pabna, Faridpur, Jessore, Maimansingh and Dhaka in the eastern and northern parts of Bengal having a total land area of 21,976 sq. miles could have only 21 towns. The said number was 47 in the districts like Malda, Murshidabad, Nadia, Hooghli, Burdwan, Howrah and the 24 Parganas all of which together covering an area of 13,344 sq. miles.[5]

The frequent changes in the course of the Bhagirathi, particularly in the district of Murshidabad, certainly had their effects on the people residing on either side of the river. But loss in one part was always compensated by another. Moreover, the annual floods also provided certain fertility to the topsoil. Hence loss during a flood could be neutralised by subsequent harvest.

The people residing on the both banks of river had earned the fame for Bengal as the producer of verities of artisan products including much-sought–after silk and cotton textile. For years together these artisan craft generated a lot of employments and also allured people from far and near to come in those places for permanent settlement. Similarly, from the mid-nineteenth century the railways and mechanised factory system drew people in increasing number. Immediately the industrialisation of the east started along the banks of the Hooghli which already had a certain amount of infrastructure. Not only the Europeans but the pioneers like Dwarka Nath Tagore and Tarak Nath Pramanik had already started their own enterprises along the bank of the Hooghli. This continued and flourished. In course of time the settlement pattern also changed. A good number of outsiders—non-Bengali speaking people began to gather in these industrial houses and raised there own colonies

By 1891, Calcutta was the destination of several fortune-seekers from several parts of the globe including Malta, Africa, Finland, Germany and many more.[6] "In all probability, Barabazar was already an important market place in the mid-eighteenth century." Its growth continued under the aegis of different types of traders coming from different parts of the sub-continent. Its prime position helped to generate substantial amount of wealth in Calcutta.[7] Gradually rural character of the areas surrounding Calcutta as far as Katwa and Santipur was changed. Thickness of population was remarkable.[8]

The nineteenth century witnessed a new environment, which had its origin in Calcutta. Since the beginning of the century a new urban middle class started coming.[9] They generated wealth, nurtured intellect, and developed a new culture. "The University of Calcutta directed higher education throughout Bengal and upper India. Its high court possessed the most extensive jurisdiction and dealt with the largest amount of litigation of all courts of India. It is a striking fact that more than a quarter of the city's Hindu population belonged to the bhardralok."[10] This *bhadralok* class was the fore-runner of a new life-style, a new education and a new world of politics. Gradually, these spread along the banks of the Hooghli and grasped the huge area of north and north-east India. Hence the moribund nature of the delta failed to make the people residing along the banks of the Bhagirathi-Hooghli decrepit in any manner.

NOTES

1 Kanan Gopal Bagchi, *The Ganges Delta* (Calcutta, 1944), p. 55

2 W. K. Firminger; *Affairs of the East India Company (Being the Fifth Report from the Select Committee of the House of Commons,* 27th July, 1812). (Calcutta, 1917, New Delhi, reprint, 1984), pp. 189-191

3 *Census of India, 1891*. Vol. IV., Table XVIIB

4 *Census of India, 1891,* Vol. IV., pp. 26-27

5 *Census of India, 1891*, Vol. IV., pp. 2-5

6 *Census of India, 1891,* Vol. IV., pp. 351-357

7 Sabyasachi Bhattacharya; 'Traders and Trades in Old Calcutta' in Sukanta Chaudhuri ed. *Calcutta: The Living City*. (Calcutta 1990) Vol. I, p. 204

8 *Census of Bengal, 1872*. General Statement—1A.

9 D. P. Bhattacharyya; *Growth of Middle Class in Bengal* (Calcutta, 1954); pp. 9-10

10 Anil Seal; *op. cit.*, pp. 48-49

BIBLIOGRAPHY

(A) Official Records

Available in the National Archives of India, New Delhi

Foreign Department (Political Branch)

Foreign Department (Public Branch)

Home Department (Public Branch)

Home Department (Secret Branch)

Public Works Department

Public Works Department (Irrigation)

Available in the West Bengal State Archives, Calcutta

Board of Revenue (Miscellaneous)

Board of Revenue (Police Circular)

Board of Revenue (Sayer)

Board of Revenue for Lower Provinces

Collection of Pattas; Bengali and Dutch

General Committee of the Fever Hospital and Municipal Improvement

Government of Bengal, Home Department Records Branch

Judicial Department (Judicial Branch)

Judicial Department (Municipal Branch)

Judicial Department (Police Branch)

Lt. Governor, Bengal in Revenue Department

Marine Department

Municipal Department (Municipal Branch)

Political Department (Police Branch)

Presidency Commissioner of Sundarban Records

Provincial Committee of Revenue at Murshidabad

Public Works Department (Railway)

Revenue Board Consisting of Whole Council

Sudder Board of Revenue for Lower Provinces

Sunnuds entered in the Bazee Zamin Daftar

Surathals in the Bazee Zamin Daftar

Available at the Collectorate Office, Berhampur; Murshidabad

Letters Issued and Received

Miscellaneous Letters

Nizamat Affairs

Available at the Collectorate Office, Malda

Books of Old Pattas

(B) Printed Records

Fort William India House Correspondence published by the National Archives of India. Vol. I, ed. by K. K. Datta (Delhi, 1958)

Vol. II, ed. by H. N. Sinha (....1957)

Vol. V, ed. by N. K. Sinha (.... 1949)

Vol. VI, ed. b. Prasad (....1960)

Foster, Sir William ed.; *The English Factories in India, 1618-1621* (Oxford, 1906)

Foster, Sir William ed; *The English Factories in India, 1637-1641* (Oxford, 1912)

Fawett, Sir Charles ed.; *The English Factories in India, 1670-1677* (Oxford, 1952) New series

(C) Gazetteers and Reports

The Imperial Gazetteer of India, Provincial Series: Bengal. (Calcutta, 1909) Vol. I

De. B.; ed. *West Bengal District Gazetteer; 24 Parganas*. (Calcutta, 1994)

Garrett, J. H. E: *Bengal District Gazetteer; Nadia* (Calcutta, 1910, reprint, 2001)

Lamboum, G. E.: *Bengal District Gazetteer; Malda* (Calcutta, 1918)

Peterson, J. C. K.: *Bengal District Gazetteer; Burdwan* (Calcutta, 1910)

O'Malley, L.S.S. and Chakravarti, Manmohan; *Bengal District Gazetteer: Howrah* (Calcutta, 1909)

O'Malley, L.S. S.; *Bengal District Gazetteer: Santal Pargana.* (Calcutta, 1910)

O' Malley, L. S. S. and Chakravarti, Manmohan; *Bengal District Gazetteer: Hooghly* (Calcutta, 1912)

O'Malley, L. S. S.; *Bengal District Gazetteer: Murshidabad* (Calcutta, 1914, reprint 1997)

O' Malley, L. S.S.; *Bengal District Gazetteer: 24 Parganas.* (Calcutta, 1914, reprint, 1998)

Government of West Bengal, State Gazetteer; *The Rivers of Bengal* Vol.I (Calcutta, 2001) Vol.II (Calcutta, 2002) Vol. III (Calcutta, 2001)

Kerr, Hem Chunder; *Report on the Cultivation of and Trade in Jute in Bengal and the Indian Fibres available for the Manufacture of paper* (Calcutta, 1874)

Macleod, Col. And Forbes, Major W.N.; *Report on the Rajmahal Canal dated 15 February 1841*

(D) Census and Surveys

Beverly, H.; *Report on the Census of Bengal, 1872* (Secretariat Press, Calcutta, 1872)

O' Donnell, C. J.; *Census of India, 1891: The Lower Provinces of Bengal and their Feudatories.* (Bengal Secretariat Press, Calcutta, 1893) Vol. IV

Census of India 1901: The Lower Provinces of Bengal and their Feudatories. (Bengal Secretariat Press, Calcutta, 1902)

Mitra, A.; *Census of India, 1951,: West Bengal State Report and District Handbooks* in separate and also several vols. (Calcutta, 1952-54)

Carter M.O.; *Cadastral Survey in Malda, 1928-35* (Bengal Secretariat Press, Calcutta, 1936)

(E) Published Works

Abid Ali Khan, M.; *History and Archaeology of Bengal, or Memoirs of Gour and Pandua.* H. E. Stapleton ed. Introduction, Aniruddha Ray and C. Datta (Calcutta, 1986)

Alami, Abu I Fazl; *Ain-i Akbari.* tr. Col. H. S. Jarret: J. N. Sarkar ed. (New Delhi Reprint 1978) Vol. II

Bagchi, Kanan Gopal, *The Ganges Delta* (Calcutta, 1944)

Barbosa, Durate; *The Book of Durate Barbosa.* tr.M. L. Dames. (Hakluyt Society, London: reprint 1921) Vol. II

Bernier, Francois; *Travels in the Mogul Empire, A.D. 1656-1668.* tr. A. Constable, revised by V. A. Smith (New Delhi reprint, 1989)

Blochmann, H.; *Contributions to the Geography and History of Bengal. (Muhammadan Period).* First published in the *Journals of the Asiatic Society, Bengal,* between 1873 and 1875; in book form (Calcutta, 1968, reprint 2003)

Bose, Nimai Sadhan; *Indian Awakening and Bengal.* (Calcutta, 1976)

Bowrey, Thomas; *A Geographical Account of the Countries around the Bay of Bengal, 1669-79* ed. R.C. Temple (Hakluyt Society, London. 1905)

Chandra, Satish, *Medieval India* (New Delhi, 1999) Vol. II

Chaudhuri, K. N.; *Trading World of Asia and the English East India Company, 1660-1760.* (Cambridge, 1978)

Chaudhuri, K. N.; *Trade and Civilisation in the Indian Ocean; An Economic History from the Rise of Islam to 1750* (New Delhi reprint, 1985)

Chaudhuri, Sukanta ed. *Calcutta: The Living City* (Calcutta, 1990) Vol. I

Chaudhuri, Sushil; *From Prosperity to Decline; 18th century Bengal.* (New Delhi, 1999)

Danvers, Frederick. C.; *The Portuguese in India: Being a History of the Eastern Empire.* (London, 1894). Vol. I

Darian, Steven G.; *The Ganges in Myth and History.* (Honolulu, 1978)

Das Gupta, Ashin, *Malabar in Asian Trade 1740-1800* (Cambridge, 1967)

Das Gupta, Ashin and Pearson M. N. eds.; *India and the Indian Ocean, 1500-1800.* (New Delhi, 1999)

Dimmock, Edward C. Jr, and Gupta, Pratul Chandra tr. and .eds.; *The Maharashtra Purana; An 18th Century Bengali Historical Text* (Honolulu, no date)

Eaton, Richard M.; *The Rise of Islam and the Bengal Frontier, 1204-1760.* (New Delhi reprint, 2000)

Foster, Sir William ed; *Early Travels in India, 1583-1619* (Oxford, 1921, New Delhi reprint, 1985)

Furber, Holden; *Rival Empires of Trade in the Orient,* 1600-1800. (New Delhi reprint, 1990)

Ganguli, B. N.; *Trends in Agriculture and Population in the Ganges Valley* (London, 1938)

Gole, Susan; *India Within the Ganges* (New Delhi, 1983)

Habib, Irfan; *Agrarian System of Mughal India* (New Delhi 1999)

Hamilton, Walter; *Geographical, Statistical and Historical Description of Hindostan and the Adjacent Countries.* (London, 1820) Vol.I

Hakluyt, Richard; *The Principal Navigations Voyages Traffiques and Discoveries of the English Nation* (Glasgow, MCMIV) Vol. V.

Hunter, W.W.; *A Statistical Account of Bengal* (London, 1876, New Delhi reprint, 1984) Vol. IX

Hunter, W. W.; *The Annals of Rural Bengal* (Calcutta reprint, 1996)

Hunter, W.W.; *A Statistical Account of Bengal: Sundarbans*. (Calcutta reprint, 1998)

Karam Ali; *Muzaffarnamah tr.* J. N. Sarkar in *Bengal Nawabs*. (Calcutta reprint, 1985)

Khan, Shafaat Ahmad ed.; *John Marshal in India. Notes and observations in Bengal, 1668-1672* (London, 1922)

Kopf, David ed.; *Bengal's Regional Identity* (Michigan, 1969)

Kumar, Dharma and Desai Meghnad eds.; *The Cambridge Economic History of India* (New Delhi reprint, 1984) Vol. II

Long, James; 'The Banks of Bhagirathi' *in the Selected Papers*. ed. M. P. Saha. (Calcutta, 1968)

Madan, P. L.; *River Ganga: A Cartogmphie Mystery*. (New Delhi, 2005)

Marshall, P. J.; *East Indian Fortunes: The British in Bengal in the 18th century*. (Oxford, 1976)

Master, Streynsham; *The Diaries of Streynsham Master, 1675-1680 and other contemporary papers relating thereto*. ed.; R. C. Temple (Indian Records Series, London, 1911) 2 Vols

Mohsin, K.M.; *A Bengal District in Transition: Murshidabad, 1765-1793*. (Dacca, 1973)

Moreland, W. H.; *India at the Death of Akbar: An Economic Study* (New Delhi reprint, 1990)

Moreland, W. H.; From *Akbar to Aurangzeb: A study in Indian Economic History* (New Delhi reprint, 1990)

Moreland, W. H.; *The Agrarian System of Moslem India* (New Delhi reprint, 1990)

Mukherjee, A.; *Reforms and Regeneration in Bengal*. (Calcutta, 1968)

Mukherjee, R. K; *The Changing Face of Bengal: A Study in Riverine Economy* (Calcutta, 1938)

Mukherjee, S. N.; Calcutta: *Myth and History* (Calcutta, 1968)

Prakash, Om; *The Dutch Factory in India, 1627-1623.A Collection of Dutch Company Documents Pertaining to India*. (Delhi, 1954)

Prakash, Om; *European Commercial Erterprise in Pre-Colonial India.* (New Delhi reprint, 2000)

Ray, A. K.; *A Short History of Calcutta :Town and Suburbs.* Introduction, N. R. Ray (Calcutta, 1982)

Raychaudhuri, T.; *Bengal under Akbar and Jahangir.* (Delhi, 1969)

Raychaudhuri, T. and Habib. I. eds.; *The Cambridge Economic History of India.* (New Delhi, reprint 1984) Vol. I

Rennell, James; *An Account of the Ganges and Burrumpooter Rivers.* (London, 1781)

Rennell, James; *The Journals of Major James Rennell, the first Surveyor General of India, written for the information of the Governors of Bengal during the Survey of the Ganges and Brahmaputra Rivers, 1764-1767.* ed. T. H. D. Latouche. (Calcutta edition, 1910)

Sarkar, J., N. ed.; *The History of Bengal.* (Dacca, 1976) Vol. II

Sarkar, Sumit; *Writing Social History* (New Delhi, 2009)

Seal, Anil; *The Emergence of Indian Nationaltism. Compitition and Collaboration in the later 19th century* (Cambridge, 1968)

Sen, S.N. ed.; *Indian Travels of Thevenot and Careri.* (New Delhi, 1949)

Singh, R. L. ed.; *A Regional Geography.* (National Geographic Society of India, Varanasi, 2000)

Sinha, N. K.; *The Economic History of Bengal.* (Calcutta, 1968) in 2 Vols

Sinha, N. K. ed.; *The History of Bengal (1757-1905).* (Calcutta, reprint 1996)

Spate, O. H. K, Learmonth, A. T. A. and Learmonth, A. M.; *India and Pakistan: General and Regional Geography* (Delhi, 1984)

Sreemani, Soumitra; *Anatomy of a Colonial Town: Calcutta, 1756-1794.* (Calcutta, 1994)

Subhrahmanyam, Sanjoy; *Imprevising Empire: Portuguese Trade and Settlement in the Bay of Bengal, 1500-1700.* (New Delhi, 1990)

Tavernier, Jean Baptiste: *Tavemier's Travels in India (1640-1667)* tr. V. Ball. revised, W. Crooke (London, 1925) 2 Vols

Varthema, Ludovico di; *The Travels of Ludovico di Varthema in Egypt, Syria, Arabia desert and Arabia Felix, in Persia, India and Ethiopia, A.D. 1503-08.* tr. John M. Jones. George P. Badger ed. (Hakuyt Society, London, 1863)

Webster, Anthony; *The Richest East India Merchant: The Life and Business of John Palmer of Calcutta, 1767-1836.* (New Delhi, 2009)

Wright, H. Nelson, *The Coinage and Metrology of the Sultans of Delhi.* (New Delhi, 1974)

(F) Articles

Anonymous; 'The Plains of the Lower Ganges' in the *Calcutta Review.* Vol. IX, January; 1843

Arasaratnam S.; 'The Rice Trade in Eastern India, 1650-1740' in *Modern Asian Studies..* Vol. 22. No. 3

Beveridge, H.; 'Old Places of Murshidabad' Part I, in the *Calcutta Review.* April 1892

Beveridge, H; 'Calcutta' Part II in the *Calcutta Review, October* 1892

Chatterjee Rai Bahadur Gopal Ch.; 'Overflow Irrigation in Bengal' in the *Modern Review.* May, 1935

Chaudhuri, Sushil; 'Rise and Decline of Hooghli' in the *Bengal Past-and Present.* Jan-June, 1967

Ferguson, J.; 'Delta of the Ganges' in the *Quarterly Journal of the Geographical Society of London,* 1863. Proceedings of 1 April 1863

Marshmann; 'Notes on the Left or Calcutta Bank of the Hooghly' in the *Calcutta Review.* No. VI. Vol. 3 (1845)

Marshmann; 'Notes on the Right Bank of the Hooghly' in the *Calcutta Review.* No. VI. Vol. 4 (1845)

Marshall, P. J.; 'Private British Investment in 18th century Bengal' *in the Bengal Past and Present.* Diamond Jubilee No.

Shastri, Hara Prasad; 'Notes on the Banks of the Hughi in 1495' in the *Proceeding, of the Asiatic Society, Bengal,* 1892

Timberg, T. A.; 'A Note on the arrival of the Calcutta's Marwaries' in the *Bengal Past and Present.* Vol. XC, Pt1, No. 169

Wise, James.; 'Muhammadans of Eastern Bengal' In the *Journal of the Asiatic Society of Bengal.* Vol. 63

(G) Bengali Works

Abdul Halim 'Sharar'; *Purana Lucknow.* Bengali tr. of *Guzeshta Lucknow* by Munira Khatoon and Gurudas Bhattacharya. (Calcutta, 1972)

Asit Bandopadhyay; *Bangla Sahityer Sarnpurna Itibritta.* (Calcutta, Magh 1385 B.S.)

Bipradass Pipilai; *Manasamongala*. ed. Achintya Biswas (Calcutta, 2002)

Brindabandass; *Chaitanyabhagvat*. ed. Sukumar Sen. (Sahitya Akademi 2003)

Ganga Ram; *Maharastra-Puranan* (Published in Part in *Jhar.* Sept. 2004)

Haridass Dass; *Gaudya Vaisnava Abhidhan* (Navadwip, 1956-57) Vol. IV

Jayananda; *Chaitanyamangala*. eds. Biman Bihai Majumder and Sukhomoy Mukhopadhyay. (Asiatic Society of Bengal, Calcutta, 1971), ed. S. C. Majumdar (Calcutta, 1978), Krittibas Ojha; *Ramayana*. Mukundararn Chakraborty; *Chandimargala*. ed. Sukumar Sen (Sahitya Akademi, 1985)

Nihar Ranjan Ray, *Bangalir ltihas*: *Adiparva* (Calcutta, 1980) Vol. I

Rabindra Nath Thakur; *Charitrapuja* (Centenary Vol. XI)

Satish Chandra Mitra; *Jessore Khnluer ltihaas*. ed. Shib Shankar Mitra (Calcutta, 1963) Vol. I

Sivnath Shastri; *Ramtanu Lahiri O Tatkalin Banga Samaj*. (Calcutta, 1977)

Somendra Chandra Nandy; *Bandar Kashimbazar.* (Calcutta, 1978)

Soumitra Sreemani; "*Sampattir Adhikar o Nagaryan: Astadash Shataker Sheserdhe Kolkata*" in *Aitihasik*. September, 1998

Sushil Chandhuri; *Nawabi Amale Murshilabad*. (Calcutta, 2004)

INDEX